Dry Diplomacy

AMERICA IN THE MODERN WORLD
STUDIES IN INTERNATIONAL HISTORY

Warren F. Kimball
Series Editor
Professor of History, Rutgers University

America in the Modern World is a series of books that places the United States, as both a government and a society, within the context of an evolving global arena. The series is based on the assumption that nations interact not only at the governmental level but at the social, economic, political, and cultural levels as well, and that these international relationships are conditioned by, and influence in turn, domestic forces within the individual societies.

This series has no set format. It includes both the traditional monograph and the more wide-ranging syntheses. While it will emphasize twentieth-century international history, it also will study topics that precede 1900. Although it focuses on the role of the United States in international affairs, *America in the Modern World* contains works that view this nation as only one actor among many in a worldwide context. By utilizing the widest possible range of contributions, this series will further our understanding of the forces that shaped the international system and the American role in it.

Volume 1
Lawrence Spinelli, *Dry Diplomacy: The United States, Great Britain, and Prohibition*

Volume 2
Richard V. Salisbury, *Anti-Imperialism and International Competition in Central America, 1920–1929*

Dry Diplomacy

The United States,
Great Britain,
and Prohibition

Lawrence Spinelli

A Scholarly Resources Imprint
WILMINGTON, DELAWARE

The paper used in this publication meets the minimum requirements of the American National Standard for permanence of paper for printed library materials, Z39.48, 1984.

Scholarly Resources Inc.
104 Greenhill Avenue
Wilmington, Delaware 19805-1897

Library of Congress Cataloging-in-Publication Data

Spinelli, Lawrence, 1952–
    Dry diplomacy : the United States, Great Britain, and prohibition / Lawrence Spinelli.
        p.   cm.
    (America in the modern world : v. 1)
    Bibliography : p.
        Includes index.
        ISBN 0-8420-2298-8 (alk. paper).
    1. United States—Foreign relations—1919–1921.   2. United States—Foreign relations—1921–1923.   3. United States—Foreign relations—1923–1929.   4. United States—Foreign relations—1929–1933.   4. Great Britain—Foreign relations—1910–1936.
    6. Prohibition.   I. Title.   II. Series
    E784.S68   1988   88-11610
    327.73—dc19   CIP

TO ARLENE,

WITH LOVE AND APPRECIATION

About the Author

Lawrence Spinelli received a Ph.D. in history from New York University. After working for several years within academia, including teaching positions at Drew University and American University, he now serves as press secretary for the office of Congressman Peter W. Rodino, Jr., and the House Judiciary Committee. This is Mr. Spinelli's first book.

Contents

Preface

The impact of American prohibition on Anglo-American diplomacy has received little attention from historians. Although there is a renewed scholarly interest in prohibition itself, recent studies have focused on domestic aspects or the various efforts to evade the law. Studies of interwar Anglo-American relations have concentrated on other issues of the period or briefly dismissed the prohibition problem. The only monograph that considers this topic is Robert L. Jones, *The Eighteenth Amendment and Our Foreign Relations* (1933). While the Jones work must be acknowledged for recognizing the importance of the subject, its preparation before the end of the prohibition period, its very limited use of primary sources, and the absence of British documentation reflect serious inadequacies. Considering this inattention, the effect of the prohibition issue on Anglo-American relations requires the in-depth examination with full documentation that the following study attempts to provide.

Beyond the closing of this scholarly gap, the story of the diplomatic ramifications of prohibition is significant because it is more than a singular tale of liquor and smuggling. Prohibition was a continuing source of Anglo-American disagreement that raised questions of international law, aroused domestic political interests, and complicated larger issues of transatlantic diplomacy. It endured until 1935, two years after the repeal of the Eighteenth Amendment, and challenged four American presidents and four British prime ministers. Prohibition reinforced a mutual suspicion and a feeling of distrust in both London and Washington, serving as a burden in the search for an Anglo-American accommodation in the interwar period. Although other disputes were settled, the enactment of the Eighteenth Amendment provided an additional obstacle to transforming agreement into political harmony.

The story of liquor diplomacy also provides an insight into the nature of British and American foreign policymaking. The liquor issue

encouraged British foreign policymakers to recognize strategic compromise as a valuable method for bolstering Great Britain's position
against the postwar reality of diminished resources. In the United States,
the enforcement of prohibition underscored the fact that American isolationism was more rhetoric than reality, as the liquor issue sparked a
bitter clash between the unilateral and collective elements of an independent internationalism. On both sides of the Atlantic Ocean, domestic
political pressures provided a major constraint and frame of reference
for foreign policymakers in the interwar years.

Finally, recognizing the diplomatic ramifications of prohibition is
important because it suggests the need for a more complex explanation
of the relationship between the United States and Great Britain in the
1920s. The post-World War I period was not simply the passing of
dominance from Great Britain to the United States. It was highlighted
by both the British determination to preserve a continuity in status and
the difficulties that confronted the United States in fully exploiting the
opportunities provided by its new strength. While American officials
remained hobbled by domestic concerns and bureaucratic infighting,
their British counterparts were prepared to exchange symbolic victory
for the protection of economic interests. The history of Anglo-American
liquor diplomacy is largely one of British success in retaining the advantage behind the illusion of compromise and concession. For all of these
reasons, I hope this study will contribute to a reassessment of the prohibition issue and its necessary inclusion in any discussion of Anglo-
American relations in the interwar period.

I wish to express my appreciation for the assistance and support of
a number of individuals. The suggestions of the staffs at the Library of
Congress Manuscript Division, National Archives, Public Record Office
at Kew, Ohio Historical Society, Cambridge University Library, Herbert
Hoover Presidential Library, and the University of Liverpool made my
task much easier. Particularly helpful were Ken Hall at the National
Archives, Robert Wood of the Hoover Presidential Library, and Michael
Cook at the University of Liverpool. Robert Scally and Michael Lutzker
at New York University offered careful criticism of an earlier version of
this work and encouraged me to continue the process of refinement.

Family and friends provided invaluable moral support. I am grateful
to my parents for understanding the infrequent visits and unanswered
letters. Special thanks are due to Howard Rosenthal who was a devoted
friend and trusted adviser.

It was my good fortune that Richard Hopper, acquisitions editor at Scholarly Resources, answered the telephone when I called to find the name of the history editor. His enthusiasm for this manuscript, after only a brief conversation, never diminished and was reflected in the diligent and caring efforts of Project Editor Carolyn Travers and Copy Editor Ann Aydelotte.

My profound thanks to Carl Prince for his friendship, suggestions, and belief in this project; his words of encouragement echoed during the most difficult times. He is a teacher in the truest sense of the word.

Finally, I give my deepest gratitude and appreciation to my wife Arlene, who was a patient and supportive partner throughout the writing of this book. Whether listening to prohibition stories on evening walks, enduring long separations for the sake of research, or proofreading under the pressure of deadlines, she remained my greatest supporter. The successful completion of this project is as much her achievement as it is mine.

Introduction

National prohibition became a reality of American life on January 16, 1920. The ratification of the Eighteenth Amendment to the Constitution and the subsequent passage of the Volstead Act made the manufacture, sale, and transportation of intoxicating liquor illegal in the United States. It was an extraordinary political achievement for a movement that had waged an uphill battle to transform temperance sentiment into prohibition support. The atmosphere of emergency that accompanied American entry into the First World War had provided a new momentum. Utilizing a highly effective organization and faced with token resistance from a weak opposition, the "dry" forces secured an easy victory. For the next fourteen years, prohibition was national policy, casting a shadow over every aspect of American life and creating a myriad of unexpected problems, both within and beyond the territory of the United States.[1]

At the same time, on the other side of the Atlantic Ocean, British whiskey distillers faced an uncertain future as the new decade began. The liquor industry in Great Britain, dominated by the major Scotch whiskey producers, was struggling to recover from the deleterious effects of World War I.[2] A wave of self-sacrifice had swept the British public in 1914, with temperance recast in the mold of patriotism, and this movement found a determined advocate in David Lloyd George. Inspired by his Welsh "chapel" constituency, Lloyd George boldly declared that "we are fighting Germany, Austria and drink and the greatest of these deadly foes is drink."[3] As minister of munitions, he introduced a series of emergency measures to limit the consumption and manufacture of distilled spirits. Many of these restrictions became permanent fixtures of government regulation of the industry, dashing the hopes of the Scotch whiskey producers for a quick return to the unrestrained business atmosphere of prewar Britain.[4]

After the armistice, Lloyd George, now the leader of the ruling National Coalition, focused on sumptuary taxation as both a new temperance weapon and a valuable source of revenue. His 1918 budget doubled the liquor tax to thirty shillings per proof gallon; by 1921 the tax on liquor had increased to over seventy-two shillings.[5] The result of Lloyd George's efforts was not the elimination of liquor consumption in Great Britain. Instead, his taxation program dramatically altered British drinking habits. The new duties significantly raised the cost of distilled spirits at a time when the economy was experiencing a difficult period of rising unemployment.[6] Scotch whiskey was now an expensive commodity and no longer competitive, as a large segment of the British public turned to more inexpensive beverages. When the economic situation worsened, a short-lived liquor boom was replaced by a sharp decline in domestic consumption of Scotch whiskey.[7] Pressed at home by regulation and taxation, the major British distillers looked elsewhere for a solution to their problems.

Although Great Britain was the world's largest exporter of liquor prior to 1914, domestic operations overshadowed foreign sales. The export market remained relatively untapped and offered the greatest potential for the salvation of the British liquor industry.[8] The international situation, however, offered little encouragement. The First World War had disrupted trade relations and realigned markets. The poor economic climate in Europe eliminated potential importers. The most discouraging development was the adoption of national prohibition in the United States. American officials acted quickly to freeze foreign liquor stocks already in the country, and British Customs refused to clear any liquor exports to the United States. Public reaction made any direct involvement in violating the law untenable, and the British liquor industry considered the potentially lucrative American market closed.[9] There appeared to be little hope for the industry as British liquor became a product in search of a buyer.

The British distillers did not have long to wait for a solution to their problem. In the Bahamas, a British Crown colony, local residents shrewdly recognized that the enactment of the Eighteenth Amendment would create an underground market for illegal liquor. With the islands providing a safe harbor in close proximity to the United States, the capital city of Nassau already served as the headquarters for a growing liquor-smuggling trade. Both islanders and newly arrived American adventurers, enjoying the safety of international waters under cover of British shipping registry, sold liquor along the Florida coast. But the expansion of this trade and the full exploitation of the unintended benefits of American prohibition depended upon a reliable source of quality spirits. This was a role that the British whiskey distillers were delighted to occupy. Within a year, an uninterrupted flow of liquor from Great Britain supplied a caravan of British-registered rum-running vessels stretched along the entire eastern seaboard of the United States, openly flaunting the Volstead Act. American prohibition and the British liquor industry had found each other.

The enactment of the Eighteenth Amendment in the United States also coincided with the beginning of a postwar uncertainty in the future of Anglo-American relations. Close wartime cooperation was replaced by distrust and abusive exchanges at the Paris Peace Conference. There was a considerable loss of confidence as serious differences developed between the United States and Great Britain over the difficult task of readjusting to the changes created by World War I. At the start of the war, sterling was the dominant currency, the Royal Navy guarded the seas, and the British Empire covered the world. By 1920 the American dollar represented the world's largest creditor, the United States threatened British hegemony, and the once cohesive empire was subjected to new stirrings of independence. Outstanding questions over European recovery, war debts, commercial interests, and naval parity remained unanswered.[10] Although the two nations were military victors, the underlying concern for many observers was "whether this domination is to be exercised in rivalry or in agreement, in friendship or in hostility."[11]

For foreign policymakers in the United States, the first challenge was to define the precise nature of the American role in the postwar world. The signing of the armistice in 1918 did not herald U.S. withdrawal from world affairs. American officials and many business leaders recognized that the economic strength of the United States and the complexity of new financial arrangements made this impossible. Reluctant to continue political entanglements, they embraced an independent internationalism that acknowledged the domestic advantages of limited American involvement in the reconstruction of Europe and the nurturing of a stable international environment.[12] But independent internationalism was a large umbrella under which the demand for unilateral diplomacy countered support for collective action. Within the government and the business community, the proponents of narrow national ambitions debated advocates of international initiative. In the absence of a single comprehensive diplomacy, partisan political rivalries, bureaucratic infighting, and domestic pressures emerged as important elements in American foreign policy.[13]

The primary postwar objective of British foreign policymakers was to restore the supremacy of pre-1914 Great Britain. Although they shared the American concern for rebuilding the international economy, the burden for British officials was to maintain their nation's position at a time when commitments exceeded resources. Rising unemployment and falling exports boldly demonstrated that the war had accelerated a decline in British economic power. Substantial war debts and an aging industrial plant further exacerbated the economic disparity between Great Britain and the United States. The British solution was to reduce debts, secure the position of London as an international financial center, and stabilize prices. A fundamental element in this strategy was the stimulation of foreign trade. This would relieve domestic pressures and draw upon the resources of the empire as an economic counterweight to the United States. To accomplish this goal, British officials were determined to protect Great Britain's preeminent position in world shipping and to expand commercial opportunities. By fostering trade and sustaining imperial links, the British hoped to minimize their weaknesses and maximize their strengths.[14]

The contrast in these two perspectives made the forging of a new Anglo-American relationship a formidable task. There were successful attempts to resolve specific problems, such as war debts and naval disarmament, and several areas of commercial competition were settled by the informal cooperation of private interests in the United States and Great Britain.[15] Yet these agreements did not translate into a lasting political harmony. In the United States, independent internationalism was a shifting balance between collectivists and unilateralists. Efforts to achieve transatlantic accord paralleled immigration restrictions, the Fordney-McCumber Tariff Act, the Jones Act, and the ship subsidy proposal and other manifestations of nationalist fervor. Anglophobia remained a potent force in domestic American politics and a catalyst for bureaucratic disagreement in Washington.[16] British officials continued to regard relations with the United States as part of the multilateral problems of trade, payments, and the maintenance of their nation's position. Many Foreign Office officials resented U.S. intrusion, particularly in shipping, and anti-Americanism was a popular antidote to Great Britain's problems.[17] As the United States and Great Britain wavered between initiative and self-interest, cooperation and conflict, the emergence of prohibition as an Anglo-American issue was an unwelcomed complication.

Notes

[1]Norman H. Clark, *Deliver Us from Evil* (New York, 1976); Joseph R. Gusfield, *Symbolic Crusade* (Urbana, 1963); Jack S. Blocker, Jr., *Retreat from Reform* (Westport, CT, 1976); K. Austin Kerr, "Organizing for Reform: The Anti-Saloon League," *American Quarterly* 32 (Spring 1980): 37–53; Peter H. Odegard, *Pressure Politics: The Story of the Anti-Saloon League* (New York, 1928); K. Austin Kerr, *Organized for Prohibition: A New History of the Anti-*

Saloon League (New Haven, 1985); David E. Kyvig, *Repealing National Prohibition* (Chicago, 1979), 1–19; Jack S. Blocker, Jr., "The Modernity of Prohibitionists: An Analysis of Leadership Structure and Background," in Jack S. Blocker, Jr., ed., *Alcohol, Reform and Society* (Westport, CT, 1979), 149–70. For a background of earlier scholarship on the external effects of prohibition see Robert L. Jones, *The Eighteenth Amendment and Our Foreign Relations* (New York, 1933); James H. Mannock, "Anglo-American Relations: 1921–1928" (Ph.D. diss., Princeton University, 1962), 166–200; H. C. Allen, *Great Britain and the United States* (London, 1954), 761; Bruce M. Russett, *Community and Contention* (Cambridge, MA, 1963), 11; Betty Glad, *Charles Evans Hughes and the Illusions of Innocence* (Urbana, 1966), 319–20; Merlo J. Pusey, *Charles Evans Hughes,* 2 vols. (New York, 1951), 2:575–78; Robert K. Murray, *The Harding Era* (Minneapolis, 1969), 403–7; Phillip C. Jessup, *The Law of Territorial Waters and Maritime Jurisdiction* (New York, 1927), 211–354; and William E. Masterson, *Jurisdiction in Marginal Seas* (New York, 1929), 304–74.

[2]Ross Wilson, *Scotch: The Formative Years* (London, 1970), 231–42.

[3]As quoted in Norman Longmate, *The Waterdrinkers* (London, 1968), 257. For Lloyd George's early views on temperance see Peter Rowland, *Lloyd George* (London, 1975), 78–82, 109–10, 177–78.

[4]Henry Carter, *The Control of the Drink Trade* (London, 1918); Michael Brander, *The Original Scotch* (New York, 1975), 120; Longmate, *Waterdrinkers,* 267–91; Wilson, *Scotch,* 156–67.

[5]Allen Andrews, *The Whiskey Barons* (London, 1977), 14–15; Wilson, *Scotch,* 233, 243–68; Brander, *Original Scotch,* 118–19; Robert B. Lockhart, *Scotch* (London, 1951), 131.

[6]Derek H. Aldcroft, *The Inter-War Economy: Britain, 1919–1939* (London, 1970), 36–38. For a general discussion of the British postwar economic situation see Sean Glynn and John Oxborrow, *Interwar Britain* (London, 1976).

[7]Wilson, *Scotch,* 299–305.

[8]Brander, *Original Scotch,* 120; Wilson, *Scotch,* 283.

[9]Several major British liquor firms suffered from the loss of merchandise left in the United States. Auckland Geddes to George Curzon, June 15, 1920, A4379/955/45, General Political Correspondence of the Foreign Office, Foreign Office 371, Public Record Office, Kew, London (hereafter cited as PRO, with all records in F.O. 371 unless otherwise noted). Liquor could not be withdrawn after January 16, 1920, although some reexport was allowed later. British Embassy, Washington, to Foreign Office, January 29, 1921, A1069/1069/45, PRO; Brewer's Society to Foreign Office, February 28, 1920, A955/955/45, PRO. See also Lockhart, *Scotch,* 145.

[10]Seth P. Tillman, *Anglo-American Relations at the Paris Peace Conference of 1919* (Princeton, 1961); Harold and Margaret Sprout, *Toward a New Order of Sea Power* (Princeton, 1940), 74–77; Herbert G. Nicholas, *The United States and Great Britain* (Chicago, 1975), 77; Thomas H. Buckley, *The United States and the Washington Conference, 1921–1922* (Knoxville, 1970); John Chalmers Vinson, *The Parchment Peace* (Athens, GA, 1955); Frank C. Costigliola, "Anglo-American Financial Rivalry in the 1920s," *Journal of Economic History*

37 (December 1977): 911–34; Michael J. Hogan, *Informal Entente: The Private Structure of Cooperation in Anglo-American Economic Diplomacy, 1918–1928* (Columbia, MO, 1977); Carl P. Parrini, *Heir to Empire: United States Economic Diplomacy, 1916–1923* (Pittsburgh, 1969); Michael G. Fry, *Illusions of Security: North Atlantic Diplomacy, 1918–1922* (Toronto, 1972); Mannock, "Anglo-American Relations: 1921-1928."

[11] Alfred G. Gardiner, *The Anglo-American Future* (New York, 1927), 18.

[12] Joan Hoff-Wilson, *American Business and Foreign Policy, 1920-1933* (Lexington, KY, 1971), xi–xvii; Melvyn P. Leffler, *The Elusive Quest: America's Pursuit of European Stability and French Security, 1919–1933* (Chapel Hill, 1979); Hogan, *Informal Entente,* 13. See also William A. Williams, "The Legend of Isolationism in the 1920s," *Science and Society* 18 (1954): 1–20.

[13] Arnold A. Offner, *The Origins of the Second World War: American Foreign Policy and World Politics, 1917–1941* (New York, 1975), 45; Melvyn P. Leffler, "Political Isolationism, Economic Expansionism, or Diplomatic Realism: American Policy toward Western Europe, 1921-1933," *Perspectives in American History* 8 (1974): 413–61; Joan Hoff-Wilson, *Herbert Hoover: Forgotten Progressive* (Boston, 1975), 169; Leffler, *Elusive Quest,* 362–64; Hoff-Wilson, *American Business and Foreign Policy,* 25–27, 74; Hogan, *Informal Entente,* 209; Selig Adler, *The Uncertain Giant* (New York, 1965); L. Ethan Ellis, *Republican Foreign Policy, 1921–1933* (New Brunswick, NJ, 1968).

[14] Costigliola, "Anglo-American Financial Rivalry in the 1920s," 911–14; D. L. Watt, *Personalities and Policies: Studies in the Formulation of British Foreign Policy in the Twentieth Century* (London, 1965), 38; Aldcroft, *Inter-War Economy,* 36–38; Glynn and Oxborrow, *Interwar Britain,* 56; D. Cameron Watt, *Succeeding John Bull: America in Britain's Place, 1900–1975* (Cambridge, England, 1984), 48–49; R. F. Holland, *Britain and the Commonwealth Alliance, 1918–1939* (London, 1981), 208–9.

[15] Hogan, *Informal Entente;* Buckley, *United States and the Washington Conference;* Vinson, *Parchment Peace;* Hoff-Wilson, *American Business and Foreign Policy,* 31–48; H. C. Allen, *Great Britain and the United States,* 741, 756–58.

[16] Robert K. Murray, *The Politics of Normalcy: Governmental Theory and Practice in the Harding-Coolidge Era* (New York, 1973), 64–71; Leffler, "Political Isolationism, Economic Expansionism, or Diplomatic Realism," 429; Hoff-Wilson, *American Business and Foreign Policy,* 74; Offner, *Origins of the Second World War,* 45, 62–70.

[17] Costigliola, "Anglo-American Financial Rivalry in the 1920s," 912–14; D. C. Watt, *Succeeding John Bull,* 22, 49–51; D. L. Watt, *Personalities and Policies,* 37–38.

Chapter One

The British Connection
Liquor Smuggling and the Bahamas, 1919–1921

Considering the overwhelming range of postwar Anglo-American problems, the advent of prohibition aroused little initial excitement within the British government. If there was a certain curiosity in the event, as there was in most things American, it was a detached interest that fostered private speculation rather than public concern. Prohibition was merely further evidence of the Yankee penchant for experimenting with the unusual. Unlike the nagging questions of war debts and naval parity, prohibition was regarded as an American domestic issue that posed no real threat to Great Britain's interests. Accordingly, the London government did not prepare for any difficulties and expected none.

Within one year, however, British officials were forced to abandon their complacency. The development of a profitable smuggling trade headquartered in a Crown colony, protected by British shipping documents, and supplied by Scotch whiskey distributors in London linked Great Britain with the efforts to violate the Eighteenth Amendment. This connection subjected the British government to American criticism and anglophobic outbursts. When U.S. antismuggling efforts threatened principles of international law supported by the British government, prohibition enforcement provided the catalyst for an unanticipated clash between the United States and Great Britain. Officials in London could no longer ignore this American fad; the British connection guaranteed that prohibition was an Anglo-American problem.

The center of this British connection was located in the warm waters of the Caribbean Sea, where the reaction to the triumph of American prohibitionists differed from that of government officials in London. Times were hard in the Bahaman islands, and this British Crown colony

1

desperately needed to bolster its sagging economy. The First World War had strained the islands' resources and curtailed trade, creating serious food shortages. Tourism, the mainstay of the economy, was disrupted and showed no sign of returning to prewar levels. From 1914 to 1920 the Bahaman public debt increased by 50 percent.[1]

Paradoxically, prohibition provided this financial relief. The Eighteenth Amendment succeeded in driving the liquor trade underground, and there was a strong demand in the United States for a high-quality whiskey to supplement the local moonshine and bootleg liquor already available. The Bahaman islands, because of their strategic location, were in a unique position to exploit this potential market. The capital city of Nassau provided a safe harbor only 175 miles from the United States and within easy sailing time to the major American cities along the eastern seaboard. Smuggling was a long-practiced profession in the islands, and as early as 1918 there was a small trade in illegal liquor between the islands and the "dry" state of Florida.[2] American whiskey interests, appreciating that the Bahamas were a natural base for smuggling, shipped some of their liquor stocks to Nassau prior to the enactment of national prohibition.[3] As the profitability of smuggling quality liquor was recognized, these supplies were depleted quickly and Bahaman liquor interests looked to Great Britain for assistance.

What these Bahaman merchants found in London was a British industry pressed at home by taxation and in search of an opportunity for expansion. The Scotch whiskey distillers responded immediately to the Bahaman request and adjusted their operations to exploit this new overseas trade. Even Berry Brothers, liquor purveyors to Buckingham Palace, announced plans to market Cutty Sark, the first Scotch whiskey created solely for export.[4] Many distillers sent their own agents to Nassau to manage this fledgling business and to protect product quality. The chief task of these agents was to maintain a trading partnership that provided British liquor interests with a method for legally tapping into the closed American market.[5] While there was little doubt that these exports were not consumed in the Bahamas, it was within the law to sell liquor to British agents in a British Crown colony. What happened to the liquor after it was sold was of no concern, one leading London liquor broker noted: smuggling was best left to the Americans.[6] Distillers in Great Britain maintained a technical detachment from the efforts to evade U.S. law as the successful exploitation of prohibition changed the character of the British liquor industry, cushioned the effects of a declining domestic market, and firmly established Scotch whiskey as the liquor preferred in the United States.[7]

The changes precipitated by this emerging British connection were more dramatic in the Bahamas. Nassau became the unofficial capital of the new drink trade, with its main street lined with brokerage houses selling liquor for cash or consignment and old warehouses refurbished to hold Scotch whiskey cargoes from Great Britain. The center of this activity was the Lucerne Hotel where its frail owner, affectionately known as "Mother" to her clientele of liquor dealers, rumrunners, and American bootleggers, presided over nightly brawls and shootings. The Bimini Rod and Rifle Club did a brisk business hosting tour groups of thirsty Americans, and plans were made to begin regular seaplane service from Miami. Nassau assumed all the characteristics of a mining boom-town where, according to an American enforcement official, the major business "was that of trafficking in liquor" and where no secret was made of the fact that "the whiskey is shipped there from the British Isles and it is to be sold in the United States."[8]

The initial reluctance of the Bahaman government to encourage this new industry faded when financial benefits transcended moral propriety.[9] With all imports placed into bond until payment of a government tariff, the islands' duty on liquor began to provide substantial revenue as this trade flourished. Liquor imports rose from 27,427 gallons in 1918 to a staggering 567,940 gallons in 1921, bringing a corresponding increase in the government's liquor revenue from $44,462 to $984,732.[10] The result was the economic rebirth of the islands; within two years, the Bahaman public debt was eliminated, funds were available for dredging Nassau harbor, and the government embarked on a major public works project. Considering the tangible benefits of smuggling, Bahaman authorities were willing to provide a sanctuary for this growing enterprise.[11]

For the rumrunners who transported smuggled liquor to the United States, this hospitable business climate was invaluable. But there was still an important element missing from the British connection. A majority of the ships in the smuggling fleet were owned by Americans and registered in the United States. Once they left the safety of Bahaman waters, they were subject to arrest or seizure by the U.S. Coast Guard. The only shield against American prohibition enforcement on the open seas was the international law immunity provided by foreign registry. There was a frantic effort in Nassau to secure British registry, and the net tonnage of vessels registered in the Bahamas rose from 1,798 in 1921 to 17,606 by 1922.[12] Bogus companies with Bahaman stockholders were established, British subjects were bribed to apply for transfer papers, and Americans assumed the mortgages on British ships.[13] American rumrunners, aided by liberal registry laws and the lax enforcement of shipping officials, succeeded in obtaining British registry through transfer, ownership, and fraud.[14] The smuggling fleet in the Caribbean now was sailing from a British Crown colony, with a cargo of liquor from London, under the protection of Great Britain's flag. The British connection was complete.

The diplomatic ramifications of this intimate link between British interests and the violation of U.S. law were not immediately recognized in London. David Lloyd George's government faced the broad task of maintaining Great Britain's position against the reality of diminished resources and the immediate challenge of European recovery and tension in the Near East. The future direction of Anglo-American relations was uncertain, and the unresolved problems of commercial competition, war debts, and naval rivalry preoccupied officials.[15] By comparison, prohibition was of minor importance. Foreign Office officials regarded the Eighteenth Amendment as "faddist legislation" that was ephemeral and required little attention.[16] Earlier minor incidents, precipitated by the overzealousness of U.S. prohibition enforcement, were resolved quietly and confirmed the belief that prohibition was not an Anglo-American problem. Reports of British involvement in liquor smuggling were dismissed as wild speculation and no cause for concern.[17]

The complacency of the Foreign Office abruptly ended. In April 1921 dedicated prohibitionist and former Secretary of State William Jennings Bryan focused public attention for the first time on the British connection. Bryan, speaking before the Illinois Anti-Saloon League, charged that "Bimini Island is being extensively used to smuggle liquor," and he warned that the British government would be responsible for any violent American retaliation.[18] Although Foreign Office officials suspected that Bryan's true objective was to increase pressure for the American purchase of the Bahamas, the speech received considerable press coverage and required a response.[19] The Foreign Office issued a directive to bolster the appearance of strict law enforcement.[20] The Bahaman government was requested to prosecute violators of customs laws and to upgrade supervision in the outer island of Bimini. All colonial officials were cautioned against financial involvement in any liquor operations and were warned that increased public attention required the "maintenance of a proper position" at all times.[21]

Bahaman authorities made a half-hearted attempt to implement the directive, but the results were negligible.[22] The archaic machinery of government in the islands delayed the sharing of timely information and made efficient enforcement difficult. The sizable representation of liquor interests in the Legislative Assembly prevented the passage of any anti-smuggling measures. The economic stakes were too high; widespread corruption and the tangible benefits of rum-running dulled any enthusiasm for stricter enforcement.[23] The Bahaman attitude was unchanged and, without stronger pressure from London, the British government remained vulnerable to American criticism.

Three months later, the British connection was again in the headlines. The British-registered vessel *Pocomoke* was seized by the Coast Guard for smuggling liquor in American waters. A search of the vessel uncovered duplicate cargo clearances, obtained from Bahaman officials, that provided a legitimate cover for rum-running. One set of clearances established that the vessel was legally transporting distilled spirits from Nassau to Canada and explained the presence of liquor cargo. The other documents, to be used after the liquor was sold, claimed that the ship was sailing empty to the United States.[24] The *Pocomoke* incident could not be ignored because the issuance of more than one shipping clearance violated British customs laws. The Bahaman government was ordered to investigate the case, an ineffective effort since it was unlikely that government officials would acknowledge corruption in their own ranks, and the final report found no evidence of impropriety. Regardless of this official disclaimer, the *Pocomoke* evidence strengthened public suspicion that Bahaman officials were in direct collusion with liquor smugglers.[25]

American criticism over the *Pocomoke* incident and reports of widespread abuse of clearance regulations in Nassau forced the Foreign Office to reconsider the situation in the Caribbean.[26] Rowland Sperling, chief of the American Department, argued that some ineffective gesture was necessary to strengthen the British position in the West Indies. But the liquor trade brought unexpected benefits, easing Great Britain's financial burdens in the Bahamas and doubling British exports to the islands, and prohibition was still regarded with contempt at the Foreign Office.[27] Ongoing Anglo-American tension over naval parity aroused strong anti-American feelings, and most officials refused to support even a weak response to the smuggling problem in the Bahamas.[28] The formidable colonial secretary, Winston Churchill, concluded that the approval of any new measure was an admission of guilt, and he refused to adopt an apologetic attitude toward the United States, a view endorsed by the foreign secretary.[29] Overruled in his own department, Sperling prophetically warned that "some day or another smuggling will make real trouble between the two countries."[30]

Throughout the summer of 1921 smugglers continued to evade the efforts of U.S. prohibition enforcement.[31] When Bill McCoy, known as the "real McCoy" because of the untainted quality of his Scotch whiskey, returned to Nassau with stories of the potential profits of the New York market, rum-running operations shifted north. The waters off the New Jersey and Long Island coasts became the new center of smuggling in the Atlantic. Safely anchored beyond the three-mile limit, British-registered ships from the Bahamas formed a "Rum Row" of floating liquor warehouses, and a steady traffic of small boats from the shore carried liquor buyers out to the ships at night.[32]

Life on Rum Row, at least initially, was pleasant. There was a strong sense of fraternity among smugglers; most early rumrunners were former mariners and fishermen, not hardened criminals, and they regarded themselves as the aristocrats of the liquor trade.[33] Unlike bootleggers on land, the rumrunners benefited from a positive public image. A panic over the appearance of mysterious ships off the New Jersey coast quickly subsided when it was discovered that these vessels were only new arrivals to Rum Row.[34] The rumrunners became celebrities, interviewed by leading newspapers and portrayed as contemporary pirates carrying on the American tradition of free enterprise. This sympathetic attitude guaranteed good shore contacts for bringing liquor safely to land and provided rumrunners with a daily supply of provisions and information.[35]

All of these advantages enjoyed by the rumrunners only added to the frustration within the Coast Guard, the agency responsible for enforcing prohibition in U.S. territorial waters. Few enforcement officials anticipated the magnitude of the smuggling problem, and the Coast Guard was both undermanned and poorly equipped. Forced to use former rescue boats as revenue cutters, the fleet was too slow and cumbersome to chase the faster rumrunners, and smugglers sailing under foreign registry could not be seized beyond the three-mile limit. Bribery and corruption were constant concerns, and the dismissal of several officers who were in the employ of liquor interests jarred the service. The absence of coordination between the Treasury Department's three divisions involved in prohibition further reduced the effectiveness of anti-smuggling operations. As rum-running flourished, the Coast Guard was under increasing pressure to eliminate Rum Row.[36]

The Coast Guard concentrated its renewed effort to end rum-running on American vessels smuggling liquor beyond the three-mile limit. On August 4, 1921, a cutter was dispatched to investigate a suspicious vessel unloading liquor nine miles off the New Jersey coast. Although the suspected ship did not display a name or flag, a 1920 Coast Guard registry listed it as the American-registered *Henry L. Marshall.* The vessel was immediately boarded, and a search uncovered duplicate clearances issued in the Bahamas and a cargo manifest proving that liquor was landed in the United States. The commander of the cutter towed the rumrunner into New York harbor according to standard procedures.[37]

The seizure of the *Marshall*, however, was far from routine. When the ship arrived in port, it was discovered that the vessel was transferred to British registry earlier in the year and the *Marshall* was now the first foreign rumrunner seized beyond American waters. The U.S. attorney in New York, William Hayward, ignored the implications of this action and moved quickly against the ship and its crew. Doubting that the Volstead Act extended beyond the three-mile limit, Hayward libeled the ship, which was the standard legal procedure for condemning property used in illegal activities. He also arrested the crew for violating the provisions of the U.S. customs law prohibiting vessels bound for the United States from unloading cargo within twelve miles of the coast.[38] With the legal process initiated, any tactical American retreat or apology for this violation of international law was impossible. Hayward, through his zeal and efficiency, contributed generously to the transformation of prohibition into an Anglo-American problem.

The diplomatic significance of the *Marshall* seizure was that it challenged a major tenet of British diplomacy. Great Britain was the most consistent and vocal supporter of a three-mile limit to a nation's jurisdiction over adjacent waters and led the effort in the nineteenth century to elevate the three-mile limit to the level of international law. Domestically, the replacement of the Hovering Acts with the Customs Consolidation Act in 1876 reconciled British municipal law with this principle and, two years later, judicial authority was restricted to the same distance.[39] The British government was the guiding force behind both the adoption of a three-mile limit in the North Seas Fisheries Convention of 1882 and subsequent efforts to prevent the Russian government from extending fishing claims to twelve miles.[40] Foreign Secretary Edward Grey confidently asserted in 1908 that the national policy was "to protest against and resist by every means in our power the pretentions of any foreign country to enforce its own jurisdiction beyond the three-mile limit."[41]

Underlying the British defense of this traditional principle was the fundamental concept of the freedom of the seas. The restriction of territorial rights to a modest, uniform measure provided the widest possible latitude for the area recognized as open ocean. With its naval and merchant shipping superiority, Great Britain exploited this freedom to defend the empire and to exert influence over vital sea-lanes and trade passages. These historical concerns remained important elements in postwar British foreign policy. Emotionally, the three-mile limit was intimately linked to the pre-1914 supremacy of Great Britain. Practically, the restoration of this supremacy was also connected to an expansion of international commerce and the promotion of imperial resources. A stagnant domestic economy, high unemployment, and an underutilized merchant fleet made the British even more dependent on imports and trade. Challenged by new commercial competition, the three-mile limit was perceived as a valuable restraint on any potential rival.[42]

The *Marshall* seizure, therefore, presented a dilemma to Foreign Office officials. They were determined to prevent the incident from serving as a precedent for the general weakening or abandonment of the three-mile limit. Recent Soviet demands for a twelve-mile fishing zone and the Norwegian Parliament's extension of customs jurisdiction encouraged other nations to threaten similar action.[43] Unfortunately, the *Marshall* case was not the strongest basis for a defense of international law. The vessel was not engaged in legitimate shipping, and the discovery of duplicate clearances exposed the glaring inadequacies of Bahaman authorities.[44] In a secret affidavit presented to the British consul in New York, American Bill McCoy affirmed that he was the owner of the *Marshall* and had paid a British front to obtain a registry transfer. This raised serious doubts in London regarding the wisdom of defending a vessel that was not entitled to any protection under the British flag.[45]

To resolve this difficulty, the Foreign Office decided to lodge a general protest without specifically mentioning the *Marshall*. On August 11, Great Britain's ambassador in Washington, Sir Auckland Geddes, presented Secretary of State Charles Evans Hughes with a formal protest objecting to the exercise of U.S. jurisdiction over British vessels on the high seas, except when in continuous pursuit from within three miles.[46] The following month a second note was delivered, confirming the original protest. British Chargé Henry Chilton verbally assured Secretary Hughes that his government was acting only to defend international law and not to protect smuggling.[47] In November, Hughes requested the suspension of discussions on the case pending further inquiries. American Department officials, relieved because subsequent investigations confirmed the invalidity of the *Marshall's* British registry, quickly agreed.[48]

Although British officials were satisfied with the success of their strategy in defending the three-mile limit, the *Marshall* controversy created an uneasiness within the Foreign Office. The seizure demonstrated the difficulty of reconciling the absolute necessity to protect international law with the undesirability of officially defending smugglers. There was neither a new sympathy for the prohibition cause nor any inclination to disrupt the economic benefits of the liquor trade. Instead, Foreign Office officials recognized that the dubious registry of what were primarily American-financed smugglers was both a weak foundation for further British action and potentially embarrassing. The support of rumrunners might tarnish the British image and, considering Great Britain's recent criticism of gunrunning to Ireland, it was inconsistent to defend lawbreakers. Protecting smugglers, for many Foreign Office officials, challenged a belief in the moral superiority of British foreign policy.[49]

No one carried the daily pressures of this dilemma more than Geddes. While equally critical of prohibition, he regarded the defense of rumrunners as a "humiliating position for any British Ambassador."[50] Following the *Marshall* incident, Geddes exercised his influence as a prominent Conservative political appointee to persuade the government to adopt a flexible seizure policy.[51] He suggested that the circumstances of each incident, particularly the extent of any international law violations, dictate the nature of the official response. The Foreign Office accepted the proposal, and Geddes was instructed to consider a vessel's guilt and the details of each case before determining a response to future seizures.[52] The ambassador exercised caution, carefully investigating each incident, and at least avoided the discomfort of defending non-British interests.[53]

Great Britain's policy of restraint did little to ease the burdens of the British smuggling connection. The link between British interests and a smuggling network that openly violated U.S. law remained intact. The Scotch whiskey industry exported its product to the Caribbean, and the quiet streets of Nassau were bustling reflections of the economic benefits of the liquor trade. The *Marshall* seizure challenged strategically important principles of international law, and a minor irritation was transformed into a potential source of diplomatic tension. The temporary calm created by Ambassador Geddes's moderation would continue only if the three-mile limit was not threatened. Foreign Office officials concluded that this now depended on the future policy of the United States.

Notes

[1]Michael Craton, *A History of the Bahamas* (London, 1962), 263–64.

[2]Paul Albury, *The Story of the Bahamas* (New York, 1975), 148–54; Craton, *History of the Bahamas,* 217–38; Horace J. Seymour, Minutes, April 28, 1920, A2598/2276/45, PRO; William Craig to Charles Evans Hughes, July 21, 1920, 811.114/BWI, General Records of the Department of State, Record Group 59, National Archives, Washington, DC (hereafter cited as RG 59, NA); *New York Times,* February 20, 1920.

[3]Herbert Asbury, *The Great Illusion: An Informal History of Prohibition* (Garden City, NY, 1950), 248.

[4]Andrews, *Whiskey Barons,* 130.

[5]Herbert W. Allen, *Number Three Saint James's Street* (London, 1950), 218–19; American Consulate, London, to State Department, May 30, 1923, 811.114/1559, RG 59, NA.

[6]Andrews, *Whiskey Barons,* 118; Wilson, *Scotch,* 144–45.

[7]Wilson, *Scotch,* 295–305; Brander, *Original Scotch,* 119–26; Percy Chaplin to Foreign Office, May 16, 1922, A3264/3264/45, PRO; Auckland Geddes to Hughes, July 27, 1922, A5096/3264/45, PRO; Geddes to Foreign Office, August 24, 1922, A5539/3264/45, PRO; Foreign Office, Memorandum, September 29, 1922, A6281/3264/45, PRO; Leslie Reed to Hughes, November 1, 1923, 811.114/3020, RG 59, NA.

[8]R. O. Matthews to Roy A. Haynes, March 24, 1922, copy in 811.114/954a, RG 59, NA; Hugh M. Bell, *Bahamas: Isles of June* (New York, 1934), 184–85, 194–99; Asbury, *Great Illusion,* 249; Ronald C. Lindsay to Foreign Office, April 16, 1920, A2609/2276/45, PRO; *New York Tribune,* May 16, 1920; *New York Times,* February 20,

[9]Lorin A. Lathrop to Hughes, June 9, 1921, 811.114/BWI/4, RG 59, NA; Bell, *Bahamas,* 185.

[10]Lathrop to Hughes, April 22, 1922, 811.114/BWI/70, RG 59, NA; Great Britain, Colonial Office, *Colonial Reports Annual–Bahamas, 1922–23* (no. 1192, London, 1924). There was no measurable increase in the islands' population during this period to account for any changes in domestic consumption of these imports.

[11]Craton, *History of the Bahamas,* 266–67; Asbury, *Great Illusion,* 180–81; Bell, *Bahamas,* 199-200; Lathrop to Hughes, October 15, 1921, 811.114/BWI/20, RG 59, NA.

[12]Statistical Department, Board of Trade, *Statistical Abstract for the Several Overseas Dominions and Protectorates, 1909-1923* (London, 1926), 40.

[13]William Hayward to Harry M. Daugherty, January 9, 1922, 23/3962/5, Classified Subject Files of the Department of Justice, Record Group 60, National Archives, Suitland, Maryland (hereafter cited as RG 60, NAS).

[14]Frederic F. Van de Water, *The Real McCoy* (Garden City, NY, 1931), 15; H. E. S. Cordeaux to Winston Churchill, October 3, 1921, copy in A2971/170/45, PRO; Lathrop to Hughes, October 6, 1921, copy in 23/1905/31, RG 60, NAS.

[15]D. L. Watt, *Personalities and Policies,* 38; Costigliola, "Anglo-American Financial Rivalry in the 1920s," 911-14; D. C. Watt, *Succeeding John Bull,* 48-49; Charles L. Mowat, *Britain between the Wars: 1918-1940* (London, 1955), 112-19.

[16]Rowland Sperling, Minutes, August 10, 1921, A5891/3560/45, PRO.

[17]The *Sarah E. Douglas,* a British-registered vessel, was boarded by Florida officials and the ship's deck was damaged. The British government was satisfied with the American explanation that the action was provoked by the crew. Colville Barclay to Frank L. Polk, May 8, 1919, 811.114/Great Britain/1, RG 59, NA. In 1920 an American bootlegger was kidnapped at Bimini by U.S. officials and brought to Baltimore to stand trial for illegal liquor activities. The British immediately protested but were appeased by a formal American apology. Colonial Office, Nassau, to Colonial Office, April 6, 1920, copy in A2276/2276/45, PRO; Lindsay to Foreign Office, April 16, 1920, A2609/2276/45, PRO; Foreign Office to Lindsay, April 17, 1920,

A2276/2276/45, PRO; Bainbridge Colby to Geddes, May 15, 1920, A3453/2276/45, and June 10, 1920, A4380/2276/45, PRO; Horace J. Seymour, Minutes, April 14, 1920, A2276/2276/45, and June 2, 1920, A3454/2276/45, PRO.

[18]Geddes to Foreign Office, May 11, 1921, A3560/3560/45, PRO; *New York Times,* April 14, 1921; *Times* (London), April 26, 1921.

[19]Sperling, Minutes, May 11, 1921, A3560/3560/45, PRO. See his comments in Minutes, April 14, 1920, A2276/2276/45, PRO.

[20]Foreign Office, Minutes, May 11, 1921, A3560/3560/45, PRO.

[21]Foreign Office to Colonial Office, June 2, 1921, A3560/3560/45, PRO; Geddes to Foreign Office, May 19, 1920, A3454/2276/45, PRO.

[22]Authorities in Bermuda did respond and curtailed a small smuggling operation on that island. Bermuda, *The Liquor Control Act of 1921* (no. 37—1921, Bermuda, 1922); Albert Swarm to State Department, October 18, 1921, 811.114/BWI/22, and July 1922, 811.114/89, RG 59, NA. Smuggling did not return to the island until after 1924.

[23]Lathrop to Hughes, October 15, 1921, 811.114/BWI/20, RG 59, NA, and October 6, 1921, copy in 23/1905/32, RG 60, NAS; Bell, *Bahamas,* 199–200; Craton, *History of the Bahamas,* 266–67; Lathrop to State Department, November 9, 1922, 811.114/BWI/117, RG 59, NA.

[24]Foreign Office, Report on the Seizure of British Vessels, July 13, 1922, A4512/170/45, PRO; *New York Times,* July 21, 1921.

[25]Cordeaux to Churchill, October 30, 1921, copy in A297/170/45, PRO; Colonial Office to Foreign Office, February 28, 1922, A1435/170/45, PRO.

[26]Gerald Campbell to Geddes, July 22, 1921, A5845/3560/45, PRO.

[27]Board of Trade, *Statistical Abstract,* 322.

[28]Foreign Office, Minutes, August 10, 1921, A5891/3560/45, PRO; D. C. Watt, *Succeeding John Bull,* 49–51; D. L. Watt, *Personalities and Policies,* 37–38.

[29]Sperling, Memorandum on Meeting, July 26, 1921, A4664/3560/45, PRO; Colonial Office to Foreign Office, August 10, 1921, A5891/3560/45, PRO.

[30]Sperling, Minutes, August 10, 1921, A5891/3560/45, PRO.

[31]For contemporary accounts of rum-running see James Barbican, *The Confessions of a Rum-Runner* (London, 1927); Gertrude C. Lythgoe, *The Bahama Queen* (New York, 1964); Van de Water, *Real McCoy.* Also *Grace and Ruby,* Box 31, *Henry L. Marshall,* Box 33, *Marion Mosher,* Box 50, all in Seized Vessels Files, Records of the United States Coast Guard, Department of the Treasury, Record Group 26, National Archives, Washington, DC (hereafter cited as Entry 291, RG 26, NA).

[32]Customs Memorandum, August 18, 1921, 811.114/BWI/9, RG 59, NA; Asbury, *Great Illusion,* 247–48; Lythgoe, *Bahama Queen,* 82; Harold Waters, *Smugglers of Spirit* (New York, 1971), 50–51. McCoy claimed that on one voyage to Rum Row he sold his cargo for a $150,000 profit. This same cargo would be sold on shore for double the value, and the profits finally would exceed $1.5 million after the liquor was cut and bottled. Van de Water, *Real*

McCoy, 26, 151. For a description of Rum Row see also Malcolm F. Willoughby, *Rum War at Sea* (Washington, DC, 1964); Robert Carse, *Rum Row* (New York, 1959).

[33]*Times* (London), July 29, 1921; Everett S. Allen, *The Black Ships* (Boston, 1965); Barbican, *Confessions of a Rum-Runner,* 18–19; Waters, *Smugglers of Spirit,* 52–53; Lythgoe, *Bahama Queen,* 93–99.

[34]*Times* (London), July 25, 1921; *New York Times,* July 21, 1921.

[35]Hayward to Daugherty, November 5, 1921, 23/1905/40, RG 60, NAS; E. S. Allen, *Black Ships,* 30–34.

[36]Enforcement was vested in the Treasury Department's Prohibition Unit, Customs Service, and Coast Guard. Willoughby, *Rum War,* 34; E. S. Allen, *Black Ships,* 46; Waters, *Smugglers of Spirit,* 55–56; Asbury, *Great Illusion,* 183.

[37]*Henry L. Marshall,* Box 33, Entry 291, RG 26, NA; Daugherty to Hughes, August 24, 1921, 311.4153/H39/3, RG 59, NA; Geddes to Foreign Office, August 4, 1921, A5728/3560/45, PRO; *New York Times,* August 4, 1921.

[38]Daugherty to Hughes, August 24, 1921, 311.4153/H39/3, RG 59, NA; *New York Times,* August 7, 1921.

[39]Foreign Office, Memorandum on Customs Act, January 18, 1922, A7298/903/45, PRO; C. John Colombos and Alexander P. Higgins, *The International Law of the Sea* (London, 1943), 64; Sayre A. Swarztrauber, *The Three Mile Limit of Territorial Seas* (Annapolis, 1972), 65, 70–71.

[40]Foreign Office, Memorandum respecting Maritime Jurisdiction, May 1918, copy in A7298/903/45, PRO; Swarztrauber, *The Three Mile Limit,* 85–86.

[41]Quoted in Foreign Office, Memorandum respecting the Seizure of Vessels outside the Three Mile Limit, March 2, 1923, A1297/65/45, PRO.

[42]Jessup, *Law of Territorial Waters,* 10, 18 n. 52; Colombos and Higgins, *Law of the Sea,* 45–46; Mowat, *Britain between the Wars,* 125–32, 259–83; D. C. Watt, *Succeeding John Bull,* 48–49; D. L. Watt, *Personalities and Policies,* 38; Costigliola, "Anglo-American Financial Rivalry in the 1920s," 911–14.

[43]Foreign Office, Memorandum of Customs Acts, January 18, 1922, A7298/903/45, PRO; Robert P. Skinner to Hughes, May 23, 1923, 811.114/1512, RG 59, NA; *Times* (London), May 23, 1923. See also Foreign Office, Report of Interdepartmental Committee, June 1923, T6883/69/350, F.O. 372, Foreign Office General Treaty Files, Public Record Office, Kew, London (hereafter cited as F.O. 372).

[44]Eyre Crowe, Minutes, September 1, 1921, A6381/3560/45, PRO; Robert Hadow, Minutes, September 1, 1921, ibid.

[45]Geddes to Foreign Office, August 8, 1921, A5776/3560/45, PRO; Gloster Armstrong to Geddes, August 3, 1921, copy in A5981/3560/45, PRO.

[46]Geddes to Hughes, August 11, 1921, A5998/3560/45, PRO. See also the Minutes in this file.

[47]"Memorandum relative to the *Henry L. Marshall,*" 1921, Folder 76A, Box 175, Charles Evans Hughes Papers, Manuscript Division, Library of Congress, Washington, DC (hereafter cited as Hughes Papers).

[48]Cordeaux to Churchill, October 3, 1921, copy in A297/170/45, PRO; Board of Trade to Foreign Office, October 13, 1921, A7499/3560/45, PRO; Seymour, Minutes, April 11, 1922, A2428/170/45, PRO. On June 1, 1922, the Foreign Office decided that the transfer of the *Marshall* was fraudulent and dropped further representations. Foreign Office, Report on Seizures, July 13, 1922, A4512/170/45, PRO; Lathrop to Daugherty, October 6, 1921, 23/1905/32, RG 60, NAS.

[49]Crowe, Minutes, September 1, 1921, A6381/3560/45, PRO; Foreign Office, Minutes, August 10, 1921, A5891/3560/45, PRO; Maurice Peterson, Minutes, November 16, 1922, A6956/903/45, PRO.

[50]Frank B. Kellogg to Hughes, March 6, 1924, 711.419/106, Microfilm Group M581, Roll 13, Record Group 59, General Records of the Department of State, National Archives, Washington, DC (hereafter cited as M581, RG 59, NA).

[51]Allen, *Great Britain and the United States,* 731; Beckles Willson, *Friendly Relations* (Boston, 1934), 329; Auckland Geddes, *The Forging of a Family* (London, 1952), 324–33.

[52]Foreign Office, Report on Seizures, July 13, 1922, A4512/170/45, PRO.

[53]Geddes to Foreign Office, October 10, 1921, A7728/3560/45, and December 30, 1921, A243/170/45, PRO; Geddes to Foreign Office, January 30, 1922, A1035/170/45, PRO; Foreign Office to Geddes, February 10, 1922, A933/170/45, PRO; Foreign Office, Report on Seizures, July 13, 1922, A4512/170/45, PRO; Geddes to Hughes, April 20, 1922, 311.4153/B46/5, RG 59, NA; Henry Chilton to State Department, August 31, 1922, 311.4153/B46/13, and February 2, 1923, 311.4153/B46/22, RG 59, NA; *New York Times,* November 3, 1921.

Chapter Two

American Uncertainty
The Harding Administration and Prohibition Enforcement 1921–1923

If the future direction of American antismuggling efforts was uncertain following the seizure of the *Henry L. Marshall*, Secretary of State Charles Evans Hughes at least indicated the course he would follow as the guardian of American foreign policy. At the Washington Naval Disarmament Conference, convened in November 1921 to resolve the question of Anglo-American naval rivalry, he clearly acknowledged that the new administration of Warren G. Harding was prepared to serve as a participant in world affairs. Under the banner of independent internationalism, Hughes advanced his notion of a collective and legalistic diplomacy, one in which decisions and agreements were made within the restrictions of logic, precedent, and the canons of international law. In securing naval parity with Great Britain and encouraging the end of the Anglo-Japanese alliance, Hughes demonstrated both his commitment to this idea and his desire to remove the obstacles to Anglo-American harmony. The success of the conference, hailed as a personal triumph for Hughes, restored to the State Department its lost initiative over foreign affairs and reestablished, after the disaster of Versailles, American respect for the collective efforts and legal obligations of international practice.[1]

The enforcement of the Eighteenth Amendment, however, threatened all of these achievements. The Coast Guard's seizure of foreign vessels beyond territorial waters ignored international law and diminished the legal foundations of American policy. As prohibition became a diplomatic problem, the involvement of advocates of unilateral action in the Treasury and Justice departments fostered bureaucratic disagreements that challenged the State Department's control of foreign affairs. The first seizure of a British-registered rumrunner created a new source of tension between the United States and Great Britain and discouraged harmony. Convinced that his intercession was essential, Secretary Hughes assumed an active role in the formulation of prohibition guidelines to ensure that American enforcement was consistent with foreign policy goals.

Hughes's decision to involve himself in prohibition enforcement was prompted by the seizure of the *Marshall*. The incident placed the secretary of state in the awkward position of defending an action taken without State Department approval. Justice Department officials acknowledged that the case "raises a question not apparently heretofore definitely settled, namely, whether any government has the right by legislation to extend its jurisdiction for any purpose beyond the limits of its territorial law." [2] But there was no interdepartmental discussion, and the vessel was libeled before the State Department was even informed of the seizure. Unable to reverse the legal condemnation, Hughes was forced to respond to the British protest. He firmly maintained that the libel was proper because it was based on laws similar to Great Britain's Hovering Acts. [3]

Behind this outward appearance of certainty, State Department officials expressed concern that the *Marshall* seizure was inconsistent with international law. Although U.S. support for the three-mile limit wavered throughout the nineteenth century, American claims never included a general denial of this principle. [4] As the United States became a stronger maritime power, its foreign policymakers, like their British counterparts, recognized the benefits of acknowledging a precise limit to a nation's territorial waters. In the Bering Sea controversy of 1911 and the North Atlantic Coast Fisheries arbitration, the United States signed agreements upholding the three-mile limit. [5] Secretary Hughes inherited a legacy that placed his country, at least since 1900, in a position second only to Great Britain in defending this principle.

With the diplomatic record challenging the validity of the *Marshall* action, Hughes postponed Anglo-American discussions on the incident and instructed his staff to reconsider the case. [6] In March 1922, State Department Solicitor Frank Neilson presented an evaluation of the *Marshall* seizure. Neilson concluded that the action was invalid under both international and domestic law because U.S. revenue laws allowed only for the searching of a vessel, and the British Hovering Acts were repealed in 1876. He recommended the adoption of new seizure guidelines that conformed with international law and urged Hughes to restrain enforcement officials from pursuing an indefensible policy. [7]

Secretary Hughes needed little convincing that the United States should respect international law. A former Supreme Court Justice, he reflected in his professional career a lifetime of legal study and an acceptance that justice transcended morality as the tradition that would bring order to society.[8] Hughes believed that international law provided this same rationale for the conduct of foreign affairs:

> Proof of the greatness of a state is sometimes manifested by the respect which it pays for the restraints of international law. The value of that respect as a salutary influence on the society of nations is enhanced in proportion to the power of the state concerned to do what it believes the law permits at a time when inaction seems harmful to local interests.[9]

Whatever the practical or political consequences, the precedent of American support for the three-mile limit and Neilson's report clearly outlined the secretary of state's responsibility. Hughes must assume the guardianship of the liquor issue, either as paternalistic educator or strict taskmaster, to ensure that prohibition enforcement recognized these restraints.

Before Hughes could act, the seizure of the British rumrunner *Grace and Ruby* provided the State Department with a clarification of policy. The Coast Guard had seized the vessel nine miles off the Massachusetts coast as the ship's crew members were transporting liquor to shore in a small boat.[10] When Solicitor Neilson drafted a rejection of libel proceedings because the vessel was beyond American waters, he discovered a precedent in international law supporting the Coast Guard's action. The *Araunah* arbitration decision, written by British statesman Lord Salisbury in 1888, had accepted the legality of seizing a vessel beyond the three-mile limit if its own equipment—that is, the ship's small boats—entered territorial waters. Salisbury argued that this did not challenge the validity of the three-mile principle. The concept of "constructive presence," which regarded any equipment as an extension of the ship itself, placed the primary vessel, by proxy, within territorial waters. Subsequent decisions in English law supported this definition and contributed to the general acceptance of Salisbury's precedent.[11]

Hughes agreed with Neilson that the *Araunah* precedent was significant, and he requested the Justice Department to proceed with the *Grace and Ruby* libel. Ambassador Geddes, informed of the legal action taken by the U.S. attorney in Boston against the *Grace and Ruby* and its owners, informed Hughes that the British government was not prepared to recognize either the *Araunah* precedent or this claim of extended jurisdiction. Privately, Foreign Office officials acknowledged that the American arguments, supported by English law, were difficult to refute, and Geddes did not lodge a formal protest.[12]

The British government's silence over the *Grace and Ruby* seizure strengthened the belief within the State Department that the *Araunah* arbitration provided a solid legal base for the new guidelines recommended by Solicitor Neilson. Although Secretary Hughes was prepared to accept an absolute adherence to the three-mile limit, this would have effectively prevented the seizure of all foreign rumrunners since these vessels operated beyond American waters. The *Araunah* decision, as applied in the *Grace and Ruby* case, suggested a wider interpretation of the circumstances for seizing foreign smugglers. Admittedly, this excluded rumrunners transferring liquor to independent small boats, yet it offered the best legal precedent that also ameliorated some of the practical difficulties encountered by enforcement officials in upholding international law. Hughes recognized the dual advantages of this, and he embraced the seizure limits established by Lord Salisbury as the State Department's definitive guideline for American prohibition enforcement.[13]

The secretary of state's acceptance of the *Araunah* precedent did not guarantee its adoption as the official policy of the Harding administration. The president allowed his cabinet secretaries to exercise considerable autonomy in their respective areas of responsibility; Harding rarely interfered and was reluctant to intervene when they disagreed.[14] While Hughes believed the seizure issue was a diplomatic problem, the perspective was markedly different at the Justice Department. Attorney General Harry M. Daugherty, charged with prosecuting rumrunners seized by the Coast Guard, recognized the political necessity of curtailing smuggling, and the goal of department officials was the establishment of a public record of successful prohibition convictions.[15] Consequently, the *Araunah* guideline was regarded as a shift in policy that restricted enforcement and placed many rumrunners, like the *Henry L. Marshall*, outside the Justice Department's jurisdiction. This sharp difference regarding the nature of American prohibition enforcement made interdepartmental warfare inevitable and provided a major barrier to the development of a consistent and cohesive antismuggling policy.

The State Department's major adversary in this battle was Assistant Attorney General Mabel Walker Willebrandt. A former California prosecutor and the first woman appointed to a subcabinet position, Willebrandt dominated the prohibition activities of the Justice Department with the support and confidence of Attorney General Daugherty.[16] Willebrandt's unflagging devotion to enforcing the Eighteenth Amendment and her flair for publicity won her the admiration of prohibitionists throughout the United States. With this dry support, Willebrandt exercised an influence over prohibition policy that extended beyond the corridors of the Justice Department and made her both a highly visible and formidable opponent.[17]

Willebrandt was determined to block State Department participation in the formulation of liquor policy. As an enforcement zealot, she advocated unilateral action and blamed the British government for the smuggling problem. She believed that Hughes's support for international law made effective prohibition enforcement impossible, and she criticized the State Department's willingness "to give 'aid and comfort' to the British Embassy."[18] Willebrandt urged the attorney general to request President Harding to settle the seizure debate. Confident of victory, she argued that "the time is ripe to thrash it out."[19] But Daugherty, lacking Willebrandt's zeal, was unwilling to confront the secretary of state.

Unable to gain total control over smuggling enforcement, Willebrandt decided to challenge Hughes on his own terms. She vigorously presented her own interpretation of international law, arguing that U.S. revenue laws provided the authority for the Coast Guard to seize foreign smugglers hovering beyond the three-mile limit. Willebrandt supported this claim with the legal precedent of *Church v. Hubbart* in which Chief Justice John Marshall supported the validity of jurisdiction over foreign vessels in marginal waters. Although international law scholars questioned the authority of this decision and it was repudiated by subsequent actions of the State Department, Willebrandt maintained that neither the revenue laws nor Marshall's opinion were ever decisively overruled by the courts or Congress. The Justice Department was obligated to support these precedents, she tersely noted in a memorandum to Daugherty, because diplomatic correspondence did not repeal a statute.[20]

State Department officials were now on the defensive. Despite the fact that Secretary Hughes asked the Justice Department to dismiss all cases not conforming with the *Araunah* precedent, these instructions were not followed and foreign rumrunners, not in contact with American waters through their own equipment, were still seized by the Coast Guard.[21] The secretary of state's difficulty in asserting his control over antismuggling policy was further compounded by developments on Capitol Hill. The expansion of the British smuggling connection aroused anglophobes and encouraged drys in Congress to attack this "national scandal."[22] Responding to the demand for stricter enforcement, Senator Thomas Sterling introduced an amendment to the Fordney-McCumber tariff bill to extend the jurisdiction of prohibition laws fifteen miles beyond U.S. territorial waters. After Hughes warned that passage of this amendment would have grave diplomatic consequences, Sterling offered a substitute measure.[23] The new provision, which was approved by Congress in September as part of the Tariff Act of 1922, authorized the Coast Guard to board and search all foreign vessels up to a distance of twelve miles from the coast, whether or not the vessel was bound for the United States, and to seize any vessel illegally unloading cargo.[24]

This was the first significant change in the seizure provisions of U.S. revenue laws since 1799. The net result differed little from Sterling's initial challenge to international law. It extended prohibition beyond the *Grace and Ruby* limits, a development that was equally unacceptable to State Department officials.[25]

Confronted with this congressional abrogation of international law, the besieged Hughes was prepared to force a resolution of the seizure question. Seven months of interdepartmental infighting produced an erratic and confusing policy. The passage of the Tariff Act of 1922 challenged the *Araunah* precedent, and its nationalistic overtones threatened Hughes's larger foreign policy goal of collectivism. Hughes needed to act quickly, and he received an unexpected endorsement from the U.S. District Court in Boston. On September 20, Judge James Morton announced his opinion in the *Grace and Ruby* libel, the first judicial consideration of extraterritorial seizures under the Eighteenth Amendment. Morton upheld Hughes's contention that a foreign vessel, hovering beyond three miles and in contact with the shore through its own equipment, could be seized.[26] State Department officials regarded the decision as a repudiation of Assistant Attorney General Willebrandt's claim that the courts had never considered the extraterritorial question.[27]

With this legal support, Hughes decided to secure a public clarification of the Harding administration's official enforcement policy. He raised the seizure issue at the next cabinet meeting, six days after the *Grace and Ruby* decision. Using his influence as the most respected member of the cabinet, Hughes persuaded President Harding to abandon his preferred role as conciliator and to choose between the State Department's and Willebrandt's positions.[28] Although the curtailment of the Coast Guard's antismuggling jurisdiction would have political repercussions, Hughes convinced Harding that the Justice Department's activities were inconsistent with American diplomacy and might force a direct confrontation with Great Britain. After the meeting, the president announced that U.S. revenue laws were not in harmony with international law and "could cause diplomatic embarrassments."[29] He instructed all Coast Guard personnel not to enforce the tariff act and to seize only those foreign vessels beyond the three-mile limit and in contact with the shore through their own boats, as in the *Grace and Ruby* case. Hughes monitored the implementation of the cabinet directive and forced the Justice Department to release foreign rumrunners seized outside the guidelines. The public spectacle of the U.S. government releasing known smuggling vessels demonstrated the extent of the secretary of state's success in anchoring American prohibition enforcement to international law.[30]

The true measure of Hughes's ability to resolve the seizure problem was the willingness of the British government to accept the *Araunah* precedent. Prior to the cabinet decision, British moderation on the seizure issue was based on the State Department's ability to restrict enforcement zeal and on the belief that Hughes was "thoroughly convinced of the necessity of Anglo-American cooperation."[31] But this conviction was shaken by months of American vacillation. Ambassador Geddes reported that President Harding's weak leadership encouraged independent action within the executive branch and allowed the schism over seizure guidelines to widen.[32] The passage of the Tariff Act and the expansion of Coast Guard activities persuaded the Foreign Office that prohibitionists in the United States were ascendant, dominating policy and encouraging the violation of international law. Foreign Office officials concluded that Hughes, incapable of withstanding the internal and external pressures of the drys, was now a lone voice of reason and they could no longer depend upon his tenuous leadership.[33]

This changed attitude was reflected in the Foreign Office reaction to the Harding administration's adoption of the *Araunah* precedent. Skeptical officials were convinced that the cabinet ruling was only the latest chapter in the bureaucratic struggle over prohibition enforcement, and they did not believe that their abandonment of Hughes was premature. Unable to deny the validity of the *Araunah* case and fearing Coast Guard abuse of the cabinet restrictions, the Foreign Office was determined to remove any certainty from the British position on extraterritorial seizures.[34] The formal response, delayed by the parliamentary elections in October that brought Bonar Law's Conservative government to power, was delivered in January 1923. The British refused to acknowledge the legality of the *Grace and Ruby* seizure and reserved the right to protest the capture of any British vessel under the new American guidelines.[35]

Throughout the spring, Hughes continued to belie the British perception of his declining leadership, and there were no serious seizure disputes. British officials, however, remained steadfast in the belief that American prohibition enforcement was the captive of domestic political pressures. The Harding administration's decision to base antismuggling limits on international law came too late to provide the foundation for an Anglo-American accord on the seizure question. By the time the secretary of state finally secured American restraint, British tolerance had waned. The failure to translate this potential into agreement guaranteed that the seizure of British ships beyond the three-mile limit remained an unresolved source of Anglo-American disagreement.

In many respects, Foreign Office officials overestimated the influence of the prohibition movement in the United States. The adoption of the Eighteenth Amendment was the climax of the dry crusade and largely a symbolic victory. Prohibitionist organizations could not sustain this momentum and proved incapable of coping with their success in achieving a legally dry America. Few prohibition leaders anticipated the monumental enforcement problems, and they were not prepared to maintain a vigilance against a resurgence of the liquor traffic. Without the capacity to continue to command a well-funded and broadly supported movement, dry groups were subjected to internal problems, a loss of public enthusiasm, and a decline in real power. Even the Anti-Saloon League, the most powerful dry organization in the United States, was subjected to financial difficulties and factional disputes over strategies for enforcing the Eighteenth Amendment.[36]

The British, however, accurately recognized that American liquor diplomacy was not free from the constraints of dry influence. Although support for prohibition began to decline in the early 1920s, this was hidden behind a facade of political power. The master of this illusion was Wayne B. Wheeler, the legislative superintendent of the Anti-Saloon League. He regarded the Eighteenth Amendment as a coercive weapon, and his zeal for law enforcement was unmatched. By helping to write the Volstead Act, Wheeler guaranteed that enforcement responsibility rested with elected officials, rather than with civil servants, whom the League could pressure. Wheeler, from his Washington office, worked diligently to maintain the political influence of the dry movement. He helped his dry friends in Congress, brilliantly used the press to attack his enemies, and nurtured a reputation as America's dry boss. Under Wheeler's guidance, the national political clout of the Anti-Saloon League still appeared awesome, and the League remained one of the most feared organizations in Washington.[37]

The development of an extensive smuggling network along the Atlantic seaboard placed Wheeler in an awkward position. During the debate over ratification of the Eighteenth Amendment, he steadfastly maintained that prohibition was an easily enforceable law and that policing costs would not exceed $5 million.[38] By 1921 it was already apparent that the public thirst for liquor did not disappear overnight. An extensive bootlegging operation flooded the illegal market with domestic liquor, and large quantities of foreign spirits were smuggled into the United States. Federal enforcement was an organizational nightmare, and Treasury officials announced that they would need 35,000 more enforcement officers to guard the coast and the borders. Daily press reports detailed the triumph of rumrunners and the growing frustration of the Coast Guard. National prohibition was quickly acquiring the image of a law that was widely ignored.[39]

The simple solution was to increase enforcement expenditures, but Wheeler recognized that to suggest that the law was unenforceable without a substantial injection of money was to deny its legitimacy. A full-scale enforcement campaign would repudiate his optimistic predictions and also might reveal the intensity of opposition to the Eighteenth Amendment. Consequently, Wheeler sought a public acknowledgment of temperance instead of the tangible reality of a dry society.[40] He used his clout on Capitol Hill to block any expansion of enforcement appropriations and diverted attention away from the inherent defects of the Eighteenth Amendment by highlighting the Harding administration's ineffective enforcement efforts. If only the Treasury Department vigorously enforced the law, Wheeler lamented, liquor smuggling would end.[41] While the drys eliminated most of the practical alternatives, they demanded that President Harding resolve the smuggling problem.

The Harding administration was already under attack from the Anti-Saloon League and other prohibition organizations. Despite Harding's public affirmation of support for the Eighteenth Amendment in 1920, drys remained skeptical about the president's moral commitment to national prohibition, and the rumor that liquor was served in the White House encouraged these doubts.[42] The positive dry reaction to the selection of Roy Haynes, the Anti-Saloon League's candidate, to direct the Treasury Department's Prohibition Unit was offset by the appointment of several "wets" to important posts in the administration. George Harvey, Harding's ambassador to Great Britain and a key player in any effort to suppress the British smuggling connection, openly opposed the Eighteenth Amendment. His continued criticism of prohibition prompted the New York Methodist Conference to censure him, and Wheeler demanded that the president restrain Harvey because "his utterances are being used by liquor interests in England as well as in this country."[43] Treasury Secretary Andrew Mellon, responsible for anti-smuggling operations, was an avowed wet and received the harshest condemnations for his enforcement failures.[44] Convinced that the administration lacked the zeal to defend the Eighteenth Amendment, the Anti-Saloon League and its dry supporters maintained their pressure on President Harding to enforce prohibition on land and sea.[45]

As Rum Row expanded during the spring of 1922, criticism of the Harding administration's antismuggling efforts intensified. Secretary Hughes's attempts to restrict American seizure policy, the absence of coordination between enforcement agencies, and corruption within the Coast Guard brought new charges of inadequate law enforcement. On Capitol Hill, Congress debated the smuggling issue, and Senator Sterling introduced his amendment to the Tariff Act. It was now politically necessary for President Harding to propose some measure to eliminate rum-running, yet the major enforcement handicap remained inadequate funding. Harding was unwilling to prod a disinterested Congress for more money or to challenge the Anti-Saloon League on this issue. Confronted with these obstacles and recognizing the liability of inaction, he sought an acceptable solution to an intractable problem.[46]

Harding focused on a proposal first broached by Senator Park Trammell in April. Writing to the president, Trammell recommended that the United States negotiate an agreement with Great Britain to end liquor exports from the Bahamas. His suggestion of British cooperation was not a new idea; anglophobes and unilateralists such as Assistant Attorney General Willebrandt had long placed the responsibility for smuggling with the British government.[47] But the externalization of enforcement problems offered a viable alternative to the administration's dilemma. Harding sent Trammell's letter to Secretary of State Hughes, acknowledging that "the illegal traffic in the transportation of intoxicating liquors from the Bahama Islands to the United States is growing to proportions of a national scandal" and reminding Hughes that a diplomatic agreement limiting exports "would be a helpful and much applauded accomplishment."[48]

For State Department officials, the major drawback of the president's suggestion was that it placed an unfair burden on Great Britain. The dry United States could not offer a similar ban on liquor exports; without any American concession, the British would not approve the agreement.[49] Appreciating Harding's desire for a diplomatic initiative, Hughes redrafted the recommendation to incorporate the ongoing Anglo-American disagreements over international law. In June he presented Ambassador Geddes with a proposal for negotiating an antismuggling agreement to allow the reciprocal searching of ships up to twelve miles from the coast. Hughes also requested that the British government investigate suspected rumrunners, carefully supervise the issuance of clearances, and deny registry transfers to Americans unless they possessed a U.S. Shipping Board certificate.[50]

The secretary of state's hope for a favorable response quickly faded when his treaty proposal was leaked to the press in July. The press reaction on both sides of the Atlantic was overwhelmingly negative, and several American newspapers criticized the State Department for requesting British assistance to enforce an American law.[51] The London *Sunday Times* concluded that it was "somewhat in the nature of a tall order when they suggest we should assist them by allowing our merchant vessels outside the three-mile limit to be seized," and the *Westminster Gazette* chided the United States for reversing its wartime support for the freedom of the seas.[52] Public debate was further encouraged by Prime Minister Lloyd George's initial refusal to acknowledge the proposal. When pressed in the House of Commons, he finally admitted that the Hughes request was under consideration.[53]

Privately, the British government had already dismissed the American treaty offer without discussion. Officials were not prepared to weaken the three-mile limit, and they did not believe that Hughes could protect the treaty against enforcement abuse. The arrival of Ambassador Geddes in late July delayed an immediate reaction, and Geddes convinced his colleagues to consider an alternative gesture to appease American public opinion.[54] Considering parliamentary criticism, drafting new legislation was politically impossible. Foreign Office attention focused on the request for stricter law enforcement in the Bahamas, the least defensible target of American criticism. Existing laws allowed questionable claims for British registry, and the Bahaman courts had adopted a narrow definition of collusion in registry cases, making it difficult to prevent Americans from obtaining British shipping papers.[55] Foreign Office and Board of Trade officials were prepared to accept Hughes's suggestion to deny British registry to any American without a Shipping Board certificate, but Bahaman authorities maintained that they were enforcing existing laws and Colonial Secretary Winston Churchill refused to consider this "excessive measure."[56] Unconvinced that it was necessary to assist the United States, Foreign Office officials were not prepared to force the issue.

In October, Ambassador Geddes presented the formal British reply to the American treaty offer. Although Great Britain was willing to cooperate in strictly enforcing all existing laws in the Bahamas, it had consistently opposed the extension of the three-mile limit, and the temporary nature of the smuggling trade did not justify the exceptions embodied in Hughes's proposal.[57] With the draft treaty rejected, the secretary of state lowered his expectations and attempted to enlist British assistance in sharing customs information, but this request also was denied.[58] Ambassador Geddes was prepared only to offer sympathy without substance. For the Harding administration, this was not enough to provide relief from criticism of the Anti-Saloon League.

Secretary Hughes's failure to secure a diplomatic solution to the smuggling problem was preordained. Unable to sustain the larger goals of Anglo-American harmony and a respect for international law that he espoused at the Washington Conference, Hughes could not convince the British that the United States was a responsible member of the international community. The protracted debate within the Harding administration over seizure limits, the congressional extension of the tariff laws, and the Anti-Saloon League's criticism of enforcement failures undermined the secretary of state's leadership. British officials continued to regard American foreign policy as inconsistent and subject to the demands of domestic political pressures.

Hughes also contributed to his own failure by adopting a narrow and legalistic posture. Raising the specter of extended territorial waters, he challenged a cardinal principle of British foreign policy. Hughes relied too heavily upon his false perception of the desire of British officials for American goodwill. The political difficulties inherent in any concession from London outweighed a concern for the American reaction to the rejection of smuggling cooperation. There was little recognition within the Foreign Office that enforcement assistance was necessary to protect British interests. Until this perspective changed, there was no compelling incentive for the British government to participate in a diplomatic solution to the smuggling problem.

Notes

[1]John Chalmers Vinson, "Charles Evans Hughes," in Norman A. Graebner, ed., *An Uncertain Tradition: American Secretaries of State in the Twentieth Century* (New York, 1961), 128–48; H. C. Allen, *Great Britain and the United States,* 733–41; Buckley, *United States and the Washington Conference*; Hoff-Wilson, *American Business and Foreign Policy,* 31–48; Leffler, *Elusive Quest,* 79; Offner, *Origins of the Second World War,* 74–84.

[2]Harry M. Daugherty to Charles Evans Hughes, August 24, 1921, 311.4153/H39/3, RG 59, NA; Robert Goff to Hughes, October 14, 1921, 23/1905/20, RG 60, NAS.

[3]Foreign Office, Report on Seizures, July 13, 1922, A4512/170/45, PRO; Goff to Hughes, October 14, 1921, 23/1905/20, RG 60, NAS.

[4]In the first Bering Seal Arbitration, the State Department argued that control, rather than strict jurisdiction, should go beyond three miles in the Bering Sea to protect the seal population. The claims were denied by the arbitration commission. Jessup, *Law of Territorial Waters,* 54–55. For a discussion of the American attitude toward the three-mile limit prior to 1900 see "The Three Mile Limit as a Rule of International Law," *Columbia Law Review* 23 (1923): 472–76; Swarztrauber, *Three Mile Limit,* 57–59, 92.

[5]Swarztrauber, *Three Mile Limit,* 117–21; "Foreign Liquor Ships outside the Territorial Belt," *Harvard Law Review* 36 (1923): 609–15.

[6]During the interim, the State Department pressed for the release of any foreign rumrunner seized beyond the three-mile limit. Justice Department, Memorandum for Assistant Attorney General Willebrandt, December 17, 1921, 23/1905/50, RG 60, NAS.

[7]Frank K. Neilson to Hughes, March 11, 1922, 311.4153/H39/23, RG 59, NA.

[8]For a discussion of Hughes's legal career see Glad, *Charles Evans Hughes*; Robert F. Wesser, *Charles Evans Hughes: Politics and Reform in New York, 1905-10* (Ithaca, 1967); Pusey, *Charles Evans Hughes,* vol. 1.

[9]Hughes to Phillip Marshall Brown, May 29, 1923, 811.114/1604, RG 59, NA; Charles Evans Hughes, *The Pathway of Peace* (New York, 1925); Vinson, "Charles Evans Hughes," 132–33, 148; Charles Cheney Hyde, "Charles Evans Hughes," in Samuel Flagg Bemis, ed., *The American Secretaries of State and Their Diplomacy,* 14 vols. (New York, 1958), 10:234; Herbert Hoover, *The Memoirs of Herbert Hoover,* 3 vols. (New York, 1952), 2:58.

[10]Mabel Walker Willebrandt to Daugherty, March 7, 1922, 23/2780/8, RG 60, NAS.

[11]William Vallance, Memorandum, March 15, 1922, 811.114/800, RG 59, NA; Willebrandt, Memorandum, March 15, 1922, 23/2780, RG 60, NAS.

[12]Foreign Office, Report on Seizures, July 13, 1922, A4512/170/45, PRO; Memorandum of Meeting with Auckland Geddes, January 4, 1923, Folder 77a, Box 175, Hughes Papers.

[13]In a later account of the liquor controversy, Hughes was silent on this shift in seizure definition. Charles Evans Hughes, "Recent Questions and Negotiations," *Foreign Affairs* 2 (February 1924): 1–7.

[14]Eugene P. Trani and David L. Wilson, *The Presidency of Warren G. Harding* (Lawrence, KS, 1977), 44–45; Francis Russell, *The Shadow of Blooming Grove* (New York, 1968), 448–50; Murray, *Harding Era,* 107–9.

[15]Willebrandt to Robert Wheat, July 9, 1923, 23/1905/171, RG 60, NAS; Dorothy M. Brown, *Mabel Walker Willebrandt: A Study of Power, Loyalty, and Law* (Knoxville, 1984), 80.

[16]Daugherty to Willebrandt, March 12, 1922, 23/2780/48, RG 60, NAS; Brown, *Mabel Walker Willebrandt,* 50, 73–76.

[17]Mabel Walker Willebrandt, *The Inside of Prohibition* (Indianapolis, 1929); Brown, *Mabel Walker Willebrandt,* 53–55, 81–116, 149–78.

[18]Willebrandt to Daugherty, October 3, 1922, copy in 811.114/1052, RG 59, NA; Brown, *Mabel Walker Willebrandt,* 80.

[19]Willebrandt to Daugherty, March 7, 1922, 23/2780/5x, RG 60, NAS; Willebrandt to Robert O. Harris, May 13, 1922, 23/2780/18, RG 60, NAS.

[20]Willebrandt to Hughes, September 28, 1922, 23/1905/119x, RG 60, NAS; Willebrandt to Daugherty, October 3, 1922, copy in 811.114/1052, RG 59, NA. Chief Justice Marshall argued in *Church v. Hubbart* that a state could exercise some control over waters beyond three miles, but Willebrandt ignored Marshall's assertion, in the same opinion, that the reasonableness of any extension would be determined by the extent to which the other nations acquiesce to it. Marshall was ambivalent over the question, denying the right of extension in *Rose v. Himley* in 1807 and then returning again to the *Church* opinion in later decisions. Jessup, *Law of Territorial Waters,* 57, 85.

[21]Willebrandt, Memorandum, March 15, 1922, 23/2780/48, RG 60, NAS; Willebrandt to Daugherty, March 7, 1922, 23/2780/5x, RG 60, NAS; Hughes to Daugherty, March 18, 1922, 23/2794/4, RG 60, NAS. A meeting was held in April to encourage interdepartmental coordination, but it was not successful. Justice Department, Memorandum, April 6, 1922, 23/2829/Part 1, RG 60, NAS; British Consulate, New York, to Foreign Office, August 4, 1922, A5249/170/45, PRO; Auckland Geddes to Foreign Office, September 22, 1922, A6085/903/45, and October 6, 1922, A6342/903/45, PRO; Vallance to Hughes, October 6, 1922, 811.114/1052, RG 59, NA.

[22]Willebrandt, Memorandum, June 1, 1922, 23/1905/276, RG 60, NAS; Willebrandt to George Tinkenham, March 9, 1922, 23/2829/18, RG 60, NAS. Ironically, Willebrandt received the brunt of the congressional criticism over seizures and the release of British rumrunners.

[23]Hughes to Thomas Sterling, August 16, 1922, 811.114/900, RG 59, NA.

[24]Sterling's bill became Section 581 of the Tariff Act of 1922 on September 21. *The Statutes at Large of the United States* (Washington, DC, 1923), 42:979; *Congressional Record,* 67th Cong., 2d sess. (August 19, 1922), 11593–96.

[25]Jessup, *Law of Territorial Waters,* 213–14; Jean Baptiste Duroselle, trans. Nancy L. Roelker, *From Wilson to Roosevelt* (Cambridge, MA, 1963), 149–50.

[26]*Federal Reporter* (St. Paul, MN, 1922), 283:475 (283 Fed 475). Morton did not mention the *Araunah* precedent. He based his opinion on the concept that the unloading of a ship continued until the cargo was landed. Jessup, *Law of Territorial Waters,* 245; *New York Times,* September 21, 1922.

[27]Willebrandt claimed in her autobiography that the *Grace and Ruby* guideline was her creation and that she convinced the State Department it was valid. Willebrandt, *Inside of Prohibition,* 244–46.

[28]Murray, *Harding Era,* 130–31; Pusey, *Charles Evans Hughes* 2:423–25; William Phillips, *Ventures in Diplomacy* (Boston, 1952), 113; Glad, *Charles Evans Hughes,* 133; Vinson, *Parchment Peace,* 75; Murray, *Politics of Normalcy,* 33.

[29]Report on the President's Press Conference, September 26, 1922, 23/2829/Part 1, RG 60, NAS; *New York Times,* September 27, 1922. Ambassador Geddes met with Hughes the day before the cabinet meeting and warned him, informally, that any more violent seizures would create serious diplomatic problems. Memorandum on Meeting with Auckland Geddes, September 25, 1922, Folder 76a, Box 175, Hughes Papers.

[30]Hughes to Justice Department, October 18, 1922, 23/3902/16, RG 60, NAS; Justice Department, Memorandum, October 19, 1922, 23/2794/19, RG 60, NAS; William Phillips to Daugherty, October 30, 1922, 23/3206/16, RG 60, NAS; Vallance, Memorandum, November 17, 1922, 811.114/*Marion Mosher*/23, RG 59, NA; Robert Lovett to William Hayward, October 26, 1922, 23/3962/12, RG 60, NAS; Hughes to Daugherty, October 26, 1922, 23/2794/17, and October 28, 1922, 23/3206/18, RG 60, NAS; Vallance, Memorandum, November 4, 1922, 811.114/*Marion Mosher*/4, RG 59, NA; Willebrandt to Hughes, September 26, 1922, 811.114/*Marion Mosher*/1, RG 59, NA; Vallance, Memorandum, September 30, 1922, 811.114/*Marion Mosher*/3, RG 59, NA; Justice Department to Hayward, October 30, 1922, 23/3206/14, RG 60, NAS. Smuggling did increase after the cabinet decision. *New York Times,* November 4, 1922.

[31]"Report of American Debt Funding Commission," 1923, File 3B, Vol. 109, Stanley Baldwin Papers, Cambridge University Library, Cambridge, England (hereafter cited as Baldwin Papers); Rowland Sperling, Minutes, September 25, 1922, A5981/903/45, PRO; Geddes, *Forging of a Family,* 328.

[32]Geddes to Foreign Office, September 23, 1922, A5926/903/45, and November 2, 1922, A6849/903/45, PRO; British Embassy, Washington, to Foreign Office, September 22, 1922, A6085/903/45, PRO; Geddes to Foreign Office, September 19, 1922, A5907/903/45, and September 25, 1922, A5891/903/45, PRO.

[33]Montague Shearman, Minutes, September 21, 1922, A5907/903/45, PRO. Foreign Office officials also were concerned that the seizure issue might be decided by the Supreme Court. Reliance on Hughes had limited the diplo-

matic record to informal representations. Memorandum on Meeting with Auckland Geddes, September 25, 1922, Folder 76a, Box 175, Hughes Papers; Maurice Peterson, Minutes, November 17, 1922, A7419/903/45, PRO.

[34]Horace Seymour, Minutes, November 2, 1922, A6849/903/45, PRO; Shearman, Minutes, September 21, 1922, A5907/903/45, PRO; Foreign Office, Minutes, November 16, 1922, A6956/903/45, PRO; Maurice Peterson, Minutes, May 2, 1922, A3211/903/45, PRO; Foreign Office, Memorandum respecting the Seizure of British Vessels, March 2, 1923, A1297/65/45, PRO.

[35]Memorandum on Meeting with Auckland Geddes, January 4, 1923, Folder 77a, Box 175, Hughes Papers; Geddes to Foreign Office, January 24, 1923, A734/65/45, PRO. For details of the 1922 parliamentary election see Robert Rhodes James, *The British Revolution: British Politics, 1880–1939*, 2 vols. (London, 1977), 2:159–66.

[36]Gusfield, *Symbolic Crusade*, 120–22; Kyvig, *Repealing Prohibition*, 26–32; Kerr, *Organized for Prohibition*, 10, 251-54.

[37]Gusfield, *Symbolic Crusade*, 119–20; Kerr, *Organized for Prohibition*, 10–11, 121, 214–16, 220–26, 242; Kyvig, *Repealing Prohibition*, 29–30; Clark, *Deliver Us from Evil*, 112–17.

[38]Kyvig, *Repealing Prohibition*, 20; Charles Merz, *The Dry Decade* (Garden City, NY, 1930), 51–52, 82–83; *New York Times*, April 15, 1920.

[39]Brown, *Mabel Walker Willebrandt*, 53–55; Kyvig, *Repealing Prohibition*, 26–32.

[40]Clark, *Deliver Us from Evil*, 157; Gusfield, *Symbolic Crusade*, 120–22.

[41]Merz, *Dry Decade*, 129; Andrew Sinclair, *Prohibition: The Era of Excess* (Boston, 1962), 273–74; Wayne B. Wheeler to Warren G. Harding, June 2, 1922, Frame 732, Roll 168 (732/168), Warren G. Harding Papers, Microfilm edition, Ohio Historical Society, Columbus, Ohio (hereafter cited as Harding Papers); *New York Times*, November 30, 1921.

[42]*Speeches of Warren G. Harding of Ohio* (Washington, DC, 1920); Sinclair, *Era of Excess*, 258; Trani and Wilson, *Presidency of Warren G. Harding*, 179; Hughes to S. George Baker, May 1, 1923, Folder "Harding," Box 24, Hughes Papers. For a discussion of Harding's earlier views on prohibition see Randolph C. Downes, *The Rise of Warren Gamaliel Harding, 1865–1920* (Columbus, 1970), 279–83, 490–502; Murray, *Harding Era*, 11.

[43]Wheeler to Harding, March 6, 1922, 182/205, Harding Papers; *New York Times*, April 4, 1922; Willis F. Johnson, *George Harvey: A Passionate Patriot* (Boston, 1929), 346–47. Wheeler also questioned Secretary of State Hughes's personal commitment to the dry cause. Wheeler to Hughes, February 6, 1922, Folder "Wh-Wi General," Box 48, Hughes Papers.

[44]Wheeler to Harding, June 2, 1922, 732/168, and April 27, 1923, 42/169, Harding Papers; Justin Steuart, *Wayne Wheeler: Dry Boss* (New York, 1928), 170–71; Kerr, *Organized for Prohibition*, 227; Brown, *Mabel Walker Willebrandt*, 54.

[45]Steuart, *Wayne Wheeler*, 172–75; Sinclair, *Era of Excess*, 257; Murray, *Harding Era*, 403–5; Russell, *Shadow of Blooming Grove*, 440–41.

[46]Murray, *Harding Era*, 406–7; Trani and Wilson, *Presidency of Warren G. Harding*, 179; Asbury, *Great Illusion*, 163; Sinclair, *Era of Excess*, 182.

Harding later considered using the U.S. Navy to assist the Coast Guard, but the plan was dropped because it required congressional approval. Harding to Augustus Seymour, April 25, 1923, 643/168, Harding Papers; Albert Ottinger to George Christian, April 17, 1923, 211/169, Harding Papers.

[47]Harding to Park Trammell, April 5, 1922, 832/168, Harding Papers; *New York Times,* March 13, 1922; New York Methodist Episcopal Conference, "Report on Temperance," April 3, 1922, copy in 718/168, Harding Papers.

[48]Harding to Hughes, April 5, 1922, 831/168, Harding Papers.

[49]Trammell to Hughes, April 3, 1922, 811.114/Great Britain/32, RG 59, NA; Solicitor's Office, State Department, to Hughes, April 6, 1922, 811.114/Great Britain/33, RG 59, NA. Hughes denied an earlier report of a pending liquor treaty. *New York Times,* March 13, 1922.

[50]Note to the British Government, June 26, 1922, Folder 47, Box 173, Hughes Papers.

[51]Phillips to Hughes, July 28, 1922, 811.114/Great Britain/26, RG 59, NA; *New York Times,* July 25, 1922; *Literary Digest* 74 (August 12, 1922): 10–11.

[52]*Sunday Times* (London), July 30, 1922; *Westminster Gazette* (London), July 28, 1922. See also *Daily Telegraph* (London), July 29, 1922; *Daily Express* (London), July 29, 1922; *Evening Standard* (London), July 27, 28, 1922.

[53]*Parliamentary Debates* (Commons), 5th series, 157:996; Hughes to American Embassy, London, July 28, 1922, 811.114/Great Britain/25a, RG 59, NA. The British did send an interim reply on August 9 stating that the matter was being carefully considered. Henry Chilton to Hughes, August 9, 1922, 811.114/Great Britain/28, RG 59, NA.

[54]Sperling to Board of Trade, July 24, 1922, A4418/903/45, PRO; Chilton to Arthur Balfour, June 30, 1922, ibid.

[55]Daniel Tudor to Colonial Governor, April 8, 1922, copy in A4806/903/45, PRO; Colonial Office, Precis on Efforts to Prevent Smuggling in the Bahamas, July 27, 1922, ibid.

[56]Churchill offered to accept the absence of the certificate as "suspicious" and subject to evaluation in London. Board of Trade to Foreign Office, July 27, 1922, A4806/903/45, PRO; Foreign Office to Colonial Office, July 27, 1922, ibid.; Board of Trade to Foreign Office, August 11, 1922, A5159/903/45, and August 29, 1922, A5452/903/45, PRO; Colonial Office to Foreign Office, August 30, 1922, A5461/903/45, PRO.

[57]Geddes to Hughes, October 13, 1922, 811.114/Great Britain/39, RG 59, NA; Foreign Office to Geddes, September 30, 1922, A5461/903/45, PRO. Bahaman officials did investigate suspected smugglers, discovering that most Americans on this list had U.S. Shipping Board certificates of "good character." Colonial Office to Foreign Office, December 18, 1922, A7597/903/45, PRO.

[58]Hughes to American Embassy, London, March 29, 1923, 811.114/1322, RG 59, NA; Post Wheeler to Foreign Office, May 31, 1923, A3258/34/45, PRO; Wheeler to Hughes, May 31, 1923, 811.114/1501, June 14, 1923, 811.114/1568, and June 1, 1923, 811.114/1558, RG 59, NA.

Chapter Three

"Puritanism Run Mad"
Shipping and Prohibition
1919–1923

In May 1922 an editorial appeared in the *Chicago Tribune* addressing the subject of prohibition and shipping. The editorial, highlighting the ongoing shipping rivalry between the United States and Great Britain, suggested that the U.S. Shipping Board's passenger liners were now part of the nation's defense. With limits placed on the size of American naval forces by the Washington Naval Disarmament Conference, these passenger ships, easily converted into cruisers and transports, were an essential auxiliary for the navy. But the operation of passenger liners, the editorial continued, depended upon wealthy travelers, and "most people of wealth will not submit to American prohibition laws when they leave the United States...not many of them will travel on American boats if on them prohibition spreads all over the seas." Therefore, the author concluded, the Shipping Board was justified in making the success of the mercantile marine its first consideration and in serving liquor on American ships "just as it is served on the ships of other flags."[1]

The *Chicago Tribune* editorial signaled that there was a new reality in Anglo-American liquor tensions. While the United States and Great Britain continued to disagree over the extension of the Eighteenth Amendment beyond the three-mile limit, the recognition that the sale of liquor on passenger ships was a financial necessity transformed the question of legal control *within* the three-mile limit into a more serious problem. The controversy revolved around two parallel concerns: whether the Volstead Act prevented British and other foreign vessels from carrying liquor in U.S. waters under any conditions, and if Eighteenth Amendment restrictions extended to American ships wherever they sailed.

This was not simply a matter of legal abstractions. Whatever compromises the British were prepared to accept in their commercial rivalry with the United States, shipping remained an important factor in the restoration of their prewar supremacy. In the United States, nationalists regarded a revitalized merchant marine as a reflection of America's power. The possibility that shipping and prohibition enforcement were incompatible radically redefined the prohibition issue and injected an economic dimension into Anglo-American liquor diplomacy.

The potential impact of national prohibition on shipping was not immediately apparent. Although the Eighteenth Amendment outlawed the transportation of liquor into U.S. territory, the geographic limits of this restriction were not defined by the vague language of the amendment. The Volstead Act prevented the import and export of distilled spirits without a permit, yet it was uncertain whether this included only duty-payable goods manifested for delivery in the United States or any liquor brought into American territory. Congress specifically exempted the Panama Canal from the prohibition laws, suggesting that there was an implied congressional intent not to interfere with foreign shipping, and the Treasury Department's regulations offered no clarification.[2]

The issue was not raised until one month after the implementation of the Volstead Act. The Chamber of Shipping of the United Kingdom requested the Foreign Office to obtain the procedures for passenger and cargo vessels bringing liquor into the United States. The Chamber was concerned because British cargo ships carrying distilled spirits to other destinations frequently refueled in American ports. Also, British law required minimum liquor sea stores for crew members and for medicinal purposes on all vessels. State Department officials informed Ambassador Geddes that all liquor on British ships placed in customs seal within the three-mile limit could enter U.S. territory. These guidelines, while inconvenient, did not impede commerce, and the British shippers willingly complied.[3]

The continued flow of liquor into the United States, whatever the restrictions, outraged the Anti-Saloon League, and Wayne Wheeler began a dry crusade to end this privilege. Wheeler claimed that the Eighteenth Amendment was framed to keep all distilled spirits out of the United States, and he used his political clout to force the Justice Department to reconsider this question.[4] During the final weeks of the Wilson administration, Acting Attorney General Frank Niebeker unexpectedly announced that carrying in-transit liquor into U.S. territory was a violation of the prohibition laws. In the absence of any expressed congressional sanction for these sealed cargoes, Niebeker concluded, they were illegal.[5]

Foreign Office officials and British shippers were angered by Niebeker's failure to hold a public hearing on this issue. Under the limits of his ruling, a British vessel carrying distilled spirits from Liverpool to Havana could no longer make a stopover in an American port. Liquor was usually only one of many types of cargoes transported in a single voyage, and the restrictions would create considerable economic burdens if shippers were forced to alter their established trade routes.[6] When the Harding administration took office in March 1921, Ambassador Geddes urged Secretary of State Hughes to reopen the transshipment question. At Hughes's request, Attorney General Daugherty agreed to hold formal hearings, and the Treasury Department rescinded the transshipment regulations until there was a new ruling.[7]

Considering the pressure from the Anti-Saloon League, the hearing was primarily an exercise in courtesy. Daugherty politely listened to the legal representatives of Cunard's Anchor Line and of the Canadian distiller Hiram Walker argue that Congress did not intend to prevent transshipments and warn of possible retaliation.[8] But on June 2 he announced that Niebeker's ruling was valid and the Eighteenth Amendment outlawed transshipment of liquor through U.S. territory. Treasury officials promptly reissued regulations forbidding this practice.[9]

Daugherty's decision was first enforced in August when customs officials in New York attempted to confiscate whiskey transferred between two Anchor Line ships that were docked in port. The Anchor Line was granted a temporary injunction against the seizure until the U.S. District Court ruled on the legality of this action. After the Hiram Walker Company filed a companion suit, Treasury officials revoked enforcement instructions to prevent additional legal challenges.[10] Although the court upheld Daugherty's ruling in October and removed the injunction, the attorneys for the Anchor Line and Hiram Walker immediately appealed the case to the U.S. Supreme Court.[11] Treasury Secretary Andrew Mellon extended the suspension of transshipment restrictions pending a final ruling on the appeal. Wheeler condemned Mellon's action and complained that "I cannot understand his position in this case...the law is clear."[12] For the present, the Harding administration was not responsible for clarifying the law.

Throughout the transshipment controversy, the Foreign Office maintained a low profile. American Department officials blamed both prohibitionists and American shipping interests for Daugherty's ruling, regarding it as an attempt "to neutralize to a large extent the advantage we enjoy at present over U.S. ships."[13] They were reluctant to protest this attack on British commerce, however, because of an appreciation of the fundamental weakness of Great Britain's position. The sole restraint

on a nation's actions in its own territorial waters was international comity, which reflected the notion that the national peculiarities of customs
and law made it essential for ships to abide by the rules of their own
flag. Both the United States and Great Britain endorsed the concept
that, within the three-mile limit, only questions of safety, health, and the
maintenance of public order brought a foreign vessel under the host
nation's jurisdiction. This practice, however, was not a principle of international law. While international law evolved from the written record
of international disputes, comity was the unwritten civility of a hand-
shake. The law was based on legal precedents and recognized principles
that could be defended before an international tribunal. Comity was
extended as a courtesy, and the sole deterrent to its withdrawal was
retaliatory action by the aggrieved nation.[14]

The seizure of the *Henry L. Marshall* in August 1921 further complicated the British government's position on the transshipment issue. In
arguing that the United States could not seize foreign vessels beyond
three miles, the British government tacitly brought the prohibition laws
to the edge of this limit and accepted the validity of American control
within this area. Whatever the dispute over enlarging enforcement jurisdiction, there was never any question of narrowing this authority. International law supported the claim that the U.S. government could exercise
the same clear title in waters extending three miles from the coast, as it
did on land. Officials at the Foreign Office and the Board of Trade
accepted this fact and remained in the background of the transshipment
debate, hoping that the legal efforts of the shippers would resolve the
problem.[15]

On May 15, 1922, the Supreme Court upheld Attorney General
Daugherty's ruling. In a 6-to-3 decision, the Court asserted that "the
Eighteenth Amendment meant a great revolution in the policy of this
country and presumably and obviously meant to upset a good many
things on as well as off the statute books."[16] Even without a specific
provision against transshipments, wrote Justice Oliver Wendell Holmes
for the majority, Congress intended to stop the whole liquor business.
The *Anchor v. Aldridge* decision raised more questions than it resolved.
The opinion did not consider the broader issue of international comity
and created uncertainty over the precise meaning of transshipments.
Daugherty and Niebeker had used the term in a general sense to include
any liquor cargoes passing through American waters. The suit brought
by the Anchor Line was based on the specific seizure of liquor transferred between two British ships in port, and this definition excluded
most British shipping from the ruling. With this key question unanswered, the transshipment question was once again subject to the
interpretation of the Treasury Department.[17]

The confusion created by the Supreme Court's opinion caused considerable concern within the British embassy in Washington. If Treasury Department regulations reflected a broad reading of the ruling, the liquor sea stores that supplied crew and passengers on transatlantic voyages would be prohibited from entering U.S. waters. Although American Department officials were unconvinced that the United States would adopt these rigid restrictions, Ambassador Geddes's warnings alarmed British shipping interests.[18] British shippers, forced to redirect their cargo trade to comply with U.S. law, were not prepared to remove all liquor from their ships. As Ashley Sparks, Cunard's agent in New York, noted, "the mere possession of wines and spirits by foreign ships in American waters has not yet been raised, but I may say that it is a possibility that is causing us some concern. Our best line of action at the moment is to keep quite still and not raise the issue."[19]

The future interpretation of the transshipment decision assumed a heightened significance because of the ongoing shipping rivalry between the United States and Great Britain. Following the First World War, there was a renewed sense of American confidence in the idea that the United States should assume its proper role as a great maritime power. The war had exposed both the inability of American shipping to provide adequate transportation for the exploitation of new markets and the futility of war preparedness without a vital merchant fleet.[20] The result was the creation of the U.S. Shipping Board (USSB) to encourage the construction and purchase of ships during the wartime emergency. When the Paris Peace Conference revealed the intensity of the British conviction to preserve shipping dominance, shipping proponents in Congress appealed for patriotic support to battle "the most determined and the fiercest competition of those long established in the business."[21] They secured the passage of legislation to extend the life of the USSB and to empower it to guarantee an American presence, either privately or by direct governmental operation, in all major sea-lanes.

By the time President Harding was inaugurated in 1921, the American challenge to British shipping hegemony had encountered serious difficulties. With new construction and the addition of former German vessels, the USSB controlled a large fleet, involved in cargo and passenger service, at a time of recession in international trade. This glut in world shipping hit the fledgling American fleet the hardest, and one-third of the vessels were idle. There was little private purchasing of ships, forcing the government to operate the bulk of the shipping lines. Moreover, the shipping program suffered from administrative mismanagement, a system of guaranteed commissions offered little incentive for profitability, and the USSB was a financial and bureaucratic nightmare.[22]

As an advocate of "America First," Harding was committed to transforming the United States into "the leading maritime nation of the world."[23] The difficult task of rebuilding the merchant marine rested with Albert Lasker, Harding's appointee to the chairmanship of the USSB. Lasker, a former campaign adviser and advertising wizard, was intemperate, cloaked his arguments in a banner of patriotism, and had no previous experience in shipping.[24] But he shared Harding's belief in the need for a viable merchant marine and developed a new plan. Lasker proposed the establishment of a fund to provide subsidies to encourage the private purchase of USSB vessels. President Harding, impressed by the promise of greater economy and a revitalized mercantile marine, submitted the ship subsidy proposal to Congress in March 1922. Rallying the shipping community and exploiting American anglophobia, Lasker embarked on a campaign to persuade Congress that the subsidy plan was the only hope for defending the merchant marine against the onslaught of Great Britain's shipping menace.[25]

The subsidy legislation sent shock waves through a British shipping industry already alarmed by the American shipping challenge. Prior to the First World War, Great Britain claimed the world's largest mercantile marine, which accounted for one-half of the world's shipping tonnage and was four times larger than its nearest rival. The wartime disruption of trade routes and the considerable loss of ships, however, seriously weakened this advantage.[26] As the leader, British shipping had the most to lose from foreign competition, and the industry was burdened by the impact of the worldwide shipping surplus and lower profits. Liner trade suffered from a decline in merchandise exports, reduced immigration, and the growth of state-assisted fleets. The rebuilding of British shipping, according to a Board of Trade report, required the London government to concentrate all its resources on this formidable challenge. British shipping, Board of Trade officials concluded, was vital to national survival, and "the maritime ascendancy of the Empire must be maintained at all costs."[27]

Working through the Liverpool Steamship Owners Association, the major shipping lines sent representatives to discuss this new American threat with Sir Charles Hipwood, director of the Board of Trade's Mercantile Marine Department and the industry's leading friend in Whitehall. The shippers expressed the concern that the Lasker plan would diminish their competitive strength, and they demanded that the Foreign Office immediately protest the proposal.[28] Foreign Office officials, fearing that the specter of British interference would aid the subsidy supporters, were reluctant to endorse any strong public response, but the government could not ignore the intensive lobbying of the shippers and the growing unemployment in the shipbuilding industry. On June 30 the British cabinet approved a provisional plan of retaliation. If necessary, the government was prepared to respond to any escalation in Anglo-American shipping tensions.[29]

A major arena in the ongoing Anglo-American shipping rivalry was the North Atlantic passenger trade. It was the most important passenger service in the world, and the Cunard Company had initiated a postwar program of new construction to expand its passenger fleet.[30] At the same time, the USSB, through its control of the United States Lines, provided new competition in the transatlantic service. Although the American lines were losing money, Lasker maintained a presence in the North Atlantic because it encouraged cargo trade and enhanced the prestige of American shipping.[31] He also anticipated the addition of a new flagship for the United States Lines, the refitted German liner *Vaterland*, scheduled for delivery in 1923. Lasker believed that the addition of this second largest passenger vessel in the world, renamed the *Leviathan*, would be "a powerful factor in the trans-Atlantic fleet so necessary for the development of an American merchant fleet."[32]

The one issue that united British shippers and the USSB was the recognition that the unrestricted sale of liquor on passenger ships was an economic necessity. The decline in immigration traffic sailing to the United States, hastened by the passage of the Emergency Quota Act in 1921, led to the conversion of empty third-class cabins into a new tourist class. With affluent Americans enthusiastically embarking on a European grand tour, carriage was out and comfort was now the accepted standard of travel. An essential component in providing shipboard amenities was a well-stocked liquor supply. For thirsty Americans, an impressive wine list on a transatlantic voyage was an appealing attraction, offering a respite from the noble experiment at home. Liquor, not patriotism or experience, emerged as an important factor in the transatlantic competition.[33]

The USSB appreciated the value of shipboard liquor. Anticipating the implementation of the Volstead Act in 1919, USSB officials began considering the impact of this law. Shipping Board members, unlike prohibitionists, entertained few illusions about the naive expectation that morally inspired Americans would flock to liquorless ships. They also recognized that the enactment of national prohibition made it both inconsistent and politically inexpedient for a governmental agency to operate wet ships and offend the Anti-Saloon League.[34]

In October the Executive Operating Committee requested the USSB's Legal Department to evaluate the legality of liquor on American ships after the Volstead Act became effective. The assistant general counsel concluded that it was probably legal, under the Eighteenth

Amendment, for ships to sell liquor on the high seas and bring these supplies, if they were sealed, into U.S. territory. The committee decided, however, to seek a more authoritative ruling from the U.S. attorney general. Until this was received, all liquor was barred from USSB ships as of January 1, 1920.[35]

USSB Chairman John Barton Payne was increasingly pessimistic about the future of passenger shipping. Discussions with congressional leaders convinced him that, even if liquor was allowed under the law, Congress would prevent government-operated vessels from sharing in this benefit.[36] At the next meeting of the board, Payne announced plans to sell the former German liners acquired by the USSB after World War I, admitting that "the Shipping Board could not compete with private firms, because of the fact that private firms could serve wines and liquors."[37] Payne's efforts, however, were frustrated by the worldwide shipping slump which dampened private interests, and the USSB remained saddled with a passenger fleet destined for certain unprofitability unless the sale of liquor on ships was made legal.

This option was eliminated in November 1920 when the Justice Department ruled that prohibition applied to American ships wherever they sailed. Private shippers appealed the decision at a Treasury Department hearing, arguing against the issuance of regulations to enforce the ruling. "The threatened enforcement of prohibition," J. Parker Kirlin of the American Steamship Owners Association testified, "is a force of overwhelming effect in deterring investors from embarking upon private ownership of property that is certain to be so hampered by it as to be unprofitable in operation."[38] Congressional supporters of shipping introduced legislation to allow liquor on American ships, but Wheeler and the Anti-Saloon League mobilized the drys in Congress to block consideration of the bill.[39] Although the Treasury Department failed to issue any regulations to enforce the ruling, USSB officials regarded it as definitive and reasserted that there was no change in their liquorless policy.[40]

This was the situation Lasker inherited when he became chairman of the USSB in June 1921. With the transshipment question still awaiting judicial review, British ships operated unfettered by regulations while USSB passenger vessels sailed without liquor. As the new chairman formulated his subsidy plan to create a strong merchant fleet, liquor was an unwelcome complication. The argument for rebuilding a potentially profitable passenger fleet through subsidies, already a tenuous proposition, was weakened further if the absence of liquor contributed to an unfair competition. Lasker needed either to guarantee that USSB ships shared equally in the amenities of liquor or that British vessels also were denied this privilege.[41]

Without seeking the approval of his fellow commissioners, Lasker decided to reinstitute the sale of liquor on USSB vessels.[42] It was an audacious decision, considering both the Harding administration's legal responsibility to enforce prohibition and the previous policy of the agency. Lasker's task was to prevent any public debate over the new policy, while making it known that USSB ships now carried liquor. Advertisements began to appear in the Paris edition of the *New York Herald* announcing that the United States Lines carried "the choicest wines and liquors."[43] Complaints about the advertisements were deflected with vagueness and misstatement. D. E. Brundage, USSB advertising manager, calmly assured Assistant Attorney General Willebrandt in October that, "of course, the Shipping Board is unalterably opposed to the sale of liquor on American ships."[44]

For almost a year, Lasker managed to sidestep this contradiction. Letters from passengers protesting the presence of liquor on USSB vessels were ignored, and Vice-Chairman J. B. Small instructed staff members not to respond to press inquiries, "for really we know nothing of the working out of the details of this item."[45] Despite this official policy of silence, the rumor of wet ships continued. In May 1922 the *Chicago Tribune, Newark Evening News, St. Louis Daily Globe-Democrat,* and the Philadelphia *Public Ledger* all published reports that liquor was sold on USSB passenger ships. The Anti-Saloon League received a growing number of complaints about liquor on these vessels, and Wheeler wrote to Lasker demanding a denial of these allegations.[46] Before he could respond, Lasker's day of reckoning finally arrived.

Ironically, the public challenge to the USSB liquor policy did not come from the prohibitionists. It was initiated by Augustus Busch, president of the Anheuser-Busch brewery and vocal opponent of the Eighteenth Amendment. Sailing to Europe on the USSB liner *George Washington*, Busch discovered:

> The Shipping Board vessels are "the wettest on the ocean." Never before have I crossed the Atlantic and found so much liquor sold as on this ship...I learn that passage on this ship has been sold with a positive guaranty that the bars for the sale of intoxicating liquors will be thrown wide open as soon as they pass outside the three mile coast line. This makes the United States incomparably the biggest bootlegger in the world.[47]

Believing his discovery offered a powerful indictment of prohibition's failure, Busch instructed his son Adolphus to publish this information. Anheuser-Busch officials carefully planned their attack, and on June 8, Adolphus Busch sent President Harding a letter denouncing the USSB policy. This was followed by the distribution of a pamphlet which included all the Busch letters, the Paris *New York Herald* advertisements, and a reproduction of the *George Washington* wine list. The following week, copies of this pamphlet were sent to every member of Congress and to all major American newspapers.[48]

The irrefutable nature of this damaging evidence made it impossible for the Harding administration to deny the charges. In a reply to Adolphus Busch which was released to the press, Lasker acknowledged that liquor was sold on USSB ships, but he claimed that this was a long-standing policy adopted by his predecessors. This practice was continued, Lasker argued, because "so long as Great Britain, Japan, France, Germany and other maritime nations continue to serve liquors...I am ashamed to state that my experience leads me to believe that there is a sufficient number of Americans...who would divert their trade to foreign flags."[49] Lasker cast himself as a dedicated patriot and attacked Busch's German ancestry, suggesting that the revelations would not "displease your German friends whose greatest hope of a restored German merchant marine is in a hurt to America's new-born merchant marine."[50] To prevent this foreign plot against American shipping, Lasker announced that he would gladly accept prohibition on all ships entering U.S. waters.

Regardless of this rationalization, Adolphus Busch precipitated a controversy that even the artful Lasker could not escape. The clear acknowledgment by the USSB chairman that liquor was a valuable part of American maritime policy unleashed an immediate public outcry. In a bold headline, the *Chicago Daily Journal* proclaimed that the Busch revelations "Link Harding to Rum Sales," and the *Washington Daily News* condemned the chairman's duplicity "as failure of some companies to make profits in operating shipping board steamers has been attributed to the belief that liquors were banned from them."[51] Lasker's action aroused both dedicated drys and unenthusiastic supporters of prohibition who believed that, whatever the shortcomings of the Eighteenth Amendment, it was a gross inconsistency for a government charged with enforcing the Volstead Act to serve as a major liquor salesman in the North Atlantic. The White House was overwhelmed by a barrage of vitriolic letters demanding Lasker's dismissal. Some irate citizens suggested that he should be prosecuted under the law as a common bootlegger.[52]

Beyond the emotion of opinion, the Busch-Lasker controversy provided a more serious problem for the Harding administration. The introduction of the ship subsidy proposal had engendered strong congressional opposition from agricultural interests and opponents of government aid. President Harding, citing the legislation as a priority, stated that he would call a special session of Congress after the July recess if the bill was not considered.[53] But the USSB liquor revelations further diminished the prospects for congressional approval. Lasker's assertion that American passenger shipping must sell liquor to remain competitive publicly exposed the link between prohibition and shipping. Unintentionally, Lasker suggested that the passage of the subsidy legislation was a futile gesture without liquor. As the maritime journal *Nauticus* concluded, law-abiders were placed in the "awful dilemma of either supporting the merchant marine and countenancing the existence of demon rum under government auspices, or refusing to compromise with Satan and give up the ships."[54] The Busch revelations provided the antisubsidy forces with an exploitable issue, and they welcomed dry support in transforming the subsidy battle into a debate over the sale of liquor on American ships.[55]

The wider impact of the liquor controversy was immediately evident in Congress where Lasker was condemned on the floor of the House and Senate. Congressman John G. Cooper argued that the "law-breaker and bootlegger in our land will be encouraged to carry on his work by reason of the policy of the Shipping Board, for it places the government in the position of admitting its inability or unwillingness to enforce its own laws."[56] Senator Frank B. Willis of Ohio, a dry and a subsidy supporter, announced that he would not support any legislation that "contemplates the paying of taxpayers' money to any organization that violates the law."[57] When the Busch allegations were published, the subsidy bill was under consideration in the House Merchant Marine Committee. On June 15 an attempt by the drys on the committee to amend the legislation to prevent subsidy payments to any passenger liners selling liquor was defeated. A compromise measure to eliminate the American disadvantage by imposing fines on any vessel selling liquor on a voyage that began or ended in a U.S. port was also defeated. Unable to reconcile the wet and dry positions, the committee sent the bill to the House without resolving this thorny issue.[58]

In the midst of this controversy, Treasury Department officials released the long-overdue regulations on transshipments. Reflecting both colossal bad timing and the lack of coordination within the Harding administration, Treasury guidelines issued on June 17 reflected a narrow interpretation of the Supreme Court's *Anchor* ruling. Transshipments of liquor in bond through the United States and the transfer of sealed liquor cargoes in port were forbidden, but liquor properly listed as passenger sea stores or destined for a foreign country on the same vessel was exempted. To the consternation of prohibitionists and American shipping proponents, the Treasury Department made it possible for foreign passenger shipping to remain untouched by prohibition and thus exacerbated an already bitter controversy.[59]

The Treasury regulations increased the pressure on the Harding administration to resolve the liquor issue. Throughout the Busch-Lasker furor, President Harding and Attorney General Daugherty offered no clarification of policy, but Republican leaders in the House demanded presidential guidance as the summer recess neared and Republican defectors joined shipping bill opponents.[60] Harding was confronted with the difficult dilemma of choosing between a prohibition clause in the subsidy bill which hampered the profitability of passenger shipping or encouraging dry opposition by allowing unrestricted liquor sales. Not knowing what to do and poorly served by his advisers, he did nothing. He finally agreed to a postponement of the subsidy debate, warning that if the shipping legislation was not considered when Congress returned, he would call a special postelection session in November. This forcefulness was hollow rhetoric; Harding conceded the advantage to the subsidy opponents when he failed to address the issues raised by the Busch-Lasker controversy.[61]

The Treasury regulations also forced Wheeler to press the administration on the liquor issue. Wheeler, unwilling to lend any support to either Augustus Busch or to the suggestion that the public preferred liquor on ships, was reluctant to condemn the liquor sales. He preferred to work behind the scenes with Lasker on a plan to bring foreign shipping under Eighteenth Amendment restrictions. When the Treasury Department's broad application of the *Anchor* ruling eliminated this possibility, he directed his wrath toward a favorite target of the drys, Treasury Secretary Mellon. Under attack from Wheeler, Mellon, after inflaming the issue, now adroitly removed his department from the center of the liquor controversy. He publicly requested that the Justice Department rule on whether or not the Eighteenth Amendment extended to American ships wherever they sailed and whether the Volstead Act prevented all liquor, including passenger sea stores, from entering the United States.[62]

Mellon's action, without prior consultation, forced the Harding administration to confront the problem it was attempting to avoid. The Justice Department was besieged with letters, petitions, and requests to testify on the USSB's liquor policy, and Assistant Attorney General Willebrandt prepared a memorandum on the question. On July 6 department officials sent Attorney General Daugherty, who was in Ohio, an urgent telegram suggesting the political importance of holding a public hearing on the Treasury Department request and recommending that he return to Washington.[63]

A week later, Daugherty met with representatives of prohibition groups and the maritime industry to discuss the geographic boundaries of the Eighteenth Amendment. The shippers, assisted by Lasker in the preparation of their case, appealed to Daugherty's patriotism and emotionally urged: "Don't give up the ship."[64] But the hearing was dominated by the prohibitionists, with opposition to the liquor sales expressed by representatives of the Anti-Saloon League, National Reform Society,

National Temperance Bureau, and Women's Christian Temperance Union. For the League, Wheeler claimed that foreign shippers sold sealed liquor to bootleggers, and he condemned the Treasury Department, which he referred to as "our opponents," for issuing regulations that conflicted with the law.[65] At the close of the three-hour meeting, Daugherty promised to give the issue careful attention.

Two important facts emerged from the hearing. First, aided by the conspicuous absence of foreign shippers, there was a general consensus that the sale of liquor on American passenger ships was linked to the transshipment issue. Second, whatever the fate of the subsidy legislation, the Harding administration had to resolve these questions. On July 20, Assistant Attorney General Willebrandt presented Daugherty with a draft ruling. She concluded that American ships, wherever they sailed, were restricted by the prohibition laws. Acknowledging the unfair competition this would create, Willebrandt recommended that foreign shipping be barred from bringing any liquor into U.S. territorial waters. Daugherty, already overwhelmed by the eruption of two national strikes, neglected to approve the draft ruling.[66]

As a result, President Harding still was unprepared to clarify the prohibition aspect of the subsidy proposal when the House reconvened in August. The industrial unrest and pending legislation further delayed consideration, and upcoming primaries forced many eastern congressmen to return home to campaign. Without their crucial support, House Republican leaders would not begin the shipping debate, and the president reluctantly accepted another postponement until November.[67] Harding, writing to Majority Leader Frank Mondell, acknowledged that the Busch-Lasker revelations affected the shipping debate and admitted that it "would be folly to ignore the development of the prohibition issue which came up so unexpectedly." Harding, however, remained inclined to let someone else resolve the problem, concluding that "we must face the fact that the friends of the bill must harmonize their views to accord with both the constitutional amendment and public opinion on this subject."[68]

Five weeks later, Harding was forced to follow his own advice. The enforcement of the Eighteenth Amendment was an issue in the upcoming midterm congressional elections, and the public acknowledgment of USSB liquor sales provided ammunition for critics who charged that the administration was "soft" on prohibition.[69] Attorney General Daugherty, coordinating campaign activities in Harding's home state of Ohio, had a firsthand appreciation of the need to diffuse these attacks. Fearing the possibility of major losses in November, he quickly returned to Washington.[70] On October 6, Daugherty announced that the prohibition laws applied to all American vessels, wherever they sailed, and prevented foreign ships from carrying all liquor, including passenger sea stores, in U.S. waters. The president immediately ordered the removal of liquor from all USSB ships. Within two days, the agency's fleet was dry.[71]

Daugherty's ruling did not immediately alarm Foreign Office officials in London. Their primary concern remained the pending subsidy legislation, and they believed that the liquor controversy eliminated the possibility of congressional approval. Although Ambassador Geddes regarded the ruling as a threat to British passenger shipping, his colleagues at the Foreign Office dismissed it as "pure politics."[72] They were confident that British shippers could either divert vessels to Canada or moor a liquor supply ship beyond the three-mile limit to evade the sealed-liquor barrier. "It should not be beyond the wit of British S/S companies," Thomas Snow of the American Department observed, "to devise means of keeping their passengers supplied with drink in spite of these regulations."[73] When the French and Spanish ambassadors suggested a joint protest, the British government refused to participate in an action that might remove a valuable restriction on other foreign shipping and the USSB fleet. The ingenuity of British shipping, they concluded, would ameliorate the effects of Daugherty's ruling.[74]

At the Cunard Company's offices in New York, Ashley Sparks did not share this confidence. He recognized the folly of attempting to avoid the liquor restrictions. Both American and British passengers would be unwilling to submit to the inconvenience of sailing from Halifax, and supplying large passenger liners with liquor beyond the three-mile limit, on the high seas in all weather conditions, was extremely difficult. Sparks also was concerned that any British subterfuge would result in a backlash of negative publicity, and he refused to indulge in "any undignified scramble or attempt any smart-aleck tricks to evade American laws."[75] Searching for a practical alternative, Sparks convened a meeting of representatives from all the foreign passenger lines, and the group unanimously agreed to cooperate in a legal effort to challenge the liquor ban. On October 17 attorneys for Cunard and the International Mercantile Marine Company requested the U.S. District Court in New York to issue a permanent injunction, based on economic hardship, against the enforcement of any restrictions on liquor sea stores.[76]

With the foreign liquor ban scheduled to begin in four days, this legal challenge created a serious problem. The Harding administration already was divided over the extension of liquor restrictions to foreign passenger ships. Secretary of State Hughes, before the ruling was released, had informed Daugherty that he disagreed with this "unnecessarily rigid construction which promises great harm to the interests of our commerce" and planned to seek a congressional exemption for foreign shipping to prevent international retaliation.[77] When the Cunard Company was granted an injunction, Hughes and Treasury Secretary Mellon opposed the enforcement of the restrictions until the courts ruled on the issue. Reluctantly, Daugherty announced that foreign ships could continue to carry sealed liquor stores until formal regulations were issued at an unspecified future date. On October 27 the District Court, upholding the attorney general's opinion, extended the injunction until the foreign shippers' announced appeal was considered by the Supreme Court.[78]

With the November elections only two weeks away, it was clear that Daugherty's ruling was disastrously ill timed and placed President Harding in a political straitjacket. As foreign ships carried sealed liquor into American ports under the protection of the courts, Harding could not rescind the announced liquor restrictions on the USSB fleet and risk the wrath of the Anti-Saloon League.[79] And Lasker was receiving overwhelming evidence that Americans preferred wet ships. From Asia to South America, passengers abandoned the government's liquorless vessels. The general manager of the United States Lines reported over 100 cancelled reservations on the transatlantic service and "the impression among our booking clerks, and those of our competitors, is that the 'booze rule' is the cause of this."[80] Lasker appealed to Harding: "We are beginning to feel the prohibition ruling at every turn." The president, however, could offer no guidance.[81]

The election results hardly justified the hardship created by the politically inspired liquor ruling. Republican losses far exceeded the most pessimistic predictions. The *New York Times*, citing prohibition as a leading factor in these results, concluded that "the demonstration of disapproval of the Administration was unmistakable."[82] Contrasted with the normal swing in midterm elections, the Republicans suffered a stinging defeat which included many of the president's supporters. In the House of Representatives, the Republicans lost 163 seats, and their majority in the Senate was reduced to 51 to 43.[83]

This setback did not diminish Harding's determination to press for action on the subsidy proposal, and he addressed a special postelection session of Congress to urge approval of the plan. Lasker had met with Wheeler and persuaded him that Daugherty's ruling and the pending court challenge made it unnecessary to include a liquor clause in the subsidy bill.[84] Despite this private agreement, the House approved an amendment to prohibit subsidy payments for any ship selling liquor. Wheeler, concerned that the Supreme Court might regard this action as a de facto acceptance of sealed liquor on foreign ships, rallied the dry forces in Congress to delete the liquor amendment from the final version of the bill. With the outstanding difference between wets and drys removed, the subsidy legislation was approved by a slim margin, but the delay caused by the Busch-Lasker controversy continued to haunt the president. On February 28, 1923, after antisubsidy senators began a filibuster in the final days of the congressional session, Harding withdrew the proposal and announced that he would not resubmit it to the new Congress.[85]

For British shipping, the defeat of the subsidy legislation was a short-lived victory. On April 30 the Supreme Court presented its opinion on the legality of Attorney General Daugherty's ruling. Under the general heading of *Cunard v. Mellon*, the Court considered twelve separate appeals from foreign and private American shippers on the geographic boundaries of the Eighteenth Amendment. In a 7-to-2 decision, the Court declared that prohibition did not extend to American ships beyond the three-mile limit. But the Court also concluded that a merchant ship voluntarily entering the waters of another country subjected itself to that state's laws. Therefore, the attorney general had the authority to prevent all liquor from entering U.S. territorial waters. Unlike the *Anchor* opinion, the Court precisely interpreted international law, and legal scholars regarded it as definitive.[86]

In London, the announcement of the *Cunard* decision was greeted with a storm of protest. The British press reacted with strong anti-American editorials, and a group of Conservative backbenchers introduced legislation to require all foreign ships to carry liquor in British waters.[87] The Liverpool Steamship Owners Association held an emergency meeting and endorsed a resolution urging the British government to preserve international comity.[88] The shippers, misreading American attitudes, concluded that the *Cunard* ruling could be nullified by either broad enforcement regulations or by congressional action. They sent representatives to pressure the Foreign Office to secure a delay in enforcement until Congress could pass legislation to lift the liquor ban.[89]

Foreign Office officials did not believe that anything would moderate what Foreign Secretary George Curzon regarded as "puritanism run mad."[90] Cecil Hurst, the department's legal adviser, informed Curzon that the weakness of British claims under international comity made it impossible to challenge the Supreme Court's action. This was irritating, Rowland Sperling noted, but it was not a violation of international law and retaliation was an option only if the liquor restrictions created a serious economic hardship, a view shared by his colleagues. To appease the shipping lobby, the Foreign Office agreed to lodge a formal protest over the American denial of international comity.[91]

The members of the Liverpool Steamship Owners Association remained convinced that they could overturn the Supreme Court's ruling. In June the Treasury Department issued new regulations following the *Cunard* decision. Effective June 10, all liquor, including sea stores, was barred from American waters; the sole exemption was for medicinal liquor and essential liquor supplies required by the nation of embarkation.[92] The British shippers now planned a series of test voyages to challenge the Harding administration's commitment to enforcing these guidelines. The Cunard Company agreed to place excess liquor, in a separate compartment under seal, on the liners *Berengaria* and *Saxonia*. If the customs seals were broken, the shippers would present a friendly protest.[93] From New York, Sparks sent daily cables to Liverpool urging his superiors to abandon this defiance of U.S. territorial sovereignty. "A less act than this has ruined many a company and has brought two nations into conflict," he warned Cunard's Chairman Thomas Royden. "I cannot see the use of risking a tremendous conflagration when we know that the initial endeavor of having Eastbound alcoholic stores on board is bound to fail." But Royden and his fellow shippers were confident that this "friendly and dignified action" would succeed.[94]

On June 16 the *Berengaria* sailed from Southampton amid growing fears on both sides of the Atlantic over the potential consequences of this test voyage. Both British and American newspapers charted the liner's daily progress as it approached U.S. waters with its sealed liquor stores, and the press speculated that the sailing would result in a serious Anglo-American clash.[95] The *Berengaria's* arrival in New York harbor, however, was anticlimactic. After some initial confusion, U.S. customs officers boarded the vessel and calmly removed the sealed liquor. No fines or libels were lodged, and generous allowances were given for liquor listed as medical stores.[96] Unknown to the public speculators, Foreign Office officials strongly opposed this test voyage because it was indefensible under international law, and they attempted to stop the sailing. When the shippers filed a private protest over the cargo seizure, Ambassador Geddes was instructed not to take any action on their behalf.[97]

For the British shipping community, the failure of the *Berengaria* sailing forcefully demonstrated that the Anti-Saloon League had triumphed and the Harding administration was determined to enforce the liquor regulations. This was further confirmed in July when the new chairman of the USSB announced that the *Cunard* ruling had not altered the agency's dry policy.[98] The British shippers abided by their promise to respect the Supreme Court's ruling if the challenge was unsuccessful. Liquor was sold on all voyages from Great Britain to the United States, with sea stores limited to the requirements of the westbound trip, and remaining supplies were thrown overboard at the three-mile limit.[99] Some travelers adapted to the new requirements by bringing their own supply of distilled spirits as transatlantic drinking became an underground activity. Royden, finally resigned to the reality of the liquor restrictions, concluded: "There is not much chance of getting relief from the present situation, and we shall be in the unfortunate position of having to connive at bootlegging on a large scale to the great detriment of morale of all on board."[100]

For the first time, the full impact of the Eighteenth Amendment extended to the Liverpool docks and the corridors of Whitehall. The transformation of the Anglo-American liquor problem into an economic issue now was complete.

Notes

[1]*Chicago Tribune,* May 6, 1922.

[2]Sinclair, *Era of Excess,* 182; Jessup, *Law of Territorial Waters,* 236–40.

[3]Foreign Office to Board of Trade, February 11, 1920, A1002/1002/45, PRO; Bainbridge Colby to Auckland Geddes, April 22, 1920, 811.114/Great Britain/5, RG 59, NA; Geddes to Foreign Office, May 4, 1920, A2776/1002/45, PRO. Medicinal liquor could be dispensed within three miles by the ship's medical officer.

[4]Anti-Saloon League, Notes upon Power to Regulate Liquor in Transit through the United States Destined for Foreign Countries, May 4, 1921, Office of the General Counsel and Legislative Superintendent, Anti-Saloon League, Series 8, Microfilm edition of Temperance and Prohibition Papers, Ohio Historical Society, Columbus, Ohio (hereafter cited as Series 8, League Papers); *New York Times,* February 22, 1920; R. H. Hadow, Minutes, April 18, 1921, A2674/1069/45, PRO.

[5]Frank B. Niebeker to U.S. Shipping Board, February 4, 1921, 600/7, General Correspondence of the U.S. Shipping Board, Records of the U.S. Shipping Board, Record Group 32, National Archives, Washington, DC (hereafter cited as RG 32).

[6]Shipping Federation Limited to Board of Trade, February 10, 1921, copy in A1220/1220/45, PRO; Robert Skinner to State Department, February 15, 1921, 811.114/Great Britain/12, RG 59, NA.

[7]Geddes to Foreign Office, April 5, 1921, A2388/1069/45, PRO; Lucius H. Beers to Henry P. Fletcher, March 24, 1921, 811.114/469, RG 59, NA; Geddes to Foreign Office, April 8, 1921, A2463/1069/45, and April 23, 1921, A3288/1069/45, PRO; State Department, Memorandum, May 13, 1921, 811.114/500, RG 59, NA. Hughes believed the original decision was a valid interpretation of the prohibition laws and could not be altered without legislation, but he agreed that those parties affected by the decision should have an opportunity to voice their objections.

[8]Geddes to Foreign Office, May 16, 1921, A3779/1069/45, PRO. The Cunard attorneys argued that the British-American Customs Treaty of 1871 guaranteed the unrestricted entry of British sealed cargoes into American ports.

[9]*New York Times,* July 14, 1921; Treasury Department to State Department, June 3, 1921, 811.114/Great Britain/2, RG 59, NA; Henry Chilton to

Foreign Office, June 9, 1921, A4483/1220/45, PRO; Geddes to Foreign Office, July 7, 1921, A4955/1069/45, and July 12, 1921, A5376/1069/45, PRO; State Department to Geddes, June 3, 1921, 811.114/Great Britain/2, RG 59, NA; Treasury Department, Bulletin, July 8, 1921, copy in 811.114/597, RG 59, NA.

[10]Geddes to Foreign Office, August 18, 1921, A6068/1069/45, PRO; Treasury Department, Bulletin, August 13, 1921, copy in 811.114/597, RG 59, NA.

[11]*Grogan v. Walker* and *Anchor v. Aldridge,* U.S. District Court, Southern District, New York, 275 Fed 373; State Department, Report, October 21, 1921, 811.114/590, RG 59, NA; Geddes to Foreign Office, October 26, 1921, A7916/1069/45, PRO.

[12]Wayne Wheeler to Harry M. Daugherty, January 5, 1922, 23/1866/10X, RG 60, NAS; Cunard Company, Executive Committee, Minutes, November 9, 1921, B/4/57/61, Minutes of the Executive Committee (B/4), Cunard Company Archives, University of Liverpool Library, Liverpool, England (hereafter cited as Cunard Archives).

[13]Hadow, Minutes, August 6, 1921, A6728/1220/45, PRO; Rowland Sperling, Minutes, April 18, 1921, A2679/1069/45, PRO.

[14]Jessup, *Law of Territorial Waters,* 125–80.

[15]Hadow, Minutes, April 5, 1921, A2388/1069/45, PRO; Foreign Office, Minutes, August 2, 1921, A5702/1069/45, PRO; Board of Trade to Foreign Office, September 15, 1921, A6728/1220/45, and August 2, 1921, A5702/1069/45, PRO.

[16]*Grogan v. Walker* and *Anchor v. Aldridge, United States Reports: Cases Adjudged in the United States Supreme Court* (Washington, DC, 1923), 259:80 (259 U.S. 80).

[17]Quincy Wright, "The Prohibition Amendment and International Law," *Minnesota Law Review* 7 (1922–23): 28–39; Jessup, *Law of Territorial Waters,* 216; Sinclair, *Era of Excess,* 182; Wheeler to Warren G. Harding, June 2, 1922, 732/168, Harding Papers.

[18]Chilton to Foreign Office, June 9, 1921, A4483/1220/45, PRO; Geddes to Foreign Office, June 6, 1922, A3625/1437/45, PRO; Foreign Office, Minutes, June 6, 1922, ibid.

[19]Ashley Sparks to Gloster Armstrong, June 1, 1922, A3773/1437/45, PRO.

[20]Arthur S. Link, *Wilson: The Struggle for Neutrality, 1914–1915* (Princeton, 1961), 137–61; Samuel A. Lawrence, *United States Merchant Shipping Policies and Politics* (Washington, DC, 1966), 38–39; Arthur S. Link, *Wilson: Confusions and Crises, 1915–1916* (Princeton, 1964), 339–41.

[21]U.S. Senate, 66th Cong., 1st sess., Committee on Commerce, *Establishment of an American Merchant Marine: Hearings . . .* (Washington, DC, 1920), 323; Arthur C. Walworth, *America's Moment: 1918* (New York, 1977), 241–42; Parrini, *Heir to Empire,* 44–45, 70; Jeffrey J. Safford, *Wilsonian Maritime Diplomacy, 1913–1921* (New Brunswick, NJ, 1978), 169–97, 221–28; Paul M. Zeis, *American Shipping Policy* (Princeton, 1938), 115–23; *New York Journal of Commerce,* February 26, 1919; *New York Times,* July 23, 1920.

²²The charter rate for a transatlantic voyage declined from $10.00-per-deadweight-ton per month in 1920 to $1.10 in 1921. John H. Kemble and Lane C. Kendall, "The Years between the Wars: 1919–1939," in Robert A. Kilmarx, ed., *America's Maritime Legacy: A History of the United States Merchant Marine and Shipbuilding Industry since Colonial Times* (Boulder, 1979), 151-55; Burl Noggle, *Into the Twenties* (Urbana, 1974), 59; John G. B. Hutchins, "The American Shipping Industry since 1914," *Business History Review* 28 (June 1954): 111–13; U.S. Shipping Board, "Financial and General Facts in Regard to the U.S.S.B.," November 21, 1922, Box 15, Albert Lasker Files, Records of the U.S. Shipping Board, Record Group 32, National Archives, Washington, DC (hereafter cited as Lasker Files, NA); Frederick Emmons, *The Atlantic Liners* (New York, 1972), 56; John D. Hicks, *Republican Ascendancy, 1921–1933* (New York, 1960), 61; Zeis, *American Shipping Policy,* 95–114; Lawrence, *United States Merchant Shipping,* 42–43.

²³*Address of Senator Warren G. Harding before the Ohio Society of New York* (New York, 1920); *New York Times,* July 23, 1920; Murray, *Harding Era,* 265–66; Andrew Sinclair, *The Available Man: Warren Gamaliel Harding* (New York, 1965), 84–91; Murray, *Politics of Normalcy,* 69.

²⁴Zeis, *American Shipping Policy,* 125; Trani and Wilson, *Presidency of Warren G. Harding,* 75; John Gunther, *Taken at the Flood: The Story of Albert D. Lasker* (New York, 1960), 126–45; Albert Lasker to Frank Munson, July 12, 1922, Box 15, Lasker Files, NA.

²⁵USSB, "Special Report on Certain Phases of Influence Prejudicial to Our Mercantile Marine," September 26, 1921, Box 16, Lasker Files, NA; Lasker to Wesley L. Jones, February 11, 1922, 580/2707/Part 2, RG 32, NA; USSB, *Government Aid to Mercantile Shipping* (Washington, DC, 1922); *Address by the President of the United States on the Need for an American Merchant Marine* (Washington, DC, 1922); Lasker to Elmer Schlesinger, April 3, 1922, 580/2707/Part 2, RG 32, NA; U.S. Senate, 67th Cong., 2d sess., Committee on Commerce and House of Representatives, Committee on Merchant Marine and Fisheries, *To Amend the Merchant Marine Act of 1920: Joint Hearings...,* 2 vols. (Washington, DC, 1922), 1:2–23; Lasker to W. S. Guerin, June 9, 1922, 580/2707/Part 3, RG 32, NA; Lasker to Albert Cummins, July 13, 1922, Box 6, Lasker Files, NA; National Merchant Marine Association, Press Release, February 17, 1922, copy in Box 15, Lasker Files, NA; USSB, Press Release, October 18, 1922, 580/2707/Part 4, RG 32, NA; Murray, *Harding Era,* 289–90.

²⁶F. Lawrence Babcock, *Spanning the Atlantic* (New York, 1931), 200; Francis E. Hyde, *Cunard and the North Atlantic, 1840–1973* (London, 1975), 170.

²⁷Great Britain, Board of Trade, *Shipping and Shipbuilding Industries after the War: Reports of the Departmental Committees* (London, 1918); Aldcroft, *Inter-War Economy,* 222–27; Geddes to Foreign Office, February 6, 1922, A1133/1133/45, and March 23, 1922, A2223/239/45, PRO; Thomas Royden to Joseph L. Carozzi, July 5, 1922, S/3/13/94, Chairman's Letterbook (S/3), Cunard Archives; Royden to Hiram K. Modeswell, July 5, 1922, S/3/13/108, Cunard Archives; Royden to S. Elford, December 12, 1922, S/3/15/196, Cunard Archives.

[28]They argued that a £12-per-day per ton British operating advantage would become a £20-per-day per ton American advantage. North Atlantic Passenger Conference to Foreign Office, March 6, 1922, A1600/1133/45, PRO; Charles Hipwood to Foreign Office, March 8, 1922, A1687/239/45, PRO; Sperling, Notes on Board of Trade Meeting, March 15, 1922, ibid.; Board of Trade to Foreign Office, March 16, 1922, A2776/239/45, PRO.

[29]Foreign Office, Minutes, March 8, 1922, A1690/239/45, PRO; Sperling, Notes on Board of Trade Meeting, March 15, 1922, A1687/239/45, PRO; Board of Trade, Memorandum for the Cabinet, June 15, 1922, A3896/239/45, PRO; Foreign Office, Minutes, June 16, 1922, A4534/239/45, PRO; Foreign Office to Winston Churchill, June 24, 1922, A4114/239/45, PRO; Horace Seymour, Memorandum of Meeting with Sir Norman Hill, August 31, 1922, A5445/239/45, PRO; Minutes of the Cabinet Meeting, June 30, 1922, Cabinet 36/22, vol. 30, Conclusions of the Meetings of the Cabinet, Cabinet 23, Public Record Office, Kew, London (hereafter cited as CAB 23); Committee on Trade, Memorandum, July 31, 1922, A4845/239/45, PRO.

[30]Babcock, *Spanning the Atlantic,* 200; Emmons, *Atlantic Liners,* 11.

[31]Lasker to Martin B. Madden, January 17, 1922, Box 14, Lasker Files, NA; T. H. Rossbottom to Lasker, October 13, 1922, and February 26, 1923, Box 22, Lasker Files, NA; Rossbottom to Lasker, February 9, 1923, Box 5, Lasker Files, NA. Lasker had embarked on an aggressive campaign to expand USSB passenger carriage in the North Atlantic by appealing to the patriotic instincts of American travelers. Hyde, *Cunard and the North Atlantic,* 171-72; Geddes to Foreign Office, February 6, 1922, A1133/1133/45, and August 12, 1922, A5169/1133/45, PRO; Board of Trade to Foreign Office, June 30, 1922, A4201/1133/45, PRO; Foreign Office to George Harvey, August 28, 1922, A5222/1133/45, PRO; Foreign Office, Minutes, September 7, 1922, A5487/1133/45, PRO; Rossbottom to Lasker, February 14, 1922, Box 22, Lasker Files, NA.

[32]Lasker to Samuel Gompers, February 18, 1922, Box 9, Lasker Files, NA; Lasker to Paul Stephens, June 6, 1922, 580/2707/Part 3, RG 32, NA.

[33]Babcock, *Spanning the Atlantic,* 201–3; U.S. Treasury Department, Internal Revenue Service, *Hearings in the Matter of the Application of the National Prohibition Act to the Sale of Intoxicating Beverages on American Vessels on the High Seas* (Washington, DC, 1920); American Steamship Owners Association to Lasker, July 10, 1922, Box 14, Lasker Files, NA.

[34]L. Ames Brown to Edward N. Hurley, July 23, 1918, 600/7, RG 32, NA.

[35]USSB, Minutes of the Meeting of Executive Heads of Operations, October 28, 1919, 600/7, RG 32, NA; Assistant General Counsel to Shipping Board, November 4, 1919, ibid.; John Barton Payne to A. Mitchell Palmer, November 11, 1919, ibid.

[36]Payne to Charles F. Riordan, December 10, 1919, 580/129/Part 1, RG 32, NA; Jones to Payne, December 20, 1919, ibid.; Payne to Major Cushing, December 22, 1919, ibid.; USSB, Minutes of Conference of Executive Heads of Operations, January 27, 1920, 600/7, RG 32, NA.

[37]John J. Flaherty, Memorandum on U.S.S.B. Meeting, December 23, 1919, 600/7, RG 32, NA; *New York Times,* February 5, 1920.

[38]Treasury Department, *Sale of Intoxicating Beverages on American Vessels: Hearings*; William Frierson to Treasury Department, November 1, 1920, copy in 580/129/Part 1, RG 32, NA; Justice Department, Memorandum of Hearing, December 22, 1920, ibid.

[39]Andrew J. Volstead to William Benson, January 17, 1921, 580/129/Part 1, RG 32, NA; *New York Times,* January 6, 19, 1921; Benson to Volstead, February 23, 1921, 580/129/Part 1, RG 32, NA.

[40]Edward Hyzer to Benson, December 14, 1920, 580/129/Part 1, RG 32, NA; Benson to Frank B. Ferris, November 5, 1920, ibid. Treasury Department records on this issue are incomplete. Secretary Mellon maintained several files, entitled "Liquor on Ships," which presumably contained the papers on this topic since they do not appear elsewhere in Treasury files. These files are listed on an early inventory of Treasury Department records. However, when the files were accessioned by the National Archives, these papers were not included in the Archives list and must have been destroyed by Treasury officials in the intervening years between the two inventories. See the index of Central Subject Files, Department of the Treasury, Record Group 56, National Archives, Washington, DC (hereafter cited as RG 56, NA).

[41]J. Parker Kirlin to Schlesinger, July 15, 1921, 580/129/Part 2, RG 32, NA; H. H. Raymond to Lasker, July 15, 1921, ibid.

[42]USSB, Board Minutes, July 5, 1921, 10/3897, Minutes of the U.S. Shipping Board, Records of the U.S. Shipping Board, Record Group 32, National Archives, Washington, DC; Flaherty to W. G. Stevens, July 5, 1921, 600/7, RG 32, NA.

[43]Walter Ballinger to Warren G. Harding, October 21, 1921, copy in 580/129/Part 2, RG 32, NA; D. E. Brundage to Ballinger, November 2, 1921, Box 10, Lasker Files, NA; Jones to Lasker, November 7, 1921, ibid.; James Boring to W. J. Love, March 27, 1922, 1/E, Emergency Fleet Corporation, Executive Office, Division of Operations (1/E), Records of the U.S. Shipping Board, Record Group 32, National Archives, Washington, DC.

[44]Brundage to Mabel Walker Willebrandt, October 29, 1921, Box 11, Lasker Files, NA.

[45]J. B. Smull to A. F. Mack, June 2, 1922, Box 22, Lasker Files, NA; Le Baron B. Colt to Lasker, April 19, 1922, Box 6, Lasker Files, NA.

[46]*Chicago Tribune,* May 6, 1922; *Newark Evening News* (New Jersey), May 26, 1922; *St. Louis Daily Globe-Democrat,* May 30, 1922; *Public Ledger* (Philadelphia), May 28, 1922; Wheeler to Lasker, June 1, 1922, Box 37, Lasker Files, NA.

[47]Augustus A. Busch to Anheuser-Busch Board of Directors, May 15, 1922, Box 3, Lasker Files, NA.

[48]Adolphus Busch to Harding, June 8, 1922, Box 3, Lasker Files, NA; George Christian to Lasker, June 13, 1922, ibid.; "Prohibition Afloat," June 13, 1922, Box 22, Lasker Files, NA.

[49]Lasker to Adolphus Busch, June 13, 1922, Box 22, Lasker Files, NA.

[50]Ibid.; Schlesinger to Lasker, June 13, 1922, 600/7, RG 32, NA; Adolphus Busch to Lasker, June 14, 1922, Box 3, Lasker Files, NA.

[51]*Chicago Daily Journal,* June 14, 1922; *Washington Daily News,* June 14, 1922; *Columbus Citizen* (Ohio), June 15, 1922; Walter H. Newton to Lasker, June 14, 1922, Box 16, Lasker Files, NA.

[52]For examples of the letters received see 75/168, Harding Papers; Box 22, Lasker Files, NA; and 580/129/Part 3, RG 32, NA.

[53]Trani and Wilson, *Presidency of Warren G. Harding,* 76; Hicks, *Republican Ascendancy,* 61; Harding to Frank Mondell, June 1, 1922, 1282/176, Harding Papers; Mondell to Harding, June 12, 1922, 1320/176, Harding Papers; Edward J. Frederick to Harding, June 13, 1922, 1311/176, Harding Papers.

[54]"The Man on the Bridge," *Nauticus* 17 (June 17, 1922): 4; Lasker to John T. Flynn, June 15, 1922, Box 3, Lasker Files, NA.

[55]Mondell to Harding, June 16, 1922, 1420/176, Harding Papers; *New York Times,* June 15, 1922; *Chicago Tribune,* June 16, 1922; Kermit Roosevelt to Lasker, June 19, 1922, Box 19, Lasker Files,

[56]*Congressional Record,* 67th Cong., 2d sess. (June 15, 1922), 8777 and 9187; Clyde Kelly to Lasker, June 14, 1922, Box 3, Lasker Files, NA.

[57]Frank B. Willis to Allen L. Walton, June 19, 1922, Box 17, Papers of Frank B. Willis, MSS 325, Ohio Historical Society, Columbus, Ohio (hereafter cited as Willis Papers); *Congressional Record,* 67th Cong., 2d sess. (June 15, 1922), 8750–52; *New York Times,* June 15, 1922.

[58]*New York Times,* June 16, 17, 1922; Lasker to W. J. Conners, June 16, 1922, Box 5, Lasker Files, NA; H.R. 12062, copy in Box 3, Lasker Files, NA; U.S. House of Representatives, 67th Cong., 2d sess. (June 16, 1922), Committee on the Merchant Marine and Fisheries, *American Merchant Marine: Report;* U.S. House of Representatives, 67th Cong., 2d sess. (June 28, 1922), Committee on the Merchant Marine and Fisheries, *Minority Views: The Subsidy Bill;* George J. Duraind to Lasker, August 26, 1922, Box 7, Lasker Files, NA. Duraind suggested that Busch was a front for subsidy opponents.

[59]Treasury Department, Regulation 3350, June 17, 1922, V/B/3, General Records of the Prohibition Unit, Department of the Treasury, Record Group 58, National Archives, Washington, DC (hereafter cited as RG 58, NA).

[60]*Congressional Record,* 67th Cong., 2d sess. (June 21, 1922), 9107–8; *Congressional Record,* 67th Cong., 2d sess. (June 22, 1922), 9187; *New York Times,* June 21, 1922; Lasker to Norman B. Beecher, June 22, 1922, Box 1, Lasker Files, NA.

[61]Harding agreed to a postponement until the pending tariff bill was considered. Harding to Mondell, June 20, 1922, 602/219, Harding Papers; *Congressional Record,* 67th Cong., 2d sess. (July 26, 1922), 9456–58; *Congressional Record,* 67th Cong., 2d sess. (June 29, 1922), 9720–23; "The Man on the Bridge," *Nauticus* 17 (June 24, 1922): 3.

[62]Wheeler to Harding, June 13, 1922, 1039/151, and June 22, 1922, 1041/151, Harding Papers; Harding to Wheeler, June 23, 1922, 1038/151, Harding Papers; Daugherty to Wheeler, June 16, 1922, 23/2829/6, RG 60, NAS; Wheeler to Daugherty, June 13, 1922, ibid. Wheeler was criticized for not condemning Lasker. *Congressional Record,* 67th Cong., 2d sess. (June 15,

1922), 8750–51, 9187; Wheeler to Daugherty, June 22, 1922, 23/2829/31, RG 60, NAS.

[63]There were a few letters of support for the USSB, but the letters were overwhelmingly against the liquor sales. See 23/2829/19x, 24, 26, 32, 40, 43, 63x, and 70, RG 60, NAS; Wheeler to Willebrandt, June 22, 1922, 23/2829/Part 1, RG 60, NAS; Warren F. Martin to Daugherty, July 6, 1922, 23/2829/63, RG 60, NAS; Daugherty to Martin, July 7, 1922, 23/0/517x, RG 60, NAS; Willebrandt, Memorandum for Attorney General, June 28, 1922, 23/2829/Part 1, RG 60, NAS.

[64]American Steamship Owners Association to Lasker, July 11, 1922, Box 14, Lasker Files, NA; Roosevelt to Lasker, July 11, 1922, Box 19, Lasker Files, NA; Lasker to Daugherty, July 13, 1922, Box 11, Lasker Files, NA; Transcript of Liquor on Ships Meeting, July 13, 1922, 23/2829/142, RG 60, NAS.

[65]Wheeler, Statement before the Attorney General, July 13, 1922, Folder 23, Roll 3, Series 8, League Papers. Wheeler announced plans to send Daugherty a full brief on the *Anchor* guidelines.

[66]Willebrandt to Daugherty, July 20, 1922, 23/2829/Part 1, RG 60, NAS. In her first draft Willebrandt wrote that the prohibition laws did not apply to American ships beyond the three-mile limit. Willebrandt, Memorandum for Attorney General, June 28, 1922, ibid. Willebrandt received all the liquor sale protests sent to the Justice Department and the White House. Martin to Judge Mayne, August 19, 1922, 215000/748, and Martin to Joseph Mumerlyn, August 19, 1922, 215000/751, both in General Records of the Department of Justice, Record Group 60, National Archives, Washington, DC (hereafter cited as RG 60, NA).

[67]*Congressional Record,* 67th Cong., 2d sess. (August 16, 1922), 11459; Mondell to Harding, August 1, 1922, 609/219, Harding Papers; Lasker to Harding, August 18, 1922, 1516/176, Harding Papers.

[68]Harding to Mondell, August 23, 1922, 68/230, Harding Papers; *Washington Post,* August 23, 1922.

[69]*Literary Digest* 73 (June 17, 1922): 12–14; *New York Times,* October 7, 1922; Gusfield, *Symbolic Crusade,* 120.

[70]Daugherty to Guy D. Goff, September 20, 1922, 60/10/5/20, RG 60, NAS; Martin to Thomas Felder, September 11, 1922, 215000/799, RG 60, NA; Jess W. Smith, Memorandum for E. S. Rochester, October 17, 1922, Folder 2, Harry M. Daugherty Collection, MSS 271, Ohio Historical Society, Columbus, Ohio (hereafter cited as Daugherty Collection); Willis to Walton, June 16, 1922, Box 17, Willis Papers; *Columbus Citizen* (Ohio), June 16, November 6, 7, 1922; Lowell Fess to Lehr Fess, October 5, 1922, Box 19, Papers of Simeon D. Fess, MSS 283, Ohio Historical Society, Columbus, Ohio (hereafter cited as Fess Papers); Harding to Simeon D. Fess, October 26, 1922, Box 19, Fess Papers; Harry M. Daugherty, Memorandum for Solicitor General, September 26, 1922, 23/0/540, RG 60, NAS.

[71]Daugherty briefed Harding, Mellon, and Hughes on October 3. Daugherty to Harding, October 3, 1922, Folder 20, Harry M. Daugherty Papers, MSS 668, Ohio Historical Society, Columbus, Ohio (hereafter cited as Daugherty

Papers); Daugherty to Andrew Mellon, October 6, 1922, 23/2829/Part 1, RG 60, NAS; Lasker to Daugherty, October 6, 1922, Box 30, Lasker Files, NA; Daugherty to Lasker, October 7, 1922, ibid.; Lasker to J. M. Patterson, October 13, 1922, Box 4, Lasker Files, NA; Harding to Lasker, October 6, 1922, 998/151, Harding Papers; Lasker to Harding, October 7, 1922, 993/151, and October 9, 1922, 995/151, Harding Papers; Lasker to U.S.S.B. Staff, October 7, 1922, 580/129/Part 4, RG 32, NA.

[72]Geddes to Foreign Office, June 16, 1922, A4048/239/45, PRO; Chilton to Foreign Office, June 19, 1922, A4424/1437/45, PRO; *Morning Post* (London), June 19, 1922; Chilton to Foreign Office, July 20, 1922, A4876/239/45, PRO; Foreign Office, Minutes, August 3, 1922, A5038/239/45, and August 24, 1922, A5382/239/45, PRO; Sperling, Minutes, June 30, 1922, A4048/239/45, PRO; Hipwood to Foreign Office, August 17, 1922, A5196/239/45, PRO; Foreign Office, Minutes, August 31, 1922, A5445/239/45, PRO; Geddes to Foreign Office, October 7, 1922, A6199/1437/45, PRO; Eyre Crowe, Minutes, October 19, 1922, A6201/1437/45, PRO.

[73]Thomas Snow, Minutes, October 9, 1922, A6233/1437/45, PRO.

[74]Foreign Office, Minutes, October 17, 1922, A6491/1437/45, PRO.

[75]Sparks to Royden, October 13, 1922, C/2/270, Papers of Chairman Sir Thomas Royden (C/2), Cunard Archives.

[76]Bill of Complaint, *Cunard Steamship Company v. Andrew Mellon* and *International Mercantile Marine Company v. Henry Stuart* (Acting Customs Director), October 17, 1922, copy in 23/4002/3, RG 60, NAS. Cunard's attorneys claimed that the restrictions would make it impossible to hire non-American crew members and sail to an intermediate port of any country requiring minimum liquor supplies for passengers. They also cited the unrecoverable loss of liquor already purchased for future voyages.

[77]Charles Evans Hughes to Daugherty, October 5, 1922, "Daugherty" folder, Box 9, Hughes Papers; Geddes to Foreign Office, October 7, 1922, A6200/1437/45, PRO; *New York Times,* October 8, 1922. At Ambassador Geddes's request, Hughes also secured an extension of the original deadline for foreign shipping and persuaded sympathetic Treasury officials to allow medicinal liquor stores. Geddes to Foreign Office, October 9, 1922, A6233/1437/45, PRO; Memorandum of Meeting with Auckland Geddes, October 7, 1922, Folder 76b, Box 175, Hughes Papers; Harding to Mellon, October 7, 1922, 999/151, and October 13, 1922, 1071/151, Harding Papers; State Department, Memorandum, October 25, 1922, 811.114/1032, RG 59, NA; Solicitor's Office, State Department, Memorandum, October 13, 1922, 811.114/Great Britain/38, RG 59, NA.

[78]Justice Department, Memorandum, October 25, 1922, 23/2829, RG 60, NAS; *New York Times,* October 25, 1922; C. E. Coterell to Foreign Office, October 26, 1922, A6577/1437/45, PRO; *New York Times,* October 28, 1922.

[79]Wheeler to Harding, October 20, 1922, 898/168, Harding Papers; Justice Department to William Hayward, October 18, 1922, 23/4002/2x, RG 60, NAS; Anti-Saloon League, Memorandum, undated, Folder 66, Roll 10, Series 8, League Papers.

[80]Rossbottom to Love, October 31, 1922, 1/E, RG 32, NA; *Japan Advertiser* (Tokyo), November 4, 1922; R. M. Semmes to Love, October 11, 17, 1922, I/E, RG 32, NA; T. A Graham to Love, October 12, 1922, ibid.; Frank Munson to Love, October 11, 1922, ibid.; Rossbottom to Love, October 17, 20, 27, 1922, ibid.; Joseph E. Sheedy to Lasker, November 15, 1922, Box 18, Lasker Files, NA; Love to Lasker, October 13, 18, 19, 24, 28, November 23, December 11, 19, 1922, ibid.

[81]Lasker to Harding, October 31, 1922, 517/151, Harding Papers.

[82]*New York Times,* November 9, 1922.

[83]*Washington Post,* November 9, 1922; Trani and Wilson, *Presidency of Warren G. Harding,* 80; Russell, *Shadow of Blooming Grove,* 551; Hicks, *Republican Ascendancy,* 88–89.

[84]Shipping supporters were prepared to expand the mail payment provisions of the bill to offset the losses created by the liquor ban. George W. Edmonds to Lasker, November 10, 1922, Box 7, Lasker Files, NA; Lasker to Carl R. Chindblom, November 14, 1922, Box 6, Lasker Files, NA. Harding addressed a joint session of Congress on November 21 and called for the passage of the subsidy bill. *Congressional Record,* 67th Cong., 3d sess. (November 21, 1922), 9–11.

[85]*Congressional Record,* 67th Cong., 3d sess. (November 28, 1922), 359–60, and (November 29, 1922), 413–14, 429; *New York Times,* November 29, 30, 1922; *Congressional Record,* 67th Cong., 4th sess. (February 7, 1923), 3213–14, (February 22, 1923), 4226–68, (February 27, 1923), 4731–72, and (February 28, 1923), 4834–37; *New York Times,* February 24, 1923. See also *Congressional Record,* 67th Cong., 4th sess. (February 19, 1923), 3935; Trani and Wilson, *Presidency of Warren G. Harding,* 77; Murray, *Harding Era,* 325. For the British reaction see *Daily Chronicle* (London), March 1, 1923.

[86]*Cunard v. Mellon,* 262 U.S. 100; *Yale Law Journal* 33 (November 1923): 72–78; Jessup, *Law of Territorial Waters,* 217–20; *American Journal of International Law* 17 (July 1923): 504–7.

[87]The legislation passed on its first reading. John M. Savage to State Department, May 2, 1923, 811.114/1448, RG 59, NA; *Times* (London), May 2, 10, 1923; *Morning Post* (London), May 2, 1923; *The Outlook* 133 (May 9, 1923), 828; Post Wheeler to State Department, May 10, 1923, 811.114/1433, RG 59, NA.

[88]Prior to the Supreme Court's ruling, the shippers persuaded the Foreign Office to send the State Department a note of concern over Daugherty's ruling. H. M. Cleminson to Phillip Lloyd-Greame, October 27, 1922, copy in A6756/1437/45, PRO; P. Toppin to Armstrong, October 26, 1922, A6728/1437/45, PRO; Geddes to Foreign Office, November 10, 1922, A6830/239/45, and November 30, 1922, A7264/239/45, PRO; Foreign Office to Geddes, December 6, 1922, A7268/239/45, PRO; Geddes to Foreign Office, December 10, 1922, A7429/239/45, PRO; Crowe, Minutes, November 6, 1922, A6756/1437/45, PRO; Foreign Office to Geddes, November 21, 1922, A6982/1437/45, PRO; Geddes to Foreign Office, November 24, 1922, A7121/1437/45, PRO; "British Note on Implications of Prohibition Policy," November 30, 1922, 811.114/1142, RG 59, NA; Willebrandt to Hughes, December 21, 1922, 23/2829/72, RG 60, NAS.

[89]Liverpool Steamship Owners Association, Resolution, May 15, 1923, copy in A2930/116/45, PRO; James V. Martin to Customs House, May 4, 1923, and Customs House to Martin, May 5, 1923, copies in A2794/116/45, PRO; Royden to Crowe, May 12, 1923, A2832/116/45, and May 2, 1923, A2620/116/45, PRO; Crowe, Minutes, May 3, 1923, ibid.; Percy Bates to Sperling, May 7, 1923, A2705/116/45, PRO; Geddes to Foreign Office, May 11, 1923, A2806/116/45, and May 17, 1923, A2982/116/45, PRO; Sparks to Royden, June 7, 1923, C/2/270, Cunard Archives; Maurice Hill, Memorandum of Meeting at the Board of Trade, May 17, 1923, copy in A2981/116/45, PRO.

[90]Foreign Office, Minutes, May 3, 1923, A2620/116/45, PRO. Surprisingly, Ambassador Geddes agreed with the shippers that the ruling could be reversed. Geddes to Foreign Office, May 3, 1923, A2642/116/45, and May 14, 1923, A2856/116/45, PRO; Meeting with the British Ambassador, May 3, 1923, Folder 77a, Box 175, Hughes Papers; Geddes to Foreign Office, May 8, 1923, A2725/116/45, and June 2, 1923, A3256/116/45, PRO.

[91]Foreign Office, Minutes, May 14, 1923, A2856/116/45, May 11, 1923, A2806/116/45, and June 2, 1923, A3256/116/45, PRO; Huntington T. Morse to Smull, May 24, 1923, 1/E, RG 32, NA; Post Wheeler to State Department, May 28, 1923, 811.114/1490, RG 59, NA; Foreign Office to Geddes, May 21, 1923, A2981/116/45, PRO; Geddes to Hughes, May 25, 1923, 811.114/1488, RG 59, NA; Meeting with British Counsellor, June 2, 1923, Folder 77a, Box 175, Hughes Papers; British Embassy, Washington, DC, to Foreign Office, May 24, 1923, A3097/116/45, PRO.

[92]Treasury Department, Regulation 3484, June 4, 1923, copy in 811.114/1489, RG 59, NA; S. J. Lister to Hipwood, June 29, 1923, copy in A3894/116/45, PRO; Foreign Office to Chilton, June 29, 1923, A3905/116/45, PRO; Chilton to Hughes, June 30, 1923, 811.114/1634, RG 59, NA; Treasury Department to State Department, July 7, 1923, 811.114/1662, RG 59, NA; Chilton to Foreign Office, July 9, 1923, A4050/116/45, PRO; Sparks to Royden, June 4, 6, 7, 1923, C/2/270, Cunard Archives; Cunard Company to Sparks, June 5, 1923, ibid.; Sparks to Cunard Company, June 5, 1923, ibid.

[93]Norman Hill to Board of Trade, June 7, 1923, copy in A3417/116/45, PRO; Hipwood, Memorandum of Meeting with Norman Hill, June 13, 1923, copy in A3487/116/45, PRO; Cunard Company, Executive Committee, Minutes, June 6, 1923, B/4/60/191, Minutes of the Meetings of the Executive Committee (B/4), Cunard Archives; Cunard Company, Executive Committee, Minutes, June 13, 1923, B/4/60/205, Cunard Archives; Cunard Company to Sparks, June 8, 1923, C/2/270, Cunard Archives.

[94]Sparks to Royden, June 15, 18, 1923, C/2/270, Cunard Archives; Sparks to Cunard Company, June 13, 14, 1923, ibid.; Royden to Sparks, June 14, 1923, ibid.; Cunard Company, Board of Directors, Minutes of the Board of Directors, June 20, 1923, B/1/11, Minutes of the Meetings of the Board of Directors (B/1), Cunard Archives.

[95]The *Berengaria* was followed by the White Star liners *Baltic* and *Cedric. Morning Post* (London), June 17, 1923; *Westminster Gazette* (London), June 19, 1923; *New York Times,* June 22, 1923; Savage to State Department, June 15, 1923, 811.114/1569, RG 59, NA.

[96]William Vallance, Memorandum, June 23, 1923, 811.114/1606, RG 59, NA.

[97]Hipwood to Norman Hill, June 7, 1923, A3417/116/45, PRO; Foreign Office to Board of Trade, June 16, 1923, A3487/116/45, PRO; Foreign Office to Geddes, June 21, 1923, A3664/116/45, PRO; Chilton to Foreign Office, June 29, 1923, A4092/116/45, PRO.

[98]Harding never rescinded his October order. On July 10 the new USSB chairman, Edward Farley, announced that the president had ordered him not to deviate from the dry policy. USSB, Press Release, July 10, 1923, 1/E, RG 32, NA; Norman Beecher to Lasker, May 1, 1923, Box 1, Lasker Files, NA; L. C. Palmer to W. A. Taylor, August 20, 1924, 580/129/Part 5, RG 32, NA.

[99]Sparks to Royden, July 19, 1923, C/2/270, Cunard Archives.

[100]Royden to Sparks, July 6, 1923, S/3/17/305, Cunard Archives.

Chapter Four

Limited Options
The American Treaty Proposal
May–July 1923

By the summer of 1923, prohibition enforcement was the most visible, unsettled source of Anglo-American postwar disagreement. One year earlier the Washington Naval Disarmament Conference had ended the problematic Anglo-Japanese alliance and reduced the potential for a dispute over armaments by establishing parity as the guideline for naval policy in London and Washington. The creation of the Irish Free State in March 1922 had taken the sting out of the Irish question, a chronic source of American anglophobia. Prime Minister Stanley Baldwin, who had succeeded the ailing Bonar Law in May 1923 as the leader of the Conservative government, was the architect of Great Britain's settlement of the war debts controversy, and a repayment agreement was signed in July. An emerging pattern of cooperation between private Anglo-American interests provided the basis for a joint approach to European recovery and commercial concessions. The defeat of the subsidy bill frustrated U.S. efforts to challenge British shippers and eased the tensions of the shipping rivalry. Although these issues continued to echo throughout the remainder of the decade, they were no longer immediately pressing questions. In the midst of a once-crowded agenda, the liquor issue was a conspicuously enduring problem.[1]

Within this larger perspective, the widening Anglo-American schism over prohibition enforcement presented a significant barrier to translating agreement into harmony. The extension of liquor restrictions to British shipping confirmed the belief of Foreign Office officials that the Harding administration was the captive of domestic political interests and unreliable. The London government's unwillingness to disrupt smuggling and its commitment to principles of international law were regarded in the United States as a selfishness calculated to frustrate American aspirations. American anglophobia and British anti-Americanism, nurtured by prohibition, remained potent constraints and contributed to a diplomatic stalemate. In an atmosphere of alienation and mutual distrust, Anglo-American tensions remained unchecked, and the acceptable options for resolving the liquor problem were limited.

Secretary of State Hughes, despite these obstacles, was determined to eliminate prohibition as a diplomatic irritant. Confident of the British desire for Washington's goodwill, he prepared a proposal to resolve Anglo-American liquor tensions which he hoped would also establish the basis for subsequent agreements with other maritime powers.[2] On June 11, Hughes summoned British Chargé Henry Chilton to the State Department and unveiled his plan to restrict the impact of the *Cunard* decision and to resolve the dispute over extraterritorial seizures. Hughes proposed the ratification of a reciprocal treaty allowing sealed liquor in U.S. territorial waters in exchange for the right to search foreign vessels up to a distance of twelve miles from the shore. Citing congressional opposition to any modification of the sealed-liquor ban, Hughes warned Chilton that the draft treaty was the best practical solution to the liquor problem.[3]

The secretary of state's willingness to repeal the liquor restrictions, six weeks after the announcement of the Supreme Court's opinion, seemed a surprising reversal. Considering that the Harding administration precipitated the *Cunard* decision, Hughes's action appeared to confirm British suspicions that Attorney General Daugherty's ruling was calculated to secure Great Britain's support for extraterritorial seizures. Ambassador Geddes was convinced that Hughes personally influenced the Supreme Court to gain this valuable new pressure.[4] Cunard Chairman Thomas Royden concluded that it was "extraordinary . . . that the government has so little respect for its own laws that it offers to break them or disregard them when the quid pro quo for doing so is sufficiently attractive."[5]

The factors that influenced Hughes, however, were far more complex. Clearly, he appreciated the strength of his negotiating position, and the sealed-liquor restrictions represented a bargaining chip missing from Hughes's earlier diplomatic overture. Yet Geddes and Royden, in concluding that this was the sole determinant, attributed a nonexistent cohesiveness to the Harding administration and unfairly demeaned the secretary of state's genuine commitment to the traditional guidelines of international affairs. Since 1921, Hughes had demanded that the Justice Department accept seizure guidelines based on international law. He strongly objected to a strict interpretation of the Supreme Court's *Anchor* decision and warned Attorney General Daugherty in October that the

State Department planned to secure legislative support for the rein-statement of international comity. After the *Cunard* ruling brought strong protests from all the major maritime powers, Hughes's uneasiness increased, and the implied threat of retaliation magnified his concern over the future of U.S. commercial relations. If Hughes the lawyer respected the Court's opinion as the final word, Hughes the diplomat understood the need to ameliorate the complications created by this departure from standard international practice.[6]

The draft treaty also reflected the changing priorities of the Harding administration. The defeat of the subsidy legislation diminished the importance of the merchant marine in administration policy. The dry regulations of the U.S. Shipping Board removed the government fleet from the liquor issue, and rescinding the liquor ban on British shipping would primarily arouse the opposition of weakened and disorganized private shipping interests.[7]

As shipping concerns faded, liquor smuggling remained a glaring example of the administration's inability to enforce the Eighteenth Amendment. Anti-Saloon League pressure was unabated, and President Harding announced a renewed commitment to stricter enforcement. Harding welcomed Hughes's treaty initiative, confessing that "if it does not accomplish anything abroad it will at least serve as a fortunate gesture here at home."[8] This provided Hughes with an opportunity to reassert his leadership over all aspects of prohibition policy that extended beyond U.S. territory. While Attorney General Daugherty had led the administration down the path of expediency toward political disaster, Hughes was committed to returning the liquor issue to the diplomatic arena.

The secretary of state based his treaty proposal on the Supreme Court's *Cunard* opinion. The Court had maintained that the absence of a clear congressional intent to exempt shipping from prohibition, as in the Panama Canal exclusion, sustained Attorney General Daugherty's liquor restrictions. The corollary to this argument, according to Hughes, was that the Eighteenth Amendment was not self-executing and Congress retained the discretion to nullify the enforcement provisions of the Volstead Act. This meant that the carriage of sealed liquor in U.S. waters, still technically illegal, could be exempted from enforcement penalties by congressional action. Hughes recognized the difficulties of obtaining congressional approval, even with the promise of extraterritorial seizure rights, for a proposal to assist foreign shipping. Consequently, he framed his proposal as a treaty to confine the political debate to the Senate, where he enjoyed a good working relationship with the leadership.[9]

Although Hughes anticipated a favorable response from the British government, the initial reaction of the British press was not encouraging.

The *Morning Post,* in a highly critical editorial reflecting the general tone of the London press, focused on the extension of seizure rights and warned that the Hughes proposal would "encourage the Bolsheviks" to press their own extraterritorial claims.[10] The offensive *Cunard* ruling was a fresh source of bitterness that encouraged anti-Americanism, and the Harding administration's prohibition policy was characterized as "unfriendly," offering no basis for cooperation whatever the concessions. British shippers, preparing for the ill-fated test voyage of the *Berengaria,* believed they could successfully challenge the liquor restrictions and any serious discussion of Hughes's concession was considered premature.[11]

Surprisingly, the perspective at the Foreign Office was different. Unlike the swift and unanimous rejection of Hughes's earlier offer, not all Foreign Office officials joined in the summary dismissal of the new U.S. proposal for enforcement assistance. "The plain fact of the matter is that the liquor question is assuming a significance, in Anglo-American relations, which is out of all proportion," warned Maurice Peterson of the American Department. "We are, I submit, by attempting to regulate our relations with America by the narrow test of international law, running the risk of provoking a grave controversy on behalf of a handful of profiteers."[12] This was the first time the government's policy toward prohibition was questioned within the Foreign Office. But instead of being condemned as a heretic, Peterson received unexpected support. Ambassador Geddes, despite his cynical observations about Hughes's motives, endorsed the treaty proposal because of the intensity of American irritation over British involvement in rum-running. Legal adviser Cecil Hurst, opposed to any extension of the three-mile limit, agreed that prohibition was a serious problem that required some response, and he proposed the adoption of new restrictions to curtail liquor smuggling.[13]

The willingness of some Foreign Office officials to consider enforcement cooperation was influenced by the changing nature of the smuggling trade. After the Harding administration adopted the State Department's seizure restrictions in September 1922, the volume of activity along Rum Row steadily increased. Large, land-based bootlegging syndicates usurped the individual rumrunner and now dominated the smuggling network. A restrained Coast Guard was less able to enforce the Eighteenth Amendment and to prevent the new violence and piracy that replaced the old fraternity. With extensive financial resources, the syndicates expanded their enterprises. By the spring of 1923, Rum Row entered a period of unrivaled activity seven miles from the U.S. coast.[14]

This prosperity was not shared by liquor interests in the Bahamas. The Bahaman government, anxious to reap the maximum benefits from liquor, had regularly increased the duty on distilled spirits. The burden of this higher duty and the surcharge added by British distillers to any cargoes sent to Nassau for reexport effectively priced Bahaman brokers out of the market and diminished Nassau's attractiveness as a smuggling headquarters.[15] The French possession of St. Pierre-Miquelon, where duty requirements were lower, became the new Caribbean haven for rumrunners, while the Canadian ports of Halifax and St. John's provided a northern base for liquor interests. The loss of liquor revenue threatened the economic recovery in the Bahamas, and a tariff reduction bill was introduced in the Legislative Assembly to lure rumrunners back to Nassau.[16]

This open acknowledgment of the importance of liquor increased Foreign Office frustration over the situation in the Bahamas. Corruption in the islands was a continuous source of American criticism and an embarrassment for the British government. Two years of experience with uncooperative island officials diminished enthusiasm within the Foreign Office for defending this Crown colony, and the tariff bill heightened this resentment. Although Foreign Office officials had overlooked Bahaman incompetence, this blatant public admission of smuggling's value was indefensible. As a result, sacrificing the greedy Bahamians in order to cooperate with the United States was no longer unacceptable, and the departure of Winston Churchill from the Colonial Office further weakened the opposition to this alternative.[17]

An added consequence of the decline in the Bahaman liquor trade was the increase in the direct involvement of British interests in smuggling. High duties made the Bahamas an expensive middleman, and liquor interests utilized larger and faster boats, equipped for transatlantic crossings, to deliver their own cargo beyond U.S. territorial waters. Loaded with liquor, ships sailed from Great Britain to one of the major continental ports. Here, shippers obtained the landing certificates required by British customs and then reshipped their supplies to Rum Row. The direct sale of liquor was an attractive method of smuggling, reducing liquor prices and enlarging the margin of profit. For Foreign Office officials, it magnified the culpability of British interests in the violation of U.S. law and strengthened the Harding administration's claim that the London government should assume some responsibility for prohibition enforcement.[18]

The new character of the British liquor connection also encouraged a growing campaign in Great Britain to end smuggling. The British temperance movement, in decline since the triumphant days of wartime restrictions, regarded the direct involvement of national interests in rum-running as an issue that would rally the flagging dry cause. In April 1923 the United Kingdom Alliance initiated the antismuggling crusade by passing a resolution demanding that the government act to prevent

British involvement in liquor smuggling. When the *Glasgow Evening News* reported that liquor ships were sailing weekly from the Clyde to the United States, there were strong protests. Other temperance groups mobilized support; joined by Methodist organizations, they petitioned the Foreign Office for the adoption of antismuggling legislation.[19] Assistant Permanent Undersecretary William Tyrell warned his Foreign Office colleagues of the potential dangers of obstructing American prohibition, for "such an issue would probably give rise to protest not only of temperance associations but also from among the general public and might lead to considerable parliamentary difficulties."[20] Although anti-American sentiment in Great Britain was a strong impediment to the fulfillment of Tyrell's prediction, the domestic pressure of the temperance campaign provided a positive incentive for reevaluating British liquor policy.[21]

All of these interconnected developments encouraged the emergence of a procompromise faction in the Foreign Office. This disparate group included Peterson, Hurst, Tyrell, and the long-distance support of Ambassador Geddes. These officials, while emphasizing different concerns and endorsing different solutions, agreed in principle that the changes in the smuggling problem made it imperative that London assist Washington in enforcing prohibition. In contrast to the dismissal of the first American proposal, they now advocated the serious consideration of some substantive cooperative action by their own government.

The path to compromise, however, was blocked by a formidable obstacle: Foreign Secretary George Curzon. Tracing his formative diplomatic roots to a time when the empire was the cornerstone of British foreign policy, Curzon was an anachronistic figure in 1923. He had begun his service at the Foreign Office as Lord Salisbury's undersecretary and had become the youngest viceroy of India in 1898. Curzon remained a product of this earlier age of imperial greatness, and he tenaciously clung to values that mirrored this experience rather than the harsh realities and limitations of the postwar world. These included an unequivocal belief that the three-mile limit, a fundamental principle that helped preserve maritime links with a far-flung empire, must be defended at any cost. As a traditionalist and a nationalist, Curzon also regarded the United States with contempt and was unable to reconcile himself to American intrusion in areas of British prerogative.[22]

Curzon immediately rejected Hughes's proposal to extend territorial jurisdiction, and he prepared a sharp rebuke to this impudence. Hurst, determined to preserve the potential for compromise, warned Curzon that, unless an alternative form of cooperation was offered when the treaty was rejected, the three-mile principle might still be in jeopardy. Without British assistance, Hurst argued, the sole defense against smuggling was the unilateral extension of U.S. seizure rights. This would encourage the international abandonment of the three-mile limit as Great Britain stood alone in defense of this principle. While the foreign secretary remained steadfast in his opposition to the Hughes treaty, he reluctantly agreed to authorize the Foreign Office staff to formulate a counterproposal for limited enforcement assistance with the United States.[23]

An informal group of departmental representatives met on the morning of June 28 to discuss the feasibility of antismuggling cooperation. With Foreign Office Parliamentary Undersecretary Ronald McNeill serving as chairman, the American treaty offer was excluded from the discussion agenda.[24] Outside the Foreign Office, attitudes toward enforcement assistance were unchanged. G. E. A. Grindle presented the standard Colonial Office disclaimer of responsibility for the situation in the Bahamas, and Customs representatives extolled the virtues of existing export regulations. Board of Trade officials, embittered by the *Cunard* ruling and uncertain of the outcome of the *Berengaria* test voyage, reflected the hard-line view of the shipping industry and criticized any suggestion of cooperation. McNeill, admitting that there was no effective method of preventing smuggling, argued for some gesture, however unworkable in practice, that would relieve the British government of the stigma of aiding rumrunners. The Americans are an "emotional people," Tyrell added, "and what they would value was the evidence of goodwill."[25] Following a lengthy discussion, the representatives agreed to meet again and discuss proposals for parliamentary legislation to strengthen current export and shipping registry laws.

When the group reassembled on July 5, both the status and nature of their discussions were altered. After an initial silence, the pressure of parliamentary questions and daily press speculation had forced Foreign Secretary Curzon to comment on the American treaty proposal. While the departmental representatives were meeting for the first time on June 28, Curzon told the House of Lords that the Anglo-American liquor situation was "difficult and delicate."[26] Conceding the technical right of the United States to exclude liquor, he then abandoned delicacy and accused the State Department of using the *Cunard* ruling to coerce Great Britain into accepting responsibility for prohibition enforcement. Under no circumstances, he declared, would the government agree to any proposal which included an extension of the three-mile limit. Curzon's prepared text ended with this repudiation, but Tyrell persuaded him to add that the Baldwin government would not officially reply to the Hughes offer until it received the report of the special interdepartmental committee considering the matter.[27] Returning to the Foreign Office and reading the minutes of the group's first meeting, Curzon already regretted his impromptu creation. "The committee seems to me to have been much more concerned with finding a way out for the Americans," he tersely noted, "than with [repudiating] a grave breach of international comity."[28]

The members of this "new" committee were surprised by their elevated status. Originally, this was an informal body, without official appointment and with limited objectives. Now they were a publicly acknowledged interdepartmental committee, occupying a central position in the formulation of the government's liquor policy, and Curzon's statement appeared to widen the scope of their inquiry.[29] When the committee met on July 5, Lord Wolmer, the Board of Trade's representative, unexpectedly recommended that the group discuss the American treaty offer. By July the *Berengaria*'s test voyage had ended in failure, and the shipping industry was the British interest most seriously affected by the Eighteenth Amendment. As distillers in Great Britain continued to export spirits and the Bahamians devised new methods for recouping lost revenue, the sealed-liquor restrictions remained. Wolmer argued that the primary concern of British shippers was the lifting of the liquor ban and it might be advantageous to discuss the American concession. Board of Trade officials, still wavering between hostility toward U.S. restrictions and the potential value of compromise, were not prepared to press the issue. When Chairman McNeill declared that the treaty was beyond the committee's jurisdiction, Wolmer withdrew his request, and the committee returned to the scheduled agenda.[30]

Following the detailed consideration of proposals prepared by the respective departments, it was apparent that all of the alternatives for smuggling assistance were impractical. Requiring bond for liquor cargo leaving Great Britain did not prevent reexport from the Bahamas or continental ports, and a suggestion to restrict liquor exports to the British West Indies was dismissed because it would force smugglers to purchase supplies elsewhere. Board of Trade officials opposed the use of ship registry regulations to punish smugglers, maintaining that this was impossible to enforce. The committee also vetoed a suggestion to invite U.S. enforcement officers to visit Nassau, fearing that these officials would be assassinated, and any action that diverted resentment from Great Britain to the Bahamas might encourage American pressure for the annexation of the islands. Unable to agree on any substantive measures, the committee approved a proposal to outlaw the export of liquor to the United States. This simply gave statutory authority to the current practice of British customs officials. As the committee recognized, it was an ineffective measure that would not sever the British smuggling connection.[31]

In Washington, Secretary of State Hughes waited impatiently for an answer to his treaty offer. He was infuriated by Curzon's charges of American duplicity in the *Cunard* ruling, and the vague reference to the interdepartmental committee was discouraging.[32] Hughes maintained that his draft treaty was presented to provide the basis for bilateral discussions, but it was apparent from Curzon's remarks that British officials regarded the proposal as a formal treaty offer.

Hughes's frustration was compounded by the absence from their posts of both Ambassador Geddes and U.S. Ambassador to Great Britain George Harvey. Hughes urged Harvey to return to London, admitting that "it is very necessary now to have the advantage of personal explanations since the British government is laboring under misapprehensions."[33] Without the benefit of this firsthand information, the secretary of state was unaware of the existence of a procompromise faction in the Foreign Office. He was convinced that the British underestimated the critical nature of the smuggling problem, and he dismissed the interdepartmental committee as a delaying tactic.[34]

To pressure the British government, Hughes instructed the American chargé in London, Post Wheeler, to inform the Foreign Office of the recent U.S. Circuit Court's decision on the *Henry L. Marshall* appeal. In upholding the first seizure of a British rumrunner beyond the three-mile limit, the court expanded the concept of "constructive presence" to include the seizure of a foreign vessel if it used *any* small boats, not just its own equipment, to unload liquor in U.S. waters. This definition would effectively extend American seizure rights to the twelve-mile limit of the Tariff Act of 1922. Hughes hoped the threatened application of the ruling might prod the British government to begin discussions on a liquor treaty.[35] But Foreign Office officials were aware of the *Marshall* opinion, which they decided to ignore because the vessel's British registry was suspect, and Hughes's strategy simply succeeded in forcing the Foreign Office to lodge a formal protest over the ruling.[36]

On July 10, the day after Wheeler delivered Hughes's warning, the interdepartmental committee presented its formal report. Prefaced with the disclaimer that "nothing we can do is likely to have a material effect in preventing the smuggling of liquor into America," the report recommended the adoption of legislation to forbid the carriage of goods to destinations where those goods were prohibited.[37] This measure would apply to all nongoverning dominions, including the Bahamas, and its passage was dependent upon Congress removing the sealed-liquor restrictions when it reconvened in the fall. The committee acknowledged that even this modest proposal would be difficult to enforce because most rumrunners did not clear their cargoes for direct export to the United States. However, they concluded that it might at least pacify critics of the smuggling connection within Great Britain and dispel "the ignorant assumption of those who have given no thought to the subject that it is a perfectly simple business for the British government to put an end to British complicity with American smuggling."[38]

The deliberations of the interdepartmental committee highlighted the Baldwin government's limited options for negotiating a settlement of the Anglo-American liquor problem. Although the committee fulfilled its mandate to frame an alternative proposal to the U.S. request for antismuggling cooperation, this halfhearted and pessimistic endorsement did little to encourage the supporters of compromise. At the same time, the *Cunard* restrictions remained a glaring example of prohibition's long reach. What the committee clearly demonstrated was that there was really no substantive British proposal, requiring a minimum of sacrifice, that was attractive enough to persuade either the Harding administration or Congress to lift the *Cunard* regulations.[39]

This did not moderate Lord Curzon's opposition to the American treaty offer. Instead, it strengthened his determination "not to give way with regard to the twelve mile limit."[40] The foreign secretary, reluctantly persuaded to defer his rejection of the Hughes initiative, regarded the committee's failure as both a vindication of his hard-line position and as a powerful rebuttal against the arguments for cooperation. Exploiting this stalemate, Curzon ordered the interdepartmental representatives to reconvene and draft a plan of retaliation against American shipping. He was convinced that a direct challenge, not compromise, was the best method of convincing the Harding administration to abandon the *Cunard* restrictions.[41]

Only a month after Secretary Hughes presented his treaty proposal, Anglo-American prohibition tensions, rather than easing, had escalated. By initiating a solution to the liquor problem, Hughes hoped to improve diplomatic relations between the United States and Great Britain. He believed that, in linking transatlantic liquor sales with extended seizure rights, he was offering a mutually beneficial agreement that would establish a precedent for international antismuggling assistance. His ability to return the liquor issue to the diplomatic arena depended upon the success of this effort and the willingness of the British government to discuss his proposal.

Hughes, however, miscalculated the desire of the British officials for American goodwill. Foreign Secretary Curzon's commitment to the traditional principles of British foreign policy guaranteed his implacable opposition to any proposal which challenged the three-mile limit. Under his guidance, the Baldwin government was not prepared to barter this principle for the uncertainty of American friendship; for Curzon, prohibition enforcement remained solely an American responsibility. Although some members of the Foreign Office endorsed cooperation, they could not temper Curzon's uncompromising perspective. Concern over changes in the smuggling trade and a growing domestic opposition to the British smuggling connection were not enough to overcome the inherent difficulties of framing a solution to the liquor problem. The interdepartmental committee's exposure of the absence of acceptable alternatives for resolving prohibition tensions allowed the foreign secretary to reorder its agenda and repudiate moderation. What the supporters of compromise needed was a strong defender to challenge Curzon's control of British liquor policy. Without this, they would be unable to prevent the drift toward confrontation.

Notes

[1]Offner, *Origins of the Second World War,* 62–78; Hoff-Wilson, *American Business and Foreign Policy,* 31–48; Leffler, *Elusive Quest,* 64–70; Hogan, *Informal Entente,* 13–77; Beckles Willson, *America's Ambassadors to England* (Freeport, NY, 1928), 478; Ellis, *Republican Foreign Policy,* 135; Glad, *Charles Evans Hughes,* 300; Buckley, *The United States and the Washington Conference, 1921–1922*; Dexter Perkins, *Charles Evans Hughes and American Democratic Statesmanship* (Boston, 1956), 111; H. C. Allen, *Great Britain and the United States,* 741, 756–58; Mowat, *Britain between the Wars,* 106–7; Esme Howard, *Theatre of Life* (London, 1936), 197–98; Keith Middlemas and John Barnes, *Baldwin* (London, 1969), 137–48.

[2]Charles Evans Hughes to Warren G. Harding, June 15, 1923, 711.419/8a, M581, Roll 13, RG 59, NA; Hughes to Harding, June 16, 1923, 1255/144, Harding Papers.

[3]Memorandum on Meeting with British Chargé, June 11, 1923, Folder 77a, Box 175, Hughes Papers; British Embassy, Washington, to Foreign Office, June 12, 1923, A3456/116/45, PRO.

[4]Auckland Geddes to Foreign Office, June 12, 1923, A3477/116/45, PRO. See also *Daily Mail* (London), June 16, 1923.

[5]Thomas Royden to Ashley Sparks, July 6, 1923, S/3/17/305, Cunard Archives.

[6]Solicitor's Office, State Department, to Hughes, April 6, 1922, 811.114/Great Britain/33, RG 59, NA; Pusey, *Charles Evans Hughes* 2:577; Hughes to Harry M. Daugherty, October 5, 1922, "Daugherty" folder, Box 9, Hughes Papers; Memorandum of Henry C. Beerits, "Treaties to Prevent the Smuggling of Intoxicating Liquor into the United States," Folder 48, Box 173, Hughes Papers (hereafter cited as Beerits Memorandum). Beerits assisted in organizing the Hughes Papers and prepared subject memoranda with Hughes's participation. When Hughes prepared notes for an autobiography, he offered no new comments on the liquor controversy, acknowledging the Beerits paper as his definitive comment on the subject.

[7]Pusey, *Charles Evans Hughes* 2:577; Kemble and Kendall, "Years between the Wars," in Kilmarx, *America's Maritime Legacy,* 159–60.

⁸Harding to Hughes, June 20, 1923, 1290/144, Harding Papers; Murray, *Harding Era,* 407; *Literary Digest* 78 (July 7, 1923): 11–13; *New York Times,* June 26, 1923.

⁹Beerits Memorandum, Folder 48, Box 173, Hughes Papers; William Vallance to Hughes, May 19, 1923, 811.114/1511, RG 59, NA; Memorandum on Meeting with British Chargé, June 11, 1923, Folder 77a, Box 175, Hughes Papers; Murray, *Harding Era,* 130.

¹⁰*Morning Post* (London), June 15, 1923; Post Wheeler to Hughes, June 18, 1923, 711.419/6, M581, Roll 13, RG 59, NA.

¹¹*Times* (London), June 4, 1923; *Daily Mail* (London), June 16, 1923; Wheeler to Hughes, June 15, 1923, 711.419/5, and June 20, 1923, 711.419/8, M581, Roll 13, RG 59, NA.

¹²Maurice Peterson, Minutes, June 12, 1923, A3412/116/45, PRO.

¹³Geddes to Foreign Office, June 12, 1923, A3477/116/45, PRO; Cecil Hurst, Memorandum, June 13, 1923, A3611/116/45, PRO; Foreign Office, Minutes, June 13, 1923, ibid. Hurst proposed legislation to fine any exporters not delivering their cargo to the manifested destination, an empire-wide prohibition of liquor exports to countries where liquor was outlawed, and the refusal to protest the seizure of rumrunners from any dominion not adopting these measures. When the British government formally responded to the treaty, these measures would be offered.

¹⁴Van de Water, *Real McCoy,* 191, 211; *New York Times,* November 4, 1922.

¹⁵By January 1923 the Bahaman duty was a hefty $5.40 per case of liquor. Lorin A. Lathrop to State Department, June 4, 1923, 811.114/1241, RG 59, NA.

¹⁶Lathrop to State Department, May 2, 1923, 811.114/BWI/186, RG 59, NA; Charles Sydney to State Department, July 1, 1923, 811.114/St. Pierre-Miquelon/2, RG 59, NA; Governor Cordeaux to Colonial Office, June 7, 1923, copy in A3707/34/45, PRO.

¹⁷Peterson, Minutes, June 12, 1923, A3412/116/45, PRO; Hurst, Memorandum, June 13, 1923, A3611/116/45, PRO; Foreign Office, Minutes, July 19, 1923, A4091/34/45, July 21, 1923, A4380/34/45, and September 13, 1923, A5706/116/45, PRO; Foreign Office to Colonial Office, July 19, 1923, A3707/34/45, PRO; Colonial Office to Foreign Office, July 21, 1923, A4380/34/45, PRO.

¹⁸Treasury Department, Circular Letter, May 1923, copies in 811.114/1401–1404, RG 59, NA; A. B. Cooke to State Department, May 3, 1923, 811.114/1449, RG 59, NA; Lythgoe, *Bahama Queen,* 113; Lathrop to State Department, May 2, 1923, 811.114/BWI/186, RG 59, NA.

¹⁹Brander, *Original Scotch,* 120; Robert P. Skinner to State Department, April 4, 1923, 811.114/1374, RG 59, NA; *Glasgow Evening News,* May 16, 1923; American Embassy, London, to State Department, April 11, 1923, 811.114/1731, and June 25, 1923, 811.114/1738, RG 59, NA; Charles Smith to George Curzon, June 22, 1923, A3712/34/45, PRO.

[20]William Tyrell, Minutes, June 6, 1923, A3312/116/45, and June 13, 1923, A3611/116/45, PRO; Peterson, Minutes, June 22, 1923, A3712/34/45, PRO.

[21]*Observer* (London), July 15, 1923; Wheeler to State Department, July 30, 1923, 811.114/1809, RG 59, NA; Foreign Office, Minutes, August 24, 1923, A5655/116/45, PRO.

[22]Leonard Mosley, *The Glorious Fault* (New York, 1960), 91–147; Kenneth Rose, *A Superior Person* (London, 1969); D. C. Watt, *Succeeding John Bull,* 48–49; D. L. Watt, *Personalities and Policies,* 37–38; George Harvey to Hughes, March 29, 1923, "March–June 1923" folder, Box 46, Hughes Papers.

[23]Geddes to Foreign Office, June 12, 1923, A3477/116/45, PRO; Hurst, Minutes, June 13, 1923, A3611/116/45, PRO; Interdepartmental Report on Territorial Waters, June 1923, T6883/69/350, F.O. 372, PRO.

[24]McNeill opened the meeting by asserting that it "was impossible to negotiate on the basis of agreeing to the United States officials exercising the right of search on British vessels." Interdepartmental Committee, Minutes, June 28, 1923, A3932/116/45, PRO.

[25]Ibid. See also "Resolution of the Merseyside Conservative Committee," June 12, 1923, copy in A3510/116/45, PRO; Wheeler to Hughes, June 20, 1923, 711.419/8, M581, Roll 13, RG 59, NA.

[26]*Parliamentary Debates* (Lords), June 28, 1923, 154:715. Prior to June 28, Curzon had refused to comment on the proposal. Wheeler to Hughes, June 18, 1923, 711.419/6, and June 19, 1923, 711.419/7, M581, Roll 13, RG 59, NA.

[27]Foreign Office, Minutes, June 28, 1923, A3614/116/45, PRO.

[28]George Curzon, Minutes, June 28, 1923, A3932/116/45, PRO.

[29]Interdepartmental Committee, Minutes, July 5, 1923, A4046/116/45, PRO; Henry Chilton to Foreign Office, June 29, 1923, A3903/116/45, and June 30, 1923, A3906/116/45, PRO; Peterson, Minutes, June 29, 1923, A3903/116/45, PRO.

[30]Sparks to Royden, July 19, 1923, C/2/270, Cunard Archives; Cunard Company, Executive Committee, Minutes, July 4, 1923, B/4/60/243, Cunard Archives; Interdepartmental Committee, Minutes, July 5, 1923, A4046/116/45, PRO.

[31]Interdepartmental Committee, Minutes, July 5, 1923, A4046/116/45, PRO.

[32]Bertram D. Hulen, *Inside the Department of State* (New York, 1939), 130–32.

[33]Hughes to Harvey, June 30, 1923, "Harvey" folder, Box 25, and July 23, 1923, "July–October 1923" folder, Box 4b, Hughes Papers. Because of his poor health, Geddes never returned to Washington. Robert Cunliffe-Owen to Hughes, June 25, 1923, "Cunliffe-Owen" folder, Box 17, Hughes Papers. Although Hughes had opposed Harvey's appointment, he valued the personal relationships established by the ambassador with officials in the Baldwin government. See Glad, *Charles Evans Hughes,* 136; Post Wheeler and Hallie E. Rives, *Dome of Many-Coloured Glass* (Garden City, NY, 1955), 685; David J. Danielski and

Joseph S. Tulchin, eds., *The Autobiographical Notes of Charles Evans Hughes* (Cambridge, MA, 1973), 206.

[34]Hughes to Wheeler, July 6, 1923, 711.419/11a, M581, Roll 13, RG 59, NA; William Phillips to Chilton, July 9, 1923, 711.419/13, M581, Roll 13, RG 59, NA. The British continued to regard the proposal as a formal offer. Chilton to Foreign Office, July 9, 1923, A4066/116/45, PRO; Rowland Sperling, Minutes, July 9, 1923, A4048/116/45, PRO. See also Wheeler and Rives, *Dome of Many-Coloured Glass,* 645–713; William Castle to Harvey, December 12, 1922, File 24, Box 3, Papers of William Castle, Herbert Hoover Presidential Library, West Branch, Iowa (hereafter cited as Castle Papers); Boylston Beale to Castle, April 30, 1923, File 24, Box 3, Castle Papers.

[35]Hughes to Wheeler, June 30, 1923, 811.114/1652a, RG 59, NA; Foreign Office, Minutes, July 6, 1923, A4016/116/45, PRO; Wheeler to Hughes, July 9, 1923, 711.419/12, M581, Roll 13, RG 59, NA; *Henry L. Marshall,* 292 Fed 486; William Hayward to Mabel Walker Willebrandt, June 16, 1923, 23/1905/167x, RG 60, NAS; Chilton to Foreign Office, July 21, 1923, A4368/34/45, PRO; State Department to Chilton, August 17, 1923, 311.4154/K11/2, RG 59, NA.

[36]*Morning Post* (London), July 2, 1923; Foreign Office to Chilton, July 9, 1923, A4019/116/45, PRO; Chilton to Hughes, July 19, 1923, A4404/116/45, PRO; Hughes to Chilton, July 16, 1923, 311.4153/H39/46, RG 59, NA; Chilton to Foreign Office, July 19, 1923, A4492/116/45, PRO; Foreign Office, Minutes, July 23, 1923, A4368/34/45, PRO.

[37]Interdepartmental Committee, Memorandum, July 10, 1923, A4097/116/45, PRO.

[38]Ibid. Members of the committee expressed concern that the United States might abandon its support of the three-mile limit. They acknowledged that "there is, moreover, a powerful section of opinion in this country which is in sympathy with the American view of the question and which regards the complicity of British shipping in the smuggling trade as discreditable to the British flag."

[39]Foreign Office, Minutes, July 10, 1923, A4097/116/45, PRO.

[40]Foreign Office, Minutes, July 14, 1923, A4198/116/45, PRO.

[41]Ibid.

Chapter Five

A New Perspective
Negotiating the Anglo-American Liquor Treaty July 1923–May 1924

As Foreign Secretary Curzon prepared his plan for retaliation against the *Cunard* restrictions, he received a disturbing letter from his cabinet colleague Phillip Lloyd-Greame. As president of the Board of Trade, Lloyd-Greame wrote "personally [to] press the importance of a settlement" in the "continued impasse over the application of the United States Prohibition Act." This stalemate, he informed Curzon, created serious problems for British shipping and for the shipbuilding industry. Elaborating on the impact of the sealed-liquor restrictions, Lloyd-Greame acknowledged the interdepartmental committee's difficulty in devising a workable solution. "In these circumstances," he concluded, "unless an effective agreement can be made on other terms, which will secure the withdrawal of the United States Regulations, I shall feel bound to press the advantages of an arrangement on the lines proposed by Mr. Hughes."[1] Lloyd-Greame's warning was unmistakable; the supporters of compromise had a defender to champion their cause.

Unwittingly, Curzon himself encouraged this growing belief in the efficacy of considering the Hughes treaty and exposed the impotency of his leadership. Without a practical alternative to weaken the British smuggling connection, his call for retaliation presented a clear choice between either the continuation of rum-running or the acceptance of the American treaty. Curzon, by polarizing the issue, enhanced the attractiveness of the Hughes offer and forced the advocates of compromise to regard it as the best solution to the prohibition problem.

Curzon's decision to intensify liquor tensions also redefined the nature of the debate. Board of Trade officials now were prepared to lead the offensive against the foreign secretary's rejection of the American treaty, providing support for the procompromise faction in the Foreign Office. But these officials were less concerned with the unsavoriness of British rum-running or domestic antismuggling pressure. They focused solely on the fact that the shipping industry suffered under the *Cunard* ruling and the Hughes proposal offered relief. Dismissing Curzon's planned retaliation as a misguided effort that would further disrupt transatlantic shipping, the officials were determined to safeguard this vital economic interest.

The impetus for the Board of Trade's endorsement of the American treaty was the new attitude of the British shipping community. In practice, the *Cunard* regulations created more problems than anticipated by discouraging passenger trade and forcing cargo vessels carrying liquor to abandon refueling stopovers in American ports. Despite the defeat of the subsidy bill, the U.S. Shipping Board announced plans to expand its transatlantic fleet, the *Leviathan* was ready to embark on its maiden voyage as the flagship of the United States Lines, and British passenger ships sailed under the same restrictions as privately owned American vessels.[2] Yet it was also apparent by July that there was little hope of any immediate moderation of the restrictions from the Harding administration or Congress. Abandoning their earlier demand for retaliation, the shippers adopted a resolution urging the acceptance of the Hughes proposal.[3]

This prompted Lord Wolmer to suggest that the interdepartmental committee discuss the American offer. As pressure from the shippers intensified, the Board of Trade's support for the treaty increased. At the committee's July 9 meeting, Wolmer refused to consider any of the alternative suggestions for antismuggling assistance. When the final recommendations were presented on the following day, the Board of Trade withheld its approval because the American treaty option was not included and the report was primarily a Foreign Office document, not a statement of interdepartmental consensus.[4]

The Board of Trade's position was confirmed in the letter sent by Lloyd-Greame to Foreign Secretary Curzon on July 10. The liquor restrictions, Lloyd-Greame maintained, came at a time when British passenger ships already were suffering from the decline in emigrant traffic, and cargo shipping could not afford the additional expense of either refusing liquor consignments or rerouting to non-American ports. Further losses would undermine the Baldwin government's efforts to revitalize the depressed shipbuilding industry. Lloyd-Greame also was alarmed by press reports of the *Henry L. Marshall* appeal and the possibility that this might encourage the United States to extend seizure rights, negating the need for the sealed-liquor concession. "In these circumstances," he concluded, "it would surely be extremely unwise to close the door on Mr. Hughes's suggested arrangement which would give to the liners and the cargo boats the freedom which is essential to them."[5] He warned that he would repeat these arguments when the issue was presented to the cabinet for a final decision.

Lloyd-Greame's letter forced Curzon to cancel his instructions to the interdepartmental committee to reconvene and discuss methods of retaliation. To reassure the Board of Trade that the liquor negotiations remained open, Curzon decided to send an interim reply to the unanswered American proposal. On July 16 he informed Secretary of State Hughes that the Baldwin government was not prepared to respond formally to his offer. Condemning the twelve-mile seizure limit as unworkable and a dangerous precedent, Curzon suggested that the best solution was to wait until Congress could reconvene and rescind the *Cunard* restrictions. The negative tone of the note suggested that, rather than seeking a new basis for further negotiations, Curzon's primary motive was to confirm the need for British retaliation.[6]

Although Secretary Hughes rejected this unrealistic request as politically impossible, he did not terminate the negotiations. Hughes, encouraged by the publication in the London *Times* of a letter from the prominent Conservative politician Lord Birkenhead, was convinced that the potential for agreement existed. Endorsing the Hughes plan, Birkenhead claimed that the three-mile limit was the only obstacle to an Anglo-American liquor pact. If the treaty included a preamble upholding this principle, Birkenhead declared, it would be an acceptable compromise.[7] The secretary of state placed great faith in Birkenhead's observations, and on July 19 he informed Curzon that he was willing to include this preamble in his proposal or to consider any other suggestion for antismuggling cooperation. The same day, Post Wheeler notified Hughes of a confidential report that the interdepartmental committee would recommend the adoption of the treaty. An elated Hughes quickly cabled the good news to President Harding, who was in Vancouver.[8]

Hughes's optimism, however, was based on inaccurate assumptions. Birkenhead was part of a minority faction of Conservatives who had opposed the dissolution of the Lloyd George coalition in 1922. Birkenhead, unwilling to serve in the cabinet with Curzon, refused to join the Baldwin government, and as an outsider his influence was limited.[9] The secretary of state also misunderstood Curzon's motives in sending the interim note. Although Hughes did not reply with the blanket rejection Curzon invited, the refusal to lift the *Cunard* restrictions without any British concessions was immediately condemned by the foreign secretary.

This removed the remaining obstacle to retaliation, and Curzon reissued orders for the interdepartmental committee to meet and prepare a counterattack.[10]

When the committee reconvened on July 24, American Department chief Rowland Sperling, among the dwindling group of Curzon supporters, offered a plan of retaliation. Sperling, to win the support of the Board of Trade, announced that this was a comprehensive action targeted at all American abuses of British shipping interests "to disassociate the whole matter so far as possible from the drink question, which was one that lent itself to sentimental propaganda both in this country and elsewhere."[11] He proposed resurrecting the dormant Passenger Vessels Liquor Bill, introduced by backbenchers in the wake of the *Cunard* ruling, to close British ports to the ships of any country denying international comity. This would be incorporated into the committee's original proposal for legislation to outlaw the export of distilled spirits to destinations where liquor was prohibited.

The committee's reaction to Sperling's proposal indicated that Curzon misjudged the impact of Secretary Hughes's response. While Curzon believed that retaliation was the next logical step, the members of the interdepartmental committee did not agree. Board of Trade officials were not swayed by Sperling's concern for British shipping and, except for the liquor restrictions, they dismissed his list of grievances as minor concerns. Retaliation was not feasible, Lord Wolmer contended, and Colonial Office representatives expressed serious doubts that the dominions would cooperate in a scheme to disrupt international commerce. Chairman Ronald McNeill, acknowledging that the shipping lobby's support for the American treaty had altered opinions in the House of Commons, argued that it would be extremely difficult to secure approval for retaliation.[12]

Recognizing that the committee was at an impasse, Board of Trade officials put forward the consideration of the American proposal. Although the Board of Trade presented recent evidence of the shipping community's support for the American treaty, the financial problems of British shippers and the previous interdepartmental deliberations made further discussion unnecessary.[13] Most committee members already were convinced of the need to accept the American proposal, and only Sperling refused to support the approval of a liquor treaty.[14]

On August 22 the interdepartmental committee submitted its final report and recommended the adoption of a treaty based on the American offer to link extraterritorial seizure rights with the repeal of the sealed-liquor restrictions. The committee's version included a preamble reaffirming the three-mile principle and a Colonial Office proviso that the dominion governments would be consulted before a final agreement was signed, and it replaced Hughes's twelve-mile seizure limit with a distance based on travel time from the shore to avoid any connection with the general question of territorial jurisdiction.[15] Highlighting the need for the treaty, the report focused on the problems of shipping, rejecting both alternate antismuggling proposals and retaliation, because this would not eliminate the sealed-liquor restrictions. Members of the committee warned that the failure to reach an agreement might force the United States to abandon its support of the three-mile limit. They concluded that "a treaty on the lines suggested by Mr. Hughes offers the only satisfactory solution of the question."[16]

Despite the committee's strong statement, Foreign Secretary Curzon remained unwilling to accept this conclusion. Confronted with the opposition of interdepartmental officials, repudiated by the committee he created, and abandoned by most of his Foreign Office staff, he still believed that the British government should not "make a 'beau geste' when the U.S. violates the comity of nations."[17] In this determination, Curzon was the captive of both his links with the past and his personal pride. He was preserving a traditional British principle, regardless of its incongruity with the economic realities of the postwar world, and this clouded his judgment and strengthened his conviction to continue the fight alone. Beset by a series of humiliations in his public life, most recently when he was passed over as Bonar Law's successor for the younger and less experienced Stanley Baldwin, Curzon could not sustain another defeat. He staked his prestige and his enduring perspective against the American treaty, and this further weakened his deficient sense of proportion and made compromise unacceptable.[18]

Prior to the submission of the formal interdepartmental report on August 22, Curzon already decided to disregard the committee's recommendations. The minutes of the group's last meeting and the committee's circulating draft treaty removed any doubts about the final conclusion.[19] Acting quickly to preempt the interdepartmental report, the foreign secretary personally drafted a letter to Secretary Hughes on August 3 in which he sharply rebuffed the American treaty offer. The Baldwin government could not accept U.S. municipal law as a higher authority on the question of territorial waters, he wrote, or weaken the three-mile limit for a seemingly minor problem. Curzon claimed that no liquor was sent directly to the United States from Great Britain and it was not illegal for British subjects to sell liquor on the open seas. Concluding his draft, he refused any British assistance unless the sealed-liquor restrictions were removed.[20]

Arrogantly believing he could continue to act independently, Curzon preordained the final rejection of his hard-line policy. His note contradicted every conclusion of the interdepartmental committee and, as written, it reflected Curzon's desire to end the liquor negotiations. When Board of Trade officials discovered Curzon's calculated maneuver, Lloyd-Greame responded immediately. Writing to the foreign secretary on August 17, Lloyd-Greame warned that, if Curzon could not support the interdepartmental recommendations, the Board of Trade was prepared to bring the issue before the cabinet.[21] Curzon appreciated the political dangers of a cabinet debate in which the opposition of the Board of Trade, Admiralty, Colonial Office, Customs, and a large part of the Foreign Office was guaranteed, and he instructed British Chargé Henry Chilton not to deliver the note.

Searching for a way to avoid a cabinet showdown and certain defeat, Curzon sought refuge in the Colonial Office proviso, included in the interdepartmental committee's draft treaty, requiring consultation with the dominions before a formal liquor agreement was signed. The 1923 Imperial Conference of dominion leaders was scheduled to convene in October, and Curzon hoped to find new support at the conference. He incorporated this fabricated deference to the dominion governments in his response to Lloyd-Greame, reassuring the Board of Trade president that the note to Secretary Hughes was simply an interim reply intended to keep the negotiations open until the Imperial Conference met.[22] After Lloyd-Greame agreed to postpone any cabinet discussion, the Foreign Office sent Chilton a new ending for Curzon's original note of rejection.[23] This tactical change, stating that the British government could not officially respond to the American offer until the question was submitted to the Imperial Conference, was added to the reply presented by Chilton to the State Department on September 17.

State Department officials regarded the British note with cautious optimism. "The note," Undersecretary of State William Phillips observed, "strikes us as somewhat contradictory because up to the last paragraph it appears to be a definite rejection of the American proposals. On the other hand, the last paragraph appears to leave it still open."[24] Following the unexpected death of President Harding in August, his successor, Vice-President Calvin Coolidge, urged Secretary Hughes to continue the treaty discussions with the British government.[25] Hughes met with Lord Birkenhead at the American Bar Association conference in Minneapolis, on August 30, to discuss the treaty. When the interim British reply arrived three weeks later, Hughes erroneously credited Birkenhead for ending the stalemate.[26] Grateful for this intercession, the secretary of state decided not to respond to Curzon's critical comments, and he accepted that the fate of the proposal now rested with the Imperial Conference. At Hughes's insistence, U.S. Ambassador George Harvey returned to London and began a whirlwind lobbying effort to influence the outcome of the conference.[27]

As the dominion leaders arrived in London, Foreign Secretary Curzon planned his final attack on the liquor treaty. Curzon was convinced that he could use his chairmanship of the Territorial Waters Committee to persuade the conference to reject the American proposal. Confident of success, he instructed his parliamentary secretary, Robert Vansittart, to prepare a list of antitreaty sympathizers. But Vansittart reported that of the six countries represented on the committee, only Newfoundland and New Zealand would support the foreign secretary. Australia favored the treaty, the Canadians were unwilling to antagonize the United States, and both South Africa and Ireland were uncommitted.[28]

Curzon found little encouragement for his crusade outside the conference. A large sector of the London press, led by the *Daily Telegraph*, advocated the approval of the Hughes plan.[29] Temperance groups continued to demand that the Baldwin government ratify an antismuggling pact.[30] The fatal blow for Curzon came on October 20 when the Foreign Office staff presented its preconference memorandum on the liquor issue. For the first time, department officials unanimously recommended the adoption of the liquor treaty on the grounds that it was advantageous to British interests. "Having regard to the preference for compromise which animates shipping and commercial interests," they concluded that it was necessary to accept the American offer.[31]

On the eve of the first session of the Imperial Conference, Curzon was forced to abandon his offensive against the treaty. He had overestimated his ability to influence the conference; the strength of his opponents, the climate of opinion, and the emergence of a new perspective guaranteed defeat. To continue the fight was to transform private failure into public humiliation.[32] At the Territorial Waters Committee's first meeting on October 25, Lloyd-Greame spoke on behalf of the treaty and concluded that "the Board of Trade considers our commercial interests to be the paramount consideration in this matter."[33] The soundness of Curzon's decision to end his challenge was confirmed as all the committee members, except the Newfoundland delegate, spoke in support of the American treaty and its sealed-liquor concession.[34] Curzon was the last speaker. Although expressing his reluctance to surrender to American pressure, the foreign secretary urged the committee to endorse a liquor agreement. "If we refused this offer," Curzon warned, "we might soon reach a condition of quasi-warfare. How were we to meet that condition?"[35]

Before the liquor treaty was presented to the Imperial Conference, there was an unexpected delay. When British and American newspapers prematurely announced on October 29 that the Hughes proposal was approved, a report appeared in the *New York World* claiming that Justice Department officials considered the treaty to be unconstitutional. These unnamed sources argued that the sealed-liquor exemption violated the Eighteenth Amendment, and they expressed their intention to oppose the treaty.[36] "I will not make the concessions unless I am assured of the quid pro quo," Curzon declared after reading the story in the British press, and he refused to continue the negotiations without an American guarantee of the liquor treaty's constitutionality.[37]

Secretary Hughes was furious at the Justice Department's ill-timed remarks and blatant attempt to scuttle the agreement.[38] Hughes had planned to present the treaty to the Senate when it reconvened in December before a long winter recess. The failure to meet this deadline would postpone pending liquor negotiations with the Dutch government. Acting to calm Curzon's apprehensions, Hughes asked President Coolidge to announce that the treaty was constitutional, and he instructed Wheeler to reassure British officials that the Panama Canal exemption in the Volstead Act provided the legal basis for the liquor concession.[39]

With the Imperial Conference preparing to adjourn, Curzon was forced to leave these legal questions temporarily unsettled. On November 9 the conference approved the British draft treaty and empowered the Foreign Office to resolve any outstanding issues, subject to dominion approval of the final agreement.[40] But Foreign Office officials remained concerned over the constitutionality of the treaty. Hughes's arguments were legally untested, and the validity of the Panama Canal exemption was never confirmed by an American court. When the negotiations began, the Foreign Office proposed adding a new clause to the treaty that suspended the entire agreement if any provision was declared illegal. Although Hughes believed a formal constitutional guarantee would discredit the agreement, he had no enthusiasm for a protracted debate and agreed to the disclaimer.[41] On December 11, Curzon presented the treaty to the British cabinet, and it was forwarded to the dominions for their approval.[42]

The final text of the treaty was an amalgamation of both the British and American drafts. Hughes's original proposal provided the basic framework, the interdepartmental committee contributed the details, and the seizure limit and specific clarifications of wording were a result of the negotiations that followed the Imperial Conference. The treaty itself was a brief document, containing only six clauses and including a preamble which bound the United States and Great Britain "to uphold the principle that 3 marine miles extending from the coastline outwards and measured from low-water mark constitute the proper limits of territorial waters."[43]

Under the treaty provisions, the British government agreed not to object to the boarding and search of its vessels suspected of liquor smuggling. If there was evidence that a vessel violated prohibition laws, it could be seized and taken into port for adjudication. All of these rights were not to be exercised "at a greater distance from the coast of the United States its territories or possessions than can be traversed in one hour by the vessel suspected of endeavoring to commit the offense."[44] In exchange for this privilege, the United States, in Article 3, agreed not to enforce any penalties against British vessels bringing sealed liquor into U.S. waters. At Hughes's suggestion, the Panama Canal exemption was cited as the basis for this privilege. The treaty also specified procedures for resolving claims by British vessels arising from improper enforcement. The liquor pact was for one year and could be modified, but renewal was automatic unless there was a notice of termination. Finally, Article 6 provided for the abrogation of the agreement if either party was prevented by "judicial decision or legislative action" (Hughes's wording) from carrying out the full effects of the treaty.[45]

The remaining hurdle for the Anglo-American liquor accord was the successful completion of the ratification process.[46] Following the first reports of favorable action by the Imperial Conference, Secretary Hughes began lobbying for the treaty. President Coolidge's declaration that American ships would not share the sealed-liquor exemption assured the opposition of the shipping industry.[47] Although maritime interests were disorganized and not a serious threat, Hughes was worried that the disgruntled shippers might join with prohibitionists in an alliance of convenience against the treaty, and he focused his strategy on winning the approval of the Anti-Saloon League. Meeting with Wayne Wheeler, Hughes glossed over the liquor concession and emphasized the enforcement benefits of the treaty. His efforts were rewarded in February when the League's Legislative Committee endorsed the liquor agreement and Wheeler consented to send a personal letter of support to all the members of the Senate.[48] Hughes also courted the Senate Foreign Relations Committee's chairman, Henry Cabot Lodge, and the committee unanimously accepted the treaty. Under Lodge's experienced guidance, the Senate, by a lopsided vote of 61 to 7, ratified the treaty on March 13, 1924.[49]

In London, the Baldwin government awaited the approval of the treaty by the dominion governments. When King George V opened Parliament on January 15, India, Newfoundland, and New Zealand had endorsed the agreement and Canada and Ireland sent preliminary approvals, subject to the confirmation of their respective legislatures.[50] The king proclaimed that the treaty was on the "eve of conclusion," and Foreign Secretary Curzon, who could at least claim credit for hastening the final stages of negotiations, lauded his accomplishment in the House of Lords.[51] Prime Minister Baldwin told the Commons that the accord would "do more good between our two peoples than almost anything of which you can think."[52]

This was one of the last pronouncements of the Baldwin government; in the December parliamentary elections, the Conservatives had lost their majority. On January 25, 1924, Ramsay MacDonald became the leader of the first Labour government in British history. MacDonald, a treaty supporter, immediately issued the pending signatory instructions. On the following day, Chilton and Hughes signed the treaty.[53] MacDonald, hampered by procedural postponements in the Canadian and Irish parliaments, finally presented the agreement to the House of Commons in April, and it was approved without debate. On May 22, after eleven months of difficult negotiations and unexpected complications, the formal documents were exchanged at the State Department. The Anglo-American Liquor Treaty of 1924 went into effect.[54]

The ratification of the liquor treaty was a bitter finale in the long public career of George Curzon. He would never again occupy a prominent position in a Conservative government, and, within a year, he was dead at the age of sixty-six.[55] Curzon's defeat signaled the emergence of a new perspective in British liquor policy. In many respects, his failure to grasp the fundamental impact of the sealed-liquor ban contributed to this reappraisal. The *Cunard* decision carried the Eighteenth Amendment to the Baldwin government's front door and transformed the controversy into an economic issue. Although the primary goal of British foreign policy remained the restoration of the nation's pre-1914 supremacy, this included a strategic evaluation of priorities. The independent defense of the three-mile limit was a far different undertaking at a time when the United States enjoyed naval parity and the immediate protection of British shipping interests occupied the center of the political stage. This was the postwar reality that Board of Trade officials defended, the Foreign Office staff accepted, and dominion leaders endorsed. But Curzon, reaching public maturity during an age of imperial omnipotence, was incapable of abandoning his traditional frame of reference. He was the victim of a changing world, a world in which he no longer belonged.

Curzon's failure brought to Secretary Hughes the success he was unable to achieve alone. With the decisive intervention of the Board of Trade, Hughes received unexpected support in his effort to anchor American liquor diplomacy to the ideals he had embraced at the Washington Naval Disarmament Conference in 1921. But Curzon's defeat simply provided the foundation for Hughes's aspirations; it did not secure these goals. The future of his achievement and the ability of the signatory powers to retain their prized concessions rested on the successful operation of the treaty. The critical question was whether or not the treaty was workable. Although this was a consideration that Hughes neglected throughout the months of negotiations and discussions, the elimination of prohibition as an Anglo-American problem depended upon the answer to this untested proposition.

Notes

[1]Phillip Lloyd-Greame to Curzon, July [3], 1923, A4198/116/45, PRO.

[2]USSB, Press Release, March 3, 1923, Box 17, Lasker Files, NA; *Our Merchant Marine* (Washington, DC, March 1923), 3–5; Winthrop L. Marvin to Albert Lasker, May 23, 1923, Box 14, Lasker Files, NA; Thomas Royden to Ashley Sparks, July 6, 1923, S/3/17/305, Cunard Archives; Sparks to Royden, July 19, 1923, C/2/270, Cunard Archives; T. V. O'Connor to W. H. Pease, November 21, 1923, 580/129/Part 5, RG 32, NA.

[3]Cunard Company, Executive Committee, Minutes, July 4, 1923, B/4/60/243, Cunard Archives; Horace Lee Washington to State Department, July 6, 1923, 811.114/1702, RG 59, NA.

[4]Interdepartmental Committee, Memorandum, July 10, 1923, A4097/116/45, PRO.

[5]Lloyd-Greame to Curzon, July [3], 1923, A4198/116/45, PRO. Lloyd-Greame drafted this letter after receiving the Liverpool Steamship Owners Association's resolution, but he delayed sending it until it was apparent that there was no British counterproposal to the American offer.

[6]Foreign Office, Minutes, July 14, 1923, A4198/116/45, PRO. Curzon refused to distribute Lloyd-Greame's letter to committee members. Henry Chilton to Foreign Office, July 9, 1923, A4066/116/45, PRO; Curzon to Chilton, July 13, 1923, ibid.; "Meeting with Henry Chilton," July 16, 1923, Folder 77a, Box 175, Hughes Papers.

[7]Post Wheeler to State Department, July 12, 1923, 711.419/15, Roll 13, M581, RG 59, NA; Henry P. Fletcher to Charles Evans Hughes, July 18, 1923, 711.419/27, Roll 13, M581, RG 59, NA; *Times* (London), July 10, 1923.

[8]Hughes to British Embassy, July 19, 1923, 711.419/16, Roll 13, M581, RG 59, NA; Post Wheeler to Hughes, July 19, 1923, 711.419/19, Roll 13, M581, RG 59, NA; Hughes to Warren G. Harding, July 23, 1923, 1403/144, Harding Papers.

[9]Middlemas and Barnes, *Baldwin,* 174; James, *British Revolution,* 159–66.

[10]Interdepartmental Meeting, Minutes, July 24, 1923, A4498/116/45, PRO; Rowland Sperling, Minutes, July 25, 1923, A4432/116/45, PRO. See also Sperling, Minutes, July 10, 1923, A4097/116/45, PRO.

[11]Interdepartmental Meeting, Minutes, July 24, 1923, A4498/116/45, PRO. Other grievances included an American requirement that USSB ships transferred to foreign registry remain dry and a dispute between British crews and American shippers.

[12]Ibid.

[13]The Board of Trade's strategy was closely coordinated with the shippers. Royden to Sparks, July 31, 1923, S/3/18/62, Cunard Archives.

[14]Interdepartmental Meeting, Minutes, July 24, 1923, A4498/116/45, PRO; Eyre Crowe, Minutes, August 1, 1923, A4687/116/45, PRO. Admiralty representatives expressed reservations about granting to the United States extended seizure rights that could not be measured from land.

[15]Cecil Hurst to Ronald McNeill, July 24, 1923, A5047/116/45, PRO; Customs House to Foreign Office, August 1, 1923, A4672/116/45, PRO; Board of Trade to Foreign Office, August 2, 1923, A4671/116/45, PRO; Admiralty to Foreign Office, August 9, 1923, A4769/116/45, PRO.

[16]Interdepartmental Committee, Memorandum, August 22, 1923, A5047/116/45, PRO.

[17]Curzon, Minutes, August 1, 1923, A4687/116/45, PRO.

[18]Harold Nicolson, *Curzon: The Last Phase, 1919-1925* (New York, 1934), 14–16, 39, 49, 353–56; D. R. Thorpe, *The Uncrowned Prime Ministers* (London, 1980), 146–51; Middlemas and Barnes, *Baldwin,* 158–71; James, *British Revolution,* 131–32, 171–74.

[19]Curzon, Minutes, August 1, 1923, A4671/116/45 and A4687/116/45, PRO.

[20]Curzon to Chilton, Draft Letter, August 3, 1923, A5047/116/45, PRO.

[21]Lloyd-Greame to Curzon, August 17, 1923, A5174/116/45, PRO; Charles Hipwood to Sperling, August 18, 1923, A5047/116/45, PRO.

[22]Curzon to Lloyd-Greame, August 26, 1923, A5175/116/45, PRO.

[23]Lloyd-Greame to Curzon, August 26, 1923, A5175/116/45, PRO; Foreign Office to Chilton, September 14, 1923, A5047/116/45, PRO.

[24]William Phillips to Hughes, September 20, 1923, "Phillips" folder, Box 38, Hughes Papers; Chilton to State Department, September 17, 1923, 711.419/32, Roll 13, M581, RG 59, NA; Post Wheeler to Hughes, August 28, 1923, 711.419/30, Roll 13, M581, RG 59, NA.

[25]Calvin Coolidge to Hughes, August 17, 1923, "Coolidge" folder, Box 16, Hughes Papers; Hughes to Post Wheeler, August 25, 1923, 711.419/31a, Roll 13, M581, RG 59, NA; Phillips to Coolidge, September 19, 1923, File 48, Roll 45, Series 1 (48/45), Papers of Calvin Coolidge, Microfilm edition, Manuscript Division, Library of Congress, Washington, DC (hereafter cited as Coolidge Papers). Coolidge continued to defer to Hughes on foreign policy matters. Donald R. McCoy, *Calvin Coolidge: The Quiet President* (New York, 1967), 167–69.

[26]Beerits Memorandum, Folder 48, Box 173, Hughes Papers. Because of Hughes's erroneous belief that Birkenhead's intervention was critical, later studies, written without examination of British documents and based on the Beerits Memorandum, cited this meeting as the turning point in the negotiations. For example, see Pusey, *Charles Evans Hughes* 2:577; Hulen, *Inside the Department of State,* 132; Mannock, "Anglo-American Relations, 1921-1928," 193.

[27]Phillips, Memorandum, September 19, 1923, 711.419/32, Roll 13, M581, RG 59, NA; Phillips to Hughes, September 20, 1923, "Phillips" folder,

Box 38, Hughes Papers; Charles Cheney Hyde, Draft Reply, September 27, 1923, 711.419/43, Roll 13, M581, RG 59, NA; George Harvey to Hughes, October 2, 1923, "Harvey" folder, Box 25, Hughes Papers; Harvey to Hughes, October 24, 1923, 711.419/39, Roll 13, M581, RG 59, NA; Harvey to Stanley Baldwin, undated, Folder 3/213-14, Vol. 108, Baldwin Papers.

[28]Curzon, Minutes, September 15, 1923, A5482/34/45, PRO; Robert Vansittart to Curzon, October 20, 1923, A6384/116/45, PRO.

[29]Harvey to Hughes, October 19, 1923, 711.419/37, Roll 13, M581, RG 59, NA; *Daily Telegraph* (London), September 29, October 9, 10, 1923.

[30]Foreign Office, Minutes, August 24, 1923, A5655/116/45, PRO; American Embassy, London, to State Department, September 24, 1923, 811.144/2016, RG 59, NA; Church of England Temperance Society to Curzon, September 26, 1923, A5711/116/45, PRO; Edwin Scrymageor to Baldwin, October 4, 1923, copy in A6347/116/45, PRO.

[31]Foreign Office, Memorandum, October 20, 1923, A6384/116/45, PRO. Eyre Crowe presented the report, acknowledging that practical considerations overruled any other concerns.

[32]McNeill, Minutes, August 8, 1925, A3821/31/45, PRO.

[33]Imperial Conference, Committee on Prohibition and Liquor Smuggling in the United States, Proceedings, October 25, 1923, A6400/116/45, PRO. See also Foreign Office, "Prohibition and Liquor Smuggling in the United States," October 1, 1923, A5909/116/45, PRO.

[34]Prime Minister Warren of Newfoundland argued that the treaty would not suppress smuggling. Officials from the Agriculture and Fisheries Department also expressed the concern that the treaty might affect fishing rights. Association of British Fisheries to Foreign Office, October 12, 1923, T10759/69/350, F.O. 372, PRO.

[35]Imperial Conference, Proceedings, October 25, 1923, A6400/116/45, PRO. Curzon suggested an exchange of diplomatic notes, instead of a treaty, but Foreign Office officials feared this would not empower Secretary Hughes to lift the sealed-liquor ban. "Committee Conclusions," October 25, 1923, Vol. 9/80, Stenographic Notes of the Imperial Conference, Cabinet 32, PRO (hereafter cited as CAB 32); Foreign Office, Minutes, October 27, 1923, A6419/116/45, PRO; Hurst, Draft Treaty, October 31, 1923, and Memorandum, November 2, 1923, A6498/116/45, PRO.

[36]*New York Times,* October 27, 29, November 1, 2, 1923; *Times* (London), October 29, 1923; Harvey to Hughes, October 27, 1923, 711.419/40, Roll 13, M581, RG 59, NA; Chilton to Hughes, October 29, 1923, 711.419/42, Roll 13, M581, RG 59, NA; Post Wheeler to State Department, November 3, 1923, 711.419/45, Roll 13, M581, RG 59, NA; Curzon to Chilton, November 3, 1923, A6485/116/45, PRO; "Meeting with Henry Chilton," November 6, 1923, Folder 77a, Box 175, Hughes Papers; *Literary Digest* 79 (November 10, 1923): 12–14; *New York World,* October 31, 1923; *New York Times,* November 2, 1923; *Morning Post* (London), November 1, 2, 3, 1923; *Times* (London), November 8, 1923.

[37]Curzon, Minutes, November 1, 1923, A6470/116/45, PRO; Curzon to

Chilton, November 7, 1923, ibid.; Post Wheeler to State Department, November 6, 1923, 711.419/48, and November 8, 1923, 711.419/50, Roll 13, M581, RG 59, NA.

[38]*New York Times,* November 2, 1923; William Vallance, Memorandum, November 8, 1923, 711.419/48, Roll 13, M581, RG 59, NA.

[39]Hughes to Post Wheeler, November 19, 1923, 711.419/57, Roll 13, M581, RG 59, NA; George Warner, Memorandum on Meeting with Post Wheeler, November 9, 1923, A6646/116/45, PRO.

[40]"15th Meeting of the Imperial Conference," November 9, 1923, Vol. 9/190, CAB 32, PRO; Post Wheeler to Hughes, November 10, 1923, 711.419/54, Roll 13, M581, RG 59, NA; *Times* (London), November 12, 1923; *Roundtable* 14:1–12; *Contemporary Review* 124 (December 1923): 791.

[41]Sperling, Minutes, November 21, 1923, A6871/116/45, PRO; Chilton to Hughes, November 23, 1923, 711.419/61, Roll 13, M581, RG 59, NA; Post Wheeler to Sperling, November 23, 1923, A6928/116/45, PRO; Hughes to Chilton, November 26, 1923, 711.419/61, Roll 13, M581, RG 59, NA; Wheeler to Hughes, November 17, 1923, 711.419/57, Roll 13, M581, RG 59, NA; "Meeting with Henry Chilton," November 26, 1923, Folder 77a, Box 175, Hughes Papers. See also *Times* (London), November 17, 1923; Foreign Office, Minutes, November 29, 1923, A6992/116/45, and December 7, 1923, A7186/116/45, PRO; Foreign Office to Chilton, December 1, 1923, A6992/116/45, PRO; State Department to Chilton, December 7, 1923, 711.419/133, Roll 14, M581, RG 59, NA; Hughes to Wheeler, December 7, 1923, 711.419/68B, Roll 13, M581, RG 59, NA.

[42]Minutes of the Cabinet Meeting, December 11, 1923, 58/23, Vol. 46, CAB 23, PRO; Foreign Office to Colonial Office, December 14, 1923, A7186/116/45, PRO. The liquor treaty was the first referral under a new rule passed by the Imperial Conference. This required dominion approval of any bilateral treaty imposing obligations on more than one part of the empire. "Stenographic Notes of the Imperial Conference of 1923," Vol. 9/190, CAB 32, PRO; Foreign Office, Minutes, December 7, 1923, A7186/116/45, PRO; Howard, *Theatre of Life* 2:50. See also the letters in October 1923, File 11/141–42, Vol. 93, Baldwin Papers.

[43]Command Paper, *British Parliamentary Papers,* 1923, Vol. 12, Part 1, Command No. 1987; *Convention between the United States and Great Britain: Prevention of Smuggling of Intoxicating Liquors* (Washington, DC, 1924), Treaty Series No. 685.

[44]Ibid.

[45]Ibid.

[46]There was a last-minute complication when the Coast Guard began seizing British ships under the unratified treaty guidelines. Although the incident aroused the press, it did not delay the ratification process. Crowe to Chilton, November 20, 1923, A6864/116/45, PRO; Chilton to Foreign Office, November 30, 1923, A7274/34/45, and November 26, 1923, A6991/34/45, PRO; British Consulate, Galveston, Texas, to Chilton, November 27, 1923,

A7231/34/45, PRO; Chilton to Foreign Office, November 30, 1923, A7052/
34/45, PRO; Post Wheeler to Hughes, November 27, 1923, 311.4153/T59/11,
RG 59, NA; Phillips, Memorandum, November 30, 1923, 311.4153/T59/13,
RG 59, NA; Sperling to Post Wheeler, November 29, 1923, A6928/116/45,
PRO; *Daily Telegraph* (London), November 26, 1923; Foreign Office, Minutes,
December 23, 1923, A7547/116/45, PRO; Foreign Office to Chilton, De-
cember 4, 1923, A7021/34/45, and December 31, 1923, A7572/34/45, PRO;
Chilton to Hughes, January 2, 1924, 311.4153/T59/17, RG 59, NA; Warner,
Memorandum, January 14, 1924, A229/27/45, PRO.

[47]*New York Times,* November 11, 1923; Chilton to Foreign Office, November 10, 1923, A6962/116/45, PRO. See also *New York Times,* November
2, 1923; *Morning Post* (London), November 2, 1923; Chilton to Foreign Office,
February 1, 1924, A88/8/45, PRO.

[48]Wayne Wheeler to Hughes, November 7, 1923, "Wh-Wi" folder, Box
48, Hughes Papers; Hughes to Wheeler, November 10, 22, 1923, ibid.; State
Department to Wheeler, December 8, 1923, 711.419/70, Roll 13, M581, RG
59, NA; Wheeler to Hughes, January 30, 1924, 711.419/83, and February 2,
1924, 711.419/85, Roll 13, M581, RG 59, NA; Vallance to Wheeler, February
5, 1924, 711.419/83, Roll 13, M581, RG 59, NA.

[49]State Department to Henry Cabot Lodge, December 8, 1923,
711.419/78, Roll 13, M581, RG 59, NA; *New York Times,* February 16, 1924;
Hughes to Lodge, February 29, 1924, "La-Ma 1924" folder, Box 62, Hughes
Papers; *Congressional Record,* 68th Cong., 1st sess. (March 13, 1924), 4084–89;
New York Times, March 14, 1924; Hughes to Rollo Ogden, March 25, 1924,
"La-Ma 1924" folder, Box 62, Hughes Papers. Hughes faced a minor problem
with Congress when Representative Henry St. George Tucker introduced a
resolution requesting that the president submit the treaty to the House of Repre-
sentatives. Tucker contended that the treaty was not self-executing and would
require supplemental legislation which the House would have to approve.
Hughes tried to pacify Tucker, but Senate ratification ended the dispute. Henry
St. George Tucker to Secretary to the President, January 28, 1924, copy in
711.419/84, Roll 13, M581, RG 59, NA; Hughes to Tucker, February 8, 1924,
ibid.; Hughes to Stephen Porter, March 3, 1924, 711.419/94, Roll 13, M581,
RG 59, NA; Phillips to Porter, March 8, 1924, 711.419/95, Roll 13, M581,
RG 59, NA; U.S. House of Representatives, 68th Cong., 1st sess., Committee
on Foreign Affairs, *The Treaty between Great Britain and the United States:
Hearings* (Washington, DC, 1924); *Congressional Record,* 68th Cong., 1st sess.
(April 19, 1924), 6723–25.

[50]Foreign Office, Minutes for the following dates, all in PRO: January 18,
1924, A231/8/45; December 28, 1923, A155/8/45; December 31, 1923,
A8/8/45; January 12, 1924, A288/8/45; January 16, 1924, A392/8/45;
January 19, 1924, A498/8/45; January 23, 1924, A488/8/45.

[51]"King's Speech to Parliament," January 15, 1924, Cabinet 3/24, Vol.
46, CAB 23, PRO; *Parliamentary Debates* (Lords), January 15, 1924, 56:38;
Frank Kellogg to Hughes, January 7, 1924, Frame 128, Roll 11 (128/11),

Microfilm edition, Papers of Frank B. Kellogg, Minnesota Historical Society, Minneapolis, Minnesota (hereafter cited as Kellogg Papers).

[52]*Parliamentary Debates* (Commons), January 15, 1924, 56:114.

[53]Coolidge to Hughes, January 23, 1924, 48/45, Coolidge Papers; Chilton to Foreign Office, February 1, 1924, A888/8/45, PRO.

[54]Kellogg to Hughes, February 28, 1924, 711.419/93, March 1, 1924, 711.419/95, and April 30, 1924, 711.419/111, Roll 13, M581, RG 59, NA; Warner, Minutes, February 28, 1924, A1314/8/45, PRO; American Consulate, Dublin, to Hughes, April 10, 1924, 711.419/109, Roll 13, M581, RG 59, NA; Colonial Office to Foreign Office, April 26, 1924, A2446/8/45, PRO. British shippers also pressured MacDonald to hasten ratification. Ramsay MacDonald, Minutes, February 29, 1924, A1358/8/45, PRO; Chamber of Shipping to Board of Trade, February 6, 1924, copy in A840/8/45, PRO; Cunard Company, Board of Directors, Minutes, March 19, 1924, B/1/11/112, Cunard Archives.

[55]Nicolson, *Curzon: The Last Phase,* 378–81.

Chapter Six

An Unresolved Problem
Post-Treaty Entanglements 1924–1926

Was the liquor treaty a workable agreement? This was not a question that animated officials in Washington or London as the post-treaty period began. Immediate tensions eased, there was a general improvement in Anglo-American relations, and the successful completion of the treaty negotiations fostered the belief that the liquor problem now was resolved.[1] British officials assumed their concession guaranteed future American moderation and eliminated the source of international law disputes. Addressing the Pilgrim Society, Ambassador Geddes acknowledged that the smuggling convention was the definitive answer to what "was really as important a question as that which stood in the forefront in 1920 when I went to Washington."[2] In the United States, the American press echoed this conclusion and hailed Secretary of State Hughes for finally settling a legitimate American grievance and removing a major obstacle to smuggling prevention. "One of the most remarkable triumphs in history," the *American Review* proclaimed, "was recorded by American diplomacy in the signing of the Anglo-American treaty to stop rum-running under the British flag."[3]

This optimism was short-lived. Within a few months, there was a growing disillusionment on both sides of the Atlantic as the labors of the previous year provided little tangible improvement in either the enforcement of the Eighteenth Amendment or the protection of international law. Although the infamous Rum Row gradually disappeared, this was the outcome of changes in the smuggling trade and not a reflection of the treaty's impact. In reality, the value of distilled spirits illegally entering the United States increased by $10 million in 1924. Rum-running and seizure disagreements persisted. In a practical sense, the treaty was a failure.[4]

Contributing to this inadequacy was the fact that the smuggling convention was a hastily contrived proposal, quickly resurrected to resolve the *Cunard* controversy. Throughout the negotiating process, there was no consideration of the future operation of the suggested arrangement, and the ambiguous wording of the document left the details of enforcement unsettled. The imprecise "one hour" limit required clarification according to the intent of the signers, adjustments were necessary in U.S. statutes, and enforcement officials needed to recognize that the smuggling convention was the approved reference for prohibition enforcement.

All these issues remained unresolved, creating a myriad of problems that undermined the validity of the liquor agreement. The treaty was immediately entangled in the complexities of the American judicial process, and the British government again was confronted with an inconsistent U.S. liquor policy that substituted unacceptable interpretations of international law for the ratified agreement. The result was a continuation of Anglo-American discord over prohibition enforcement which focused on the glaring weaknesses of the treaty itself.[5]

The responsibility for the treaty's failure ultimately rested with Secretary of State Hughes. Since 1922, Hughes had dominated the liquor issue and transformed his views into administration doctrine. While this independent leadership succeeded in preserving his own perspective on international law, it was a handicap in producing an effective liquor agreement to serve as the new basis for U.S. policy. Treasury and Justice Department officials were not involved in the treaty negotiations, nor had Hughes shared the details of his reassurances to the British government that the treaty would end American reliance on disputed doctrines of international law. Removed from the practical realities of the problem, the secretary underestimated the difficulties of prohibition enforcement. Moreover, despite ambitious claims, the elimination of smuggling and Anglo-American liquor disputes by treaty alone was an unrealistic goal. For all his efforts, Hughes only secured a simplistic short-term solution for a long-range and complicated problem.

Emerging from three years of bitterness was the enduring lesson that the *practical* enforcement of the Eighteenth Amendment determined the intensity of Anglo-American liquor tensions. What was demanded was both a sustained vigilance to ensure that the treaty was properly enforced and a parallel commitment to reduce prohibition disagreements. But Hughes was unwilling to accept this guardianship, and he offered no guidance on questions of refinement or enforcement. When the Coast Guard could not obtain the maximum speed of suspected British rum-runners, information vital to the proper execution of the treaty's extended seizure clause, the State Department was silent. Furthermore, few U.S. enforcement officials were given a copy of the ratified document, and Hughes did nothing to educate them on the proper interpretation of the agreement. Ignoring his obligations as author of the smuggling convention, the secretary of state was a major contributor to its impotency and vulnerability in the postratification period.[6]

Hughes's abandonment of the treaty also began a diminution in both the willingness and the ability of State Department officials to retain their leadership of the liquor issue. With effective prohibition enforcement still an elusive goal, the primary concern of Justice Department officials was successful prosecution, not diplomacy. Assistant Attorney General Mabel Walker Willebrandt's views had not moderated to accommodate the treaty, and her zeal to uphold the law was unabated. "Of course it is embarrassing for a Department," she wrote, "which holds the Treaty in as much contempt as most of the officials do that are called upon to operate under it, to have to defend it."[7] President Coolidge, like his predecessor, preferred not to interfere in the bureaucratic struggle that created a division of purpose in enforcement policy. Unless Secretary Hughes interceded, there was little hope that strident enforcement officials would faithfully and consistently respect the treaty as the new guide for antismuggling efforts.[8]

The magnitude of the liquor treaty's problems became apparent following the first postratification seizure of a British vessel. On July 14, 1924, the Coast Guard caught a small boat unloading liquor from the rumrunner *Frances and Louise*, anchored seventeen miles off the coast of Massachusetts. After establishing the connection between the two ships, officials towed both vessels into port. Assistant U.S. Attorney Laurence Curtis in Boston immediately drafted a libel for forfeiture under Article 2 of the new smuggling convention, which empowered the United States to seize rumrunners within one hour's traveling distance of the delivery boat. Because there was no official listing of the vessel's speed, Curtis ordered a trial test. When this revealed that the *Frances and Louise* was beyond treaty limits, Curtis, with the approval of his boss, U.S. Attorney Robert O. Harris, prepared to terminate further legal action.[9]

In respecting the treaty's precedence and providing a positive beginning to the post-treaty period, Curtis did not anticipate the reaction of Assistant Attorney General Willebrandt. Despite the fact that in most cases the one-hour limit was a greater distance than Hughes's original twelve-mile proposal, Willebrandt was determined to extend the seizure jurisdiction of the United States even further. She believed that the treaty, by removing the restraining influence of the British government's protests, gave enforcement officials the unfettered right to prevent smuggling. "It certainly was not intended," she asserted, "that we should *lose* any international rights to suppress smuggling when it was the expressed purpose of the treaties to extend those rights."[10] If the treaty did not support zealous enforcement, Willebrandt would resurrect disputed doctrines of international law to provide legal justification for her policies.

As the first postratification seizure, the *Frances and Louise* case offered Willebrandt an opportunity to reclaim her influence over prohibition enforcement. She summoned Curtis to the Justice Department and attempted to persuade him not to withdraw the libel. While hotly disputing that seizure jurisdiction depended upon the treaty, Willebrandt suggested that this was a question to be resolved by the courts. When Curtis refused to abandon his plans to request a dismissal, Willebrandt enlisted the support of Attorney General Harlan Stone, who ordered Harris to proceed with the libel. Convinced that the vessel was not within the one-hour limit, Willebrandt instructed Curtis to eliminate any treaty references and to base the case on "constructive presence," a concept never accepted by the British government, which placed the *Frances and Louise* in territorial waters through the connection of the delivery boats.[11] But on September 30 the U.S. District Court dismissed the *Frances and Louise* libel, ruling that the smuggling convention was the exclusive basis for seizing British vessels and "both nations intended the treaty to deal with the matter in a complete way."[12]

The court's decision did not convince Willebrandt to restrict legal action to the guidelines established by the treaty. Three weeks later, the British-registered *Marjorie Bachman* was seized twenty miles off the Massachusetts coast after liquor was sold to undercover Coast Guard officers piloting a small boat. Curtis expressed reservations about the validity of the seizure under the treaty, but Willebrandt ordered him to proceed with the case on the basis of constructive presence.[13] Once again, the District Court dismissed the libel, declaring that if there was no case under the treaty, there was no case at all.[14]

This second rebuff forced Willebrandt to reconsider her position. Not only were her plans for a series of highly publicized smuggling prosecutions frustrated, but also the release of the rumrunners *Frances and Louise* and *Marjorie Bachman* was a visible embarrassment. The rulings were the first legal pronouncements on the treaty, and Willebrandt acknowledged that "the fatal thing is that whether it is justifiable or not legal opinions emanating from Massachusetts carry a tremendous weight."[15] Appreciating the hazards of further legal reversals, she instructed Coast Guard officials to curtail extratreaty seizures until the judicial environment improved.[16]

Notwithstanding these setbacks, Willebrandt did receive some support for her flagging crusade against the treaty. In a preliminary ruling involving the seizure of the British rumrunner *Quadra*, Judge John Partridge of the U.S. District Court in San Francisco upheld the use of "hot pursuit," a highly controversial interpretation of international law that allowed a vessel to be seized on the high seas if pursuit began within territorial waters. Partridge declared that the United States enjoyed extended seizure rights in all smuggling cases, and he questioned the need for the liquor agreement. With this endorsement, Willebrandt instructed officials to proceed quickly with a final libel, excluding all references to the treaty, and obtain a positive ruling on the use of this expanded doctrine.[17]

Willebrandt also was buoyed by Harris's dismissal. His refusal to proceed with cases outside the treaty's limits had frustrated Willebrandt's efforts to enlarge seizure jurisdiction. With Harris removed, the assistant attorney general pressured his successor to begin the appeal of the *Marjorie Bachman* and *Frances and Louise* cases. Unable to secure the early validity of her policy, Willebrandt remained determined to establish her hard-line views as the sole guide for smuggling enforcement.[18]

For the British government, Assistant Attorney General Willebrandt's attack on the liquor treaty was a surprising development. Foreign Office officials assumed that the smuggling convention resolved all outstanding disagreements over prohibition enforcement, and Prime Minister Ramsay MacDonald, concurrently serving as foreign secretary, was more sympathetic than his predecessors toward American efforts to curtail smuggling. When the *Frances and Louise* was seized, there was no immediate concern in London, and Esme Howard, Auckland Geddes's replacement in Washington, was instructed not to respond to the seizure of British vessels without Foreign Office approval.[19] But following the libel hearing, there was concern within the Foreign Office that the Justice Department's reliance on disputed doctrines of international law threatened the liquor agreement. Ambassador Howard, offering to discuss the seizure with Secretary of State Hughes, was confident that Hughes would quickly correct this misunderstanding.[20]

Considering the absence of external pressures on the State Department, Howard's optimism was not unfounded. The Anti-Saloon League's public support for the liquor treaty as a panacea for the smuggling problem muted any postratification criticism of its limitations. Wayne Wheeler, condemned by some drys for reversing his views on the sealed-liquor issue, now was obligated to defend the agreement. By 1924 the dry movement's political weaknesses also were becoming more apparent, and the opponents of the Eighteenth Amendment were gaining

strength. The repeal of state prohibition laws in New York, the establishment of the Association Against the Prohibition Amendment
(AAPA), and increased criticism in the media all reflected this shift in
public opinion. While prohibition supporters still blamed the British
smuggling connection and ineffective enforcement for the failings of the
Eighteenth Amendment, they were no longer an influential arbiter of
U.S. liquor diplomacy.[21]

The secretary of state's concern for the smuggling convention,
however, waned following ratification. During the summer Hughes had
broadened his diplomatic initiative to secure similar agreements with the
other maritime powers. When this task was completed, he lost interest
in the prohibition issue.[22] This indifference confronted Ambassador
Howard when he met with Hughes on October 7 to discuss the *Frances
and Louise* seizure. The secretary of state was not concerned with the
British government's complaint, and he was not even aware of the legal
basis for the Justice Department's libel until Howard supplied the necessary details. Hughes, admitting that the rumrunner never entered territorial waters, refused to clarify the status of the smuggling convention.
He also would neither confirm nor deny that the use of the constructive-
presence doctrine was invalidated by the treaty, and the meeting ended
on this unsatisfactory note.[23]

Howard's visit did persuade State Department Solicitor Charles
Cheney Hyde to discuss the seizure with Curtis. Concerned about the
apparent weakness of the case, Hyde recommended the release of the
vessel if the owners agreed not to press for damages. But the State
Department was not prepared to respond to Curtis's request for general
guidelines on future seizure policy under the treaty, and Secretary Hughes
squandered this early opportunity to limit smuggling enforcement. When
Ambassador Howard voiced no further objections to the *Frances and
Louise* seizure, Curtis was forced to follow the unequivocal instructions
of Assistant Attorney General Willebrandt, and he proceeded with the
appeal process.[24]

The British government's response to Secretary Hughes was delayed
by an unexpected general election in Great Britain following the Labour
government's defeat on a vote of confidence. The results returned Stanley
Baldwin and the Conservatives to office, and Austin Chamberlain became the new foreign secretary.[25] For Howard, this was an advantageous
change; as an appointee of the first Baldwin government, he had been
obliged to assume a more passive role under a Labour government.[26]
Now, with his own party in office, Howard was determined to influence
British liquor policy, and on November 6 he sent a private letter to
Chamberlain. Distressed by Secretary Hughes's indifferent attitude,
Howard warned that, without the State Department's intervention, en-

forcement officials would continue to ignore the treaty. This escalation in Anglo-American tensions could not be resolved by the weak seizure provisions of the smuggling convention, he argued, and the only viable solution was to allow the seizure and prosecution of British rumrunners based on any doctrine of international law.[27]

Foreign Office officials were both surprised and angered by Howard's letter. It was the first indication that the State Department was not prepared to defend the liquor agreement, and Foreign Secretary Chamberlain was shocked that "Great Britain's concession to the United States regarding the twelve mile limit is no sooner made than to become worthless in their eyes."[28] Foreign Office officials considered the ambassador to be an alarmist. Dismissing his suggestion that the treaty was inadequate, they cited the general absurdity of the Eighteenth Amendment and the inability of the Coast Guard to seize rumrunners within one hour as the major causes of postratification problems. Whatever the difficulties, Cecil Hurst argued, the proper recourse was for the United States to request modification of the smuggling convention when it was time for renewal.[29] Chamberlain informed Howard that the British government was not prepared to recognize disputed interpretations of international law and that further concessions were impossible.[30]

This negative response did not diminish Howard's resolve to modify British seizure policy. He sent the foreign secretary a second private letter urging acceptance of the doctrine of constructive presence. In January 1925, Howard reported that, in a meeting with the secretary of state, Hughes finally accepted the need for stricter enforcement regulations and promised to instruct the Coast Guard to confine its activities to the limits of the treaty.[31] But Foreign Office officials were not prepared to accept doctrines of international law which their own government had always vehemently opposed. Hughes's belated support for the treaty simply confirmed the belief that Howard was overreacting and that treaty enforcement problems were of American, not British, origin.[32] On March 13, Foreign Secretary Chamberlain denied the request for the adoption of constructive presence. Assuring Howard that the Baldwin government would continue, whenever possible, to allow the courts to resolve extra-treaty seizure cases, Chamberlain instructed him to defer further discussions on seizure-related issues.[33]

The Baldwin government's desire to end the seizure debate also was influenced by the announcement that Secretary of State Hughes planned to retire in March. President Coolidge's choice of Frank Kellogg, the U.S. ambassador to Great Britain, to succeed Hughes was regarded in Whitehall as a positive development. Foreign Secretary Chamberlain anticipated that Kellogg's tenure in London would guarantee a more sympathetic hearing for British concerns and resolve the tensions over the treaty.[34] When Kellogg arrived at the State Department, he immediately informed Ambassador Howard that he planned to instruct enforcement officials not to seize British vessels beyond the one-hour limit. Impressed with this decisive action, Foreign Office officials were hopeful that Kellogg would succeed in restoring American support for the smuggling convention.[35]

Judged on the basis of good intentions, the new secretary of state fulfilled his promise. Kellogg was less obsessed than was Hughes with disputed legal theories.[36] Two weeks after assuming office, he asked Hyde to prepare a memorandum on treaty enforcement. Analyzing postratification seizures, Hyde rejected the use of constructive presence and argued that the seizure of British vessels was limited to the one-hour distance. He warned that further abuse of the treaty might lead to its termination and urged Kellogg to secure the support of President Coolidge in restricting smuggling enforcement. "The point here to be observed," Hyde concluded, "is that this is a matter to be dealt with by diplomacy and by no other process."[37] Encouraged by Hyde's arguments, Kellogg prepared to reclaim control over U.S. liquor policy and to reinstate the liquor agreement as the definitive reference for smuggling enforcement.

In terms of practical achievements, Kellogg neither realized his own goals nor justified British expectations of his leadership. For almost one year Coast Guard officials had acted without restraint, and this handicapped Kellogg's efforts. Hughes's failure to defend the smuggling convention created a pattern of uncoordinated and confused enforcement and established the Justice Department as the final interpreter of seizure policy. Refocusing attention on the diplomatic concerns of the smuggling issue was a formidable challenge, and Kellogg, lacking Hughes's talents, did not dominate the Coolidge administration.[38]

Compounding Kellogg's difficult task was the reorganization of the Treasury Department in April 1925. The Customs Service, Coast Guard, and Prohibition Unit were placed under the singular authority of an assistant secretary for prohibition, and President Coolidge appointed former general Lincoln C. Andrews to the post. Andrews announced a new antismuggling campaign, and during the first months of his tenure three British rumrunners were seized beyond the one-hour limit.[39] By September it was apparent that Kellogg was unable to establish a tangible commitment to the smuggling convention. State Department officials were forced to follow rather than initiate enforcement policy, and the secretary of state's role was largely confined to repairing the diplomatic damage created by the Coast Guard's action.[40]

In addition, Kellogg failed to restrict the Justice Department's freedom to pursue legal claims contrary to the liquor treaty. In March he had informed Assistant Attorney General Willebrandt that any judicial rulings authorizing the seizure of foreign vessels at any distance from the shore were unlawful under international law. Kellogg, responding to Judge Partridge's *Quadra* decision, added that the State Department would not recognize this claim or any related legal precedent.[41] Unfortunately, Kellogg did not specifically include in his objections the State Department's opposition to the use of the constructive-presence doctrine. This provided Willebrandt with an excuse to ignore Kellogg's general support for the treaty. She now recognized that the quick and favorable appeal of the *Frances and Louise* and *Marjorie Bachman* cases offered the best opportunity for sustaining her policy of extended-seizure rights.[42]

Willebrandt's plans for judicial vindication were frustrated when the new solicitor general, William Mitchell, opposed the appeals. Mitchell, responsible for arguing the cases before the Supreme Court, questioned the validity of the seizures and requested an opinion from the State Department on the proper interpretation of the treaty.[43] Hyde prepared a draft reply which reflected his earlier conclusion that the smuggling convention limited the application of other international law doctrines, but his resignation delayed the final approval of the letter. In October, Mitchell was informed that the State Department was not prepared to offer an opinion on the seizures. Forced to resolve the issue independently, he recommended withdrawing both cases, maintaining that any seizure in violation of the liquor treaty was invalid and would not be upheld by the Supreme Court. Willebrandt, faced with Mitchell's opposition and the probability of legal defeat, reluctantly accepted the recommendation. On February 1, 1926, the libels were terminated.[44]

While Mitchell's refusal to pursue the appeals was based on his support for the liquor treaty, it was an unwelcome development for Foreign Office officials. The Baldwin government's policy was to defer any formal protests of extratreaty seizures pending the outcome of all legal proceedings. Foreign Office officials were confident that the Supreme Court would both deny the validity of extended claims and establish the primacy of the smuggling convention. Considering Secretary of State Kellogg's inability to restrict American enforcement, the Foreign Office regarded a favorable Supreme Court ruling as the sole means of forcing the Justice Department and the Coast Guard to respect the one-hour limit.[45] This anticipation moderated the British response to treaty disagreements, but the termination of the *Frances and Louise* and *Marjorie Bachman* appeals eliminated this possibility and returned the responsibility for interpreting the treaty to enforcement officials. Mitchell's action, rather than enhancing the smuggling convention's effectiveness, made the further escalation of Anglo-American liquor tensions an unsettling possibility.

Contributing to this uncertainty over the treaty's future was the question of whether or not the smuggling convention was a self-executing agreement. Principally an American concern, it indirectly affected Great Britain by encouraging the belief that the treaty was an inadequate basis for smuggling enforcement. The controversy arose because the treaty did not contain a specific provision to extend U.S. statutes to the one-hour limit. This meant that, although seizures were allowed, the laws used to condemn rumrunners and prosecute smugglers might not operate at this same distance. Many legal scholars argued that U.S. laws were not in force beyond territorial waters without the expressed authorization of Congress. The sole statute incorporating areas outside the three-mile limit was the Tariff Act of 1922, which extended customs authority to a distance of twelve miles from shore. When applied to the illegal importation of liquor, the law still left the status of rumrunners between twelve miles and the generally greater one-hour treaty limit undefined. This created a zone where seizure was proper, yet prosecution for smuggling was a legal uncertainty.[46]

State Department officials, recognizing this problem, did little to correct it. At the time of ratification, Secretary Hughes had instructed Assistant Solicitor William Vallance to prepare supplemental legislation to extend statutes to the one-hour limit. But Hughes, with his declining interest in the treaty, never approved the proposal.[47] The ramifications of this neglect were apparent when the U.S. District Courts in Connecticut and Massachusetts rejected Justice Department libels against smugglers on the grounds that there was no U.S. statutory authority beyond the twelve-mile jurisdiction of the Tariff Act.[48] When Kellogg became secretary of state, Vallance suggested that the department correct this defect. Kellogg, concerned that the difficulty of prosecuting rumrunners under the liquor agreement was encouraging extratreaty seizures, authorized Vallance to draft a bill applying the provisions of the Tariff Act to the treaty. Unable to win approval for his measure before Congress recessed, Vallance informed Assistant Attorney General Willebrandt that it now was the Justice Department's responsibility to secure the necessary legislation.[49]

Willebrandt was unenthusiastic about pressing for congressional relief. She was convinced that the self-executing nature of the liquor treaty would be upheld on appeal. Furthermore, she was equally confident that the courts would sustain her extended-seizure claims. This would eliminate the need to rely on the treaty because the doctrine of constructive presence placed rumrunners, through the delivery boats, within territorial waters and subject to American laws.[50]

By the spring of 1926, both of these predictions proved incorrect. Solicitor General Mitchell had refused to proceed with extratreaty libels, and, in two separate Circuit Court of Appeals decisions, the courts ruled that the treaty did not extend U.S. statutes to the one-hour limit.[51] Mitchell also opposed Willebrandt's plans to bring these two cases to the Supreme Court. "The accumulation of decisions in the Federal courts on this point," Mitchell argued, "is now such that the time has arrived when a wholly untenable contention should be abandoned."[52] Mitchell concluded that the passage of supplemental legislation was the only solution to this enforcement handicap. Willebrandt was forced to withdraw the libels and announce that the Justice Department no longer endorsed the opinion that the treaty was self-executing.[53]

Initially, Foreign Office officials regarded the self-executing question as an American concern. They did not oppose the extension of U.S. statutes if this was for the expressed purpose of smuggling enforcement and restricted to the treaty limits. But the repeated reliance on the Tariff Act, instead of on the smuggling convention, forced the Baldwin government to reconsider its policy of noninvolvement. In June, Ambassador Howard sent the State Department a letter requesting that enforcement officials adhere to the treaty guidelines.[54] Although there was a renewed effort by the Coolidge administration to clarify this situation through legislation, the self-executing issue was unsettled, and Foreign Office officials remained concerned that it was contributing to the continued neglect of the treaty.[55]

Anglo-American post-treaty disagreements also were exacerbated by the State Department's failure to prevent specific enforcement activities that created tensions even when the treaty was the basis for seizure. Coast Guard officials persisted in ignoring the rights of British citizens serving as crew members on seized vessels.[56] A secondary problem was the delay in releasing seized vessels pending the appeal of a dismissed libel. Under the treaty, a procedure was established for securing compensation, and the judicial declaration that a seizure was invalid offered a potential claim for damages. Secretary of State Hughes, unwilling to pay for his neglect of the treaty, had prevented the release of rumrunners on bond, prior to appeal, unless the owners waived all rights to compensation. Foreign Office officials, regarding compensation claims as a private matter except where there was a willful denial of treaty rights, resented this policy of "blackmail." Secretary Kellogg's opposition to this practice did not end the delay in the release of British vessels, and this became an ongoing source of diplomatic friction.[57]

A more contentious issue was the question of the proper interpretation of the liquor treaty's geographic limits for seizure. The British government's insistence on a distance of "one hour's sailing time" of either the smuggling vessel or smaller delivery boats created unanticipated complications. Allowing for American confusion and incompetency, this was still an inadequate measurement that was difficult to determine and far less satisfactory in practice than either a firm mileage limit or a distance based on the travel of the enforcement vessel. Since Coast Guard officials lacked detailed information on the speed of boats engaged in smuggling, it was often impossible to calculate the exact location of a rumrunner in rough waters. Confronted with this problem, the Coast Guard began operating camouflaged revenue cutters to establish contact with smugglers and using hypothetical measurements of the distance a standard rumrunner could traverse in one hour.[58]

The validity of these practices under the treaty was doubtful. The liquor agreement clearly stated that the one-hour limit applied only to those vessels intending to smuggle, and the adoption of a hypothetical guide extended American seizure rights beyond the true limits of the treaty. Citing this weakness, the U.S. District Courts in Massachusetts and Connecticut rejected seizures based on hypothetical measurements and Coast Guard entrapment.[59] This view also was shared by some Justice Department officials, including Solicitor Mitchell. Assistant Attorney General Willebrandt, recognizing that hypothetical measurements were a valuable and indirect method of expanding seizure jurisdiction, continued to support the Coast Guard's disputed policy.[60]

Although Foreign Office officials did not accept Willebrandt's liberal interpretation of the treaty, they were reluctant to protest its application. The use of hypothetical measurements, in theory, did not weaken the three-mile limit, and American courts generally had supported the Baldwin government's view of the enforcement clauses. But the continued reliance on this incorrect definition convinced the Foreign Office that it was an attempt to secure additional concessions and to extend American seizure rights. On March 30, 1926, Ambassador Howard sent Secretary Kellogg a note affirming that the Baldwin government unequivocally refused to accept any treaty measurement not based on the operation of an actual rumrunner.[61] Kellogg forwarded the note to Attorney General John Sargent, who declined to discuss the matter because of pending court action. When the Circuit Court of Appeals rejected the libel in the remaining case involving hypothetical measurements, Sargent still did not acknowledge his misreading of the treaty, and there was no Justice Department announcement of any change in this policy.[62]

The disagreements over the use of hypothetical measurements reflected both the imperfections of the liquor treaty and the reality that, two years after ratification, the full realization of Secretary Hughes's acclaimed diplomatic triumph was illusory. Prohibition enforcement efforts were restricted by the treaty's inherent flaws, and disputes over seizure limits reappeared. The treaty represented a superficial victory, rather than a substantive accomplishment, and it neither ended smuggling nor eliminated diplomatic tensions. Important questions of international law and treaty obligations remained unanswered. Without further action to resolve these issues, prohibition disagreements would continue to handicap Anglo-American relations and undermine all of the benefits secured by the diplomatic efforts of 1923.

Notes

[1]D. C. Watt, *Succeeding John Bull,* 51; Hogan, *Informal Entente,* 39, 217.

[2]Frank Kellogg to Charles Evans Hughes, March 6, 1924, 711.419/106, Roll 13, M581, RG 59, NA.

[3]George W. Hinman, "Diplomatic Victory over Rum," *American Review* 3 (1925): 418; *Literary Digest* 80 (February 9, 1924): 16.

[4]Willoughby, *Rum War at Sea,* 45–59; U.S. Department of Commerce, *The Balance of International Payments of the United States in 1924* (Washington, DC, 1925). Wayne Wheeler criticized this measurement, but Commerce Secretary Herbert Hoover responded that if he reviewed the matter, he would be inclined to increase the estimate. Wayne Wheeler to Herbert Hoover, May 19, 1925, and Hoover to Wheeler, June 8, 1925, "Prohibition, 1925, January–July" folder, Box 486, Commerce Papers (CP), Papers of Herbert Hoover, Herbert Hoover Presidential Library, West Branch, Iowa (hereafter cited as Hoover Papers).

[5]Only four weeks after ratifications were exchanged in Washington, the liquor treaty already was embroiled in legal controversy. On June 25 the Neptune Association of Masters and Mates of Ocean and Coastwise Vessels asked the U.S. District Court in New York to order the seizure of the *Berengaria's* liquor cargo because the liquor treaty violated the provisions of the Eighteenth Amendment. Cunard Company, Board of Directors, Minutes, May 21, 1924, B/1/11/193, and Executive Committee, Minutes, May 28, 1924, B/4/62/187, and July 16, 1924, B/4/62/188, Cunard Archives; R. H. Blake to Gloster Armstrong, June 26, 1924, copy in A4269/8/45, PRO. Although the court refused to act on the request, John Milliken, editor of the association's journal, filed a second suit on September 24. F. E. Garlick to Armstrong, September 26, 1924, copy in A560/8/45, PRO; *Milliken v. Stone,* September 24, 1924, copy in 711.419/130, Roll 14, M581, RG 59, NA; Esme Howard to Foreign Office, September 25, 1924, A5760/8/45, PRO; Cunard Company, Executive Committee, Minutes, October 8, 1924, B/4/63/30, and Board of Directors, Minutes, October 15, 1924, B/1/11/213, Cunard Archives. On July 13, 1925, the District Court dismissed Milliken's suit, arguing that there was no cause for equitable relief, without ruling on the constitutional question. The Circuit Court of Appeals upheld the ruling in 1927, also skirting the issue of the treaty's legality. On June 1 the Supreme Court refused a request to hear the case. *Milliken v. Stone,* October 6, 1924, copy in 23/51/214/1, RG 60, NAS; Emory Buckner to Mabel Walker Willebrandt, July 15, 1925, 23/51/214/11, and January 11, 1927, 23/51/214/15, RG 60, NAS; Willebrandt to U.S. Attorney, New York,

June 1, 1927, 23/51/214/18, RG 60, NAS.

[6]Garrad Winston to Hughes, April 3, 1924, 811.114/3478, RG 59, NA; Sterling Carr to Justice Department, October 18, 1924, 23/11/69/1, RG 60, NAS; Henry Chilton to Foreign Office, October 24, 1924, A6338/27/45, PRO; Foreign Office to Howard, June 10, 1924, A3556/8/45, PRO; Herbert Brooks to State Department, June 13, 1924, 711.419/120, Roll 13, M581, RG 59, NA; State Department to British Embassy, July 9, 1924, 711.419/122, Roll 14, M581, RG 59, NA; Treasury Department, "Regulation 3601," July 28, 1924, copy in 811.114/3708a, RG 59, NA. See also Hughes, "Recent Questions and Negotiations," *Foreign Affairs,* 5–6.

[7]Willebrandt, Memorandum, October 6, 1924, 23/51/214/1, RG 60, NAS.

[8]McCoy, *Calvin Coolidge,* 303; Calvin Coolidge to Justice Department, October 1924, 75a/56, Coolidge Papers.

[9]Laurence Curtis to Willebrandt, July 18, 1924, 23/36/59/2, and July 26, 1924, 23/36/59/3, RG 60, NAS.

[10]Willebrandt to Carr, January 20, 1925, 23/11/69/36, RG 60, NAS.

[11]Willebrandt to Attorney General, July 31, 1924, 23/36/59, RG 60, NAS; Harlan Stone to Robert O. Harris, August 1, 1924, 23/36/59/8, RG 60, NAS; Curtis to Willebrandt, August 1, 1924, 23/36/59/6x, and August 15, 1924, 23/36/59/13, RG 60, NAS; Willebrandt to Curtis, August 7, 1924, 23/36/59/10, RG 60, NAS.

[12]1 Fed. (2d.) 1004.

[13]Willebrandt to Harris, October 28, 1924, 23/100/4/2, RG 60, NAS; Curtis to Willebrandt, November 13, 1924, 23/100/4/3, RG 60, NAS. The British-registered *Astra* also was seized beyond treaty limits. Howard to Foreign Office, October 2, 1924, A5734/27/45, PRO.

[14]4 Fed. (2d.) 405.

[15]Willebrandt to Harold Williams, February 3, 1925, 23/11/69/44, RG 60, NAS; Justice Department, Memorandum to United States Attorneys, December 12, 1924, 23/013/12, RG 60, NAS.

[16]Willebrandt to Carr, January 20, 1925, 23/11/69/36, RG 60, NAS.

[17]3 Fed. (2d.) 643. The *Quadra* actually was seized within treaty limits. This was not a forfeiture libel but a hearing to determine if the ship could be used as evidence. Willebrandt to Carr, March 12, 1925, 23/11/69/55, RG 60, NAS.

[18]William Vallance to Hughes, December 10, 1924, 311.4154/F84/24, RG 59, NA; Brown, *Mabel Walker Willebrandt,* 73.

[19]Foreign Office to Treasury, June 4, 1924, A3255/8/45, PRO; Board of Trade to Foreign Office, October 24, 1924, A6086/8/45, PRO; Howard to Foreign Office, July 18, 1924, A4547/27/45, and July 25, 1924, A4751/27/45, PRO; Foreign Office, Minutes, July 18, 1924, A4547/27/45, PRO.

[20]Howard to Foreign Office, August 18, 1924, A5002/27/45, PRO; Foreign Office, Minutes, August 28, 1924, A5149/27/45, PRO; Foreign Office to Howard, August 24, 1924, A5002/27/45, and October 7, 1924, A5727/27/45, PRO; Howard to Foreign Office, September 8, 1924, A5310/27/45, and September 15, 1924, A5417/27/45, PRO.

[21]G. R. Munroe to Wheeler, July 26, 1924, Folder 25, Roll 13, Series 8, League Papers; Foreign Office, Minutes, January 9, 1925, A181/31/45, PRO; Howard to Foreign Office, January 12, 1925, A246/31/45, PRO; *New York Times,* April 2, 1925; Kyvig, *Repealing National Prohibition,* 57, 68–99; Kerr, *Organized for Prohibition,* 236, 253–55; McCoy, *Calvin Coolidge,* 303; Larry Engleman, "Organized Thirst: The Story of Repeal in Michigan," in Jack S. Blocker, Jr., ed., *Alcohol, Reform and Society* (Westport, CT, 1979), 172–74; Merz, *Dry Decade,* 183–90.

[22]Treaties were signed in May with Germany, Sweden, Norway, and Denmark, and with Italy and Panama in June; France and the Netherlands signed treaties in August. See also Jones, *Eighteenth Amendment and Our Foreign Relations,* 96–160.

[23]Howard to Foreign Office, October 7, 1924, A6005/27/45, PRO.

[24]Vallance to Hughes, October 10, 1924, 311.4154/F84/5, RG 59, NA; State Department, Solicitor's Office, Memorandum, October 22, 1924, 311.4154/F84/3, RG 59, NA.

[25]Mowat, *Britain between the Wars,* 183–90; James, *British Revolution* 2:193–95.

[26]Howard, *Theatre of Life* 2:477; Howard to Eyre Crowe, January 19, 1924, "United States" file, 24/11, Vol. 388, Private Secretary Archives, Private Office Papers, Foreign Office, F.O. 800, Public Record Office, Kew, London (hereafter cited as F.O. 800).

[27]Howard to Austin Chamberlain, November 6, 1924, A6491/8/45, PRO; Chamberlain to Stanley Baldwin, November 6, 1924, Vol. 108/222, Private Papers of Austin Chamberlain, Private Secretary Archives, Foreign Office, F.O. 800, Public Record Office, Kew, London (hereafter cited as Chamberlain Papers). See also Howard to Foreign Office, October 7, 1924, A6005/27/45, PRO.

[28]Chamberlain to Howard, November 17, 1924, Vol. 256, Chamberlain Papers. See also R. I. Campbell, Minutes, October 29, 1924, A6344/27/45, PRO.

[29]Foreign Office, Minutes, November 6, 1924, A6461/8/45, PRO.

[30]Chamberlain to Howard, December 3, 1924, A6461/8/45, PRO.

[31]Howard to Chamberlain, December 18, 1924, A52/52/45, PRO; Howard to Foreign Office, January 16, 1925, A454/31/45, PRO; "Meeting with the British Ambassador," January 15, 1925, Folder 77b, Box 175, Hughes Papers.

[32]Foreign Office, Minutes, December 31, 1924, A52/52/45, PRO; Admiralty to Foreign Office, March 10, 1925, A1285/31/45, PRO.

[33]Chamberlain to Howard, March 13, 1925, A1285/31/45, PRO.

[34]Kellogg's appointment was announced in January. Frank Kellogg to Coolidge, January 11, 1925, 42/15, Kellogg Papers; Howard to Chamberlain, February 13, 1925, Vol. 257/298, Chamberlain Papers; Chamberlain to Howard, March 13, 1925, A1285/31/45, PRO; Chamberlain, Memorandum on Final Meeting with Ambassador Kellogg, February 10, 1925, A764/52/45, PRO; Chamberlain to Howard, February 14, 1925, Vol. 257/310, Chamberlain Papers.

35Howard to Foreign Office, March 13, 1925, A1508/52/45, PRO.

36L. Ethan Ellis, *Frank B. Kellogg* (New Brunswick, NJ, 1961), 7; Kellogg to Coolidge, February 5, 1924, 712/140, Coolidge Papers.

37Charles Cheney Hyde to Kellogg, March 17, 1925, 711.419/136, Roll 14, M581, RG 59, NA; Kellogg to William Castle, August 9, 1929, Folder 35, Box 4, Castle Papers.

38McCoy, *Calvin Coolidge,* 282; Ellis, *Frank B. Kellogg,* 233, 282; British Embassy (Washington) to Foreign Office, June 17, 1925, A3317/52/45, PRO.

39Andrew Mellon to Secretary of War, February 20, 1925, Box 231, RG 56, NA; *New York Times,* April 2, 1925; Ira L. Reeves, *Ol' Rum River* (Chicago, 1931), 24. In 1925 the *Aesop* was seized on August 26, the *Fannie E. Prescott* on September 5, and the *Hazel E. Herman* on October 9. Willebrandt to State Department, October 24, 1925, 23/100/224, RG 60, NAS.

40"British Correspondence to State Department on the Arrest and Detention of Crewmembers on Rumrunners," March 30, 1927, 811.114/4614a, RG 59, NA; Kellogg, Memorandum, December 17, 1925, 711.419/138, Roll 14, M581, RG 59, NA; Kellogg to Treasury Secretary, December 21, 1925, ibid.; Lincoln C. Andrews to Kellogg, December 28, 1925, 711.419/139, Roll 14, M581, RG 59, NA; Chilton to Foreign Office, September 24, 1925, A5014/31/45, PRO.

41This forced Willebrandt to narrow the scope of the *Quadra* libel. Willebrandt to Carr, March 12, 1925, 23/11/69/55, RG 60, NAS.

42Willebrandt to Solicitor General, February 2, 1925, 23/36/59/64, RG 60, NAS.

43Willebrandt to William Mitchell, March 3, 1925, 23/100/4/33, and Mitchell to Willebrandt, June 25, 1925, 23/100/4/54, RG 60, NAS; Solicitor General to State Department, August 7, 1925, 711.419/137, Roll 14, M581, RG 59, NA.

44State Department, "Draft Reply to Solicitor General," September 14, 1925, 711.419/137, Roll 14, M581, RG 59, NA; Mitchell to Willebrandt, November 2, 1925, 23/36/59/76, and January 22, 1926, 23/100/4, RG 60, NAS.

45Foreign Office, Minutes, April 9, 1926, A1871/88/45, PRO. Willebrandt assured Howard in December 1925 that the Supreme Court would rule on this question within the next few months.

46E. D. Dickinson, "Are the Liquor Treaties Self-Executing?" *American Journal of International Law* 20 (1926): 444–52; "Self-Execution of Treaties under the Constitution," *Columbia Law Review* 26 (1926): 859–70.

47Vallance to Hyde, May 21, 1924, 711.419/117, and 711.419/118, Roll 13, M581, RG 59, NA; State Department, Solicitor's Office, Memorandum, October 22, 1924, 311.4154/F84/3, RG 59, NA.

48The first ruling was made by the Massachusetts court in the *Marjorie Bachman* case. 4 Fed. (2d.) 405. This was followed by the Connecticut opinion in the *Over the Top* seizure. 5 Fed. (2d.) 838; Willebrandt to Hughes, January 25, 1925, 23/14/46/14, RG 60, NAS. Although the U.S. District Court in New York (Eastern District) maintained that the treaty was self-executing in the *Pictonian* seizure, this was regarded as a weak precedent. 3 Fed. (2d.) 145; Jessup, *Law of Territorial Waters,* 323.

[49]Vallance to Kellogg, March 2, 1925, 311.4153/Ov2/6, RG 59, NA; Vallance, Memorandum, March 5, 1925, 311.4153/Ov2/5, RG 59, NA.

[50]Willebrandt to Solicitor General, March 5, 1925, 23/14/46/22, RG 60, NAS; Willebrandt to Andrews, February 27, 1926, 23/51/217/47, RG 60, NAS.

[51]The Circuit Court of Appeals in New York denied this claim in the *Sagatind/Diamentia* case on April 5, 1926. Vallance to Hughes, November 7, 1924, 811.114/*Sagatind*/1, RG 59, NA; Buckner to Justice Department, May 4, 1925, 23/51/217/19, RG 60, NAS; Willebrandt to Mitchell, August 18, 1925, 23/51/217/27, and Mitchell to Willebrandt, February 27, 1926, 23/51/217/44, RG 60, NAS; Justice Department, "Sagatind Brief," copy in 23/51/217/46, RG 60, NAS; 11 Fed. (2d.) 673. In the *Frances E.,* the Circuit Court of Appeals (Fifth Circuit) overturned a lower court ruling and held that the liquor treaty was not self-executing. Joseph W. John to Justice Department, August 5, 1925, 23/3/20/9, RG 60, NAS; 7 Fed. (2d.) 488; 13 Fed. (2d.) 74. Willebrandt previously had decided not to appeal the *Over the Top* case after the U.S. District Court in Connecticut ruled that the treaty did not extend the jurisdiction of the smuggling laws. John Buckley to Attorney General, March 2, 1925, 23/14/46/24, RG 60, NAS; Arthur Henderson to Willebrandt, June 23, 1925, 23/14/46/37, RG 60, NAS; Justice Department to Buckley, July 28, 1925, ibid.

[52]Mitchell, Memorandum, April 16, 1926, 23/51/217/59, RG 60, NAS.

[53]Willebrandt was prepared to order filing for certiorari, based on the recommendation of her advisers, until she received Mitchell's memorandum. Henderson to Willebrandt, April 12, 1926, 23/51/217, RG 60, NAS; Attorney General to Buckner, April 19, 1926, 23/51/217/60, RG 60, NAS; Willebrandt to Aubrey Boyles, April 24, 1926, 23/100/198/22, RG 60, NAS; Willebrandt to Kellogg, May 27, 1926, 23/3/20/46, RG 60, NAS.

[54]Howard to Chamberlain, November 6, 1924, A6461/8/45, PRO; Cecil Hurst, Minutes, November 6, 1924, ibid.; Foreign Office, Minutes, October 16, 1924, A6119/27/45, PRO; Howard to Foreign Office, April 23, 1926, A2424/88/45, and May 20, 1926, A2895/88/45, PRO; Foreign Office to Howard, May 25, 1926, A2451/88/45, PRO; British Embassy to State Department, June 10, 1926, 711.419/167, Roll 14, M581, RG 59, NA.

[55]A provision to extend Coast Guard jurisdiction to one hour was included in a comprehensive prohibition bill. Mellon to Kellogg, March 8, 1926, and Kellogg to Mellon, April 3, 1926, 811.114/4497, RG 59, NA; *New York Times,* April 20, 1926; Vallance, Memorandum, April 26, 1926, 811.114/4574, RG 59, NA; Treasury Department, Memorandum, May 1926, VI/C/4, RG 58, NA.

[56]Curtis to Henderson, November 1, 1924, 23/100/4/4, RG 60, NAS; Willebrandt to Charles Root, March 10, 1925, 23/100/4, RG 60, NAS; Howard to Foreign Office, December 4, 1925, A6300/31/45, PRO; "British Correspondence to the State Department," March 30, 1927, 811.114/4614a, RG 59, NA.

[57]Howard to Foreign Office, October 7, 1924, A6005/27/45, and December 18, 1924, A52/52/45, PRO; Howard to Chamberlain, December 18, 1924, A52/52/45, PRO; Vallance to Hughes, October 22, 1924, 811.114/Great

Britain/97, RG 59, NA; State Department, Memorandum, November 6, 1924, 311.4154/F84/12, RG 59, NA; Robert Craigie, Minutes, February 6, 1925, A2136/3/45, PRO; Chamberlain to Howard, January 22, 1926, A6540/31/45, PRO; Foreign Office, Minutes, February 26, 1926, A1296/88/45, and March 26, 1926, A1878/88/45, PRO; Foreign Office to Howard, March 25, 1926, A1149/88/45, PRO; Hurst, Memorandum, March 29, 1926, A1724/88/45, PRO; Foreign Office to Dominion Office, April 28, 1926, ibid.; R. I. Campbell, Minutes, November 28, 1924, A6791/27/45, PRO.

[58]Curtis to Willebrandt, November 13, 1924, 23/100/4/3, RG 60, NAS; Commanding Officer, Coast Guard Cutter *Tampa,* to Customs Collector, New London, Connecticut, October 20, 1924, copy in 23/14/46/1, RG 60, NAS; Vallance to Hughes, November 7, 1924, 811.114/*Sagatind*/1, RG 59, NA; Willebrandt to Secretary of State, January 25, 1925, 23/14/46/14, RG 60, NAS.

[59]11 Fed. (2d.) 1004; 5 Fed. (2d.) 838.

[60]Curtis to Willebrandt, November 13, 1924, 23/100/4/3, RG 60, NAS; Mitchell to Willebrandt, July 1, 1925, 23/14/46/37, and January 22, 1926, 23/100/4, RG 60, NAS; Buckley to Attorney General, January 13, 1925, 23/14/46/15, and January 24, 1925, 23/14/46/16, RG 60, NAS. Willebrandt did find some support in the *Frances E.* opinion when the U.S. District Court in Mobile, Alabama, maintained in two hearings that the speed of "such boats as were ordinarily used for that purpose in that locality" was sufficient evidence. 7 Fed. (2d.) 488; Willebrandt to Kellogg, December 21, 1925, 23/100/98/3, RG 60, NAS. This argument was rejected on appeal.

[61]Howard to Foreign Office, December 4, 1925, A6300/31/45, PRO; Foreign Office, Minutes, December 14, 1925, A6540/31/45, PRO; Chamberlain to Howard, January 22, 1926, ibid.; Howard to Kellogg, March 30, 1926, 711.419/142, Roll 14, M581, RG 59, NA.

[62]John Sargent to Kellogg, April 16, 1926, 23/3/20/37, RG 60, NAS; 13 Fed. (2d.) 74.

Chapter Seven

Making the Treaty Work
The London Conference
1926–1928

As disagreements over the enforcement of the liquor treaty escalated, the Baldwin government's interdepartmental committee on liquor policy quietly reconvened at the Foreign Office on October 5, 1925. It was the first meeting of the committee, which occupied such a critical position during the treaty negotiations, since the completion of its original task two years earlier. The intended purpose of this latest assembly was "to bring conviction to Sir Esme Howard" regarding the impossibility of adopting new concessions to assist the United States in the prevention of smuggling.[1] The ambassador, returning to London in the summer of 1925, had continued to urge his colleagues to resolve the problems that entangled the liquor agreement. Foreign Office officials hoped to stifle this irritating dissenter by demonstrating unanimous opposition to his suggestion.

The resurrection of the dormant committee did not temper Howard's steadfast convictions. On the contrary, Foreign Office officials were forced to modify their position when the Board of Trade strongly endorsed the ambassador's proposal for further antismuggling measures. Surprisingly, Howard, who was so quick to abandon the smuggling convention, inspired the first serious effort to make the treaty a more effective agreement.

The catalyst for this dramatic reappraisal of the prohibition issue was the recognition within the Baldwin government that the treaty clearly resolved one aspect of Anglo-American liquor tensions: the disputed right of British ships to bring liquor into U.S. waters. Only two months after ratification, Great Britain's passenger liners once again embarked on transatlantic crossings with a full complement of alcoholic beverages, and its cargo vessels, carrying in-transit liquor supplies, docked in American ports. While controversies arose over the enforcement provisions of the treaty, the practical application of the sealed-liquor concession provoked little debate. British shipping operated unfettered by the constraints of the Eighteenth Amendment, and, from an economic perspective, the liquor agreement was an unqualified bargain for Great Britain.[2]

London officials, however, were not free from the burdens of the liquor problem. The smuggling convention was a bilateral agreement based on the advantages of mutual concessions. Its benefits could not be enjoyed in isolation, and the inability of the United States to exercise its full enforcement powers under the treaty jeopardized the valuable sealed-liquor provision. Regardless of American indifference, economic self-interest demanded that the British government accept responsibility for the success of the entire agreement.

As the leading proponent of expanding Great Britain's antismuggling efforts, Ambassador Howard was the central figure in this reassessment of British liquor policy. He was motivated by a long-held belief in the importance of Anglo-American friendship and the conviction that the major obstacle to harmony was the continued involvement of British interests in rum-running.[3] Dismissing the treaty as a failure and ignoring the State Department's responsibility for postratification problems, Howard had urged Foreign Secretary Chamberlain to allow the unrestricted seizure of British rumrunners. Chamberlain's rejection of this proposal did not persuade Howard to abandon his lonely crusade. In January 1925, Secretary of State Hughes had suggested that the British government provide information on the movements of suspected rumrunners sailing from British or colonial ports. Howard immediately supported this idea and warned the Foreign Office that the absence of cooperative action encouraged anti-British sentiment in the United States.[4]

Howard's new proposal was dismissed by Foreign Office officials as an alarmist plea from "our amiable but erratic Ambassador."[5] For them, Howard's previous sympathy for American enforcement abuses compromised his objectivity. Participants in the bitter treaty debate of 1923, like Cecil Hurst and Ronald McNeill, found it incomprehensible that further British concessions were necessary. While Foreign Secretary Chamberlain and the recently appointed chief of the American Department, Robert Vansittart, were less dogmatic than their predecessors, there was scant evidence to support Howard's claim that treaty problems were inflaming American anglophobia. The political influence of the prohibitionists in the United States continued to decline, and postratification grievances were primarily British. In March, Howard's request for information sharing was denied.[6]

Howard's determination was not diminished by this latest rebuff. When he returned to London in the summer of 1925, he sent the foreign secretary a memorandum on the prohibition issue. Wisely omitting any reference to the possible extension of American seizure rights, Howard argued that the British smuggling connection encouraged support for U.S. annexation of the Bahamas and was the leading source of Anglo-American tensions. The only solution to the liquor problem, Howard concluded, was for the Baldwin government to reconvene the interdepartmental committee to consider new antismuggling legislation.[7] Foreign Office officials unanimously condemned the memorandum as useless and impractical. "No one is bothering about us now in connection with prohibition," Vansittart noted; "there is no visible danger to Anglo-American relations in a dwindling drink traffic."[8] Chamberlain decided to reassemble the interdepartmental committee to convince Howard that his proposal was unnecessary and unacceptable.

For all his misapprehensions, Howard accurately exposed the outstanding weakness of Great Britain's liquor policy. British-registered ships were involved in rum-running, and the Bahamas provided a safe refuge for smugglers.[9] The London government's failure to disrupt these operations, even to the extent of seriously enforcing existing statutes, was difficult to defend. The dangers of this vulnerability, outlined in Howard's memorandum, alarmed Board of Trade officials. Charles Hipwood, chief of the Mercantile Marine Department, feared that without further assistance American enforcement officers would consider the liquor agreement of little value. This endangered the sealed-liquor privilege and threatened British shipping interests. Having fought hard to gain a valuable concession, Hipwood was not prepared to sacrifice the one undisputed benefit of the treaty.[10]

When the interdepartmental committee reconvened on October 5, 1925, Chairman Vansittart reassured the representatives that there was no apparent demand from the United States for further enforcement assistance, but Hipwood interrupted to announce that the Board of Trade supported Howard's proposal for the adoption of new antismuggling measures. Colonial Office officials, hoping to diffuse criticism of the Bahamas, added their endorsement. Hipwood suggested enforcing all existing laws to their extreme limit, with the United States supplying evidence for legal prosecutions, and inviting an American representative to London to discuss the details of these administrative arrangements. With the Board of Trade and Colonial Office prepared to accept the burdens of a cooperative agreement with the United States, there was no basis for Foreign Office opposition. Hipwood's proposal was accepted and distributed to the departments for approval.[11]

Buoyed by his success at home, Ambassador Howard returned to Washington and began to expand the scope of British cooperation before he received the interdepartmental committee's final report. Prior to his departure, a U.S. Coast Guard cutter had illegally entered the waters near Gun Cay, a favorite hiding place for rumrunners, and the Bahaman government demanded an apology. Howard suggested that instead of a protest the Foreign Office allow the United States to send patrol boats into Bahaman territory. Unknown to the ambassador, Secretary of State Kellogg received a similar proposal from the Treasury Department, and, on November 16, Kellogg formally requested that the British government permit Coast Guard vessels to sail in the waters off Gun Cay.[12]

Without the approval of the Foreign Office, Howard met with U.S. enforcement officials to discuss this suggestion. Overwhelmed by their cordiality, he offered to broach the possibility of Coast Guard visitation rights when he visited Nassau during the Christmas holidays. He also agreed to recommend that Bahaman officials ratify an information treaty with the United States and adopt more stringent antismuggling measures.[13] In January 1926, Howard informed the State Department that Bahaman authorities approved the Coast Guard visits and were willing to accept Colonial Office instructions for information sharing.[14]

Exceeding his instructions, Howard went beyond the scope of the interdepartmental recommendations and was strongly rebuked by Foreign Secretary Chamberlain,[15] but the Foreign Office accepted the ambassador's improvisations. On March 29, 1926, he presented the State Department with an outline of British assistance. British and colonial authorities would supply U.S. officials with information on suspicious vessels, and Coast Guard cutters were permitted to visit Gun Cay. In addition, vessels owned or controlled by Americans would lose their British registration and individuals making false cargo and clearance declarations would be prosecuted. Stressing that these measures were informal, the Baldwin government invited the United States to send a representative to London to aid in "the efficient execution of this offer of cooperation which it is hoped that the United States will accept as proof of the desire of His Majesty's government to render such assistance as within their power to give."[16]

With his own determination and the crucial support of the Board of Trade, Howard secured his goal of enlarging Great Britain's involvement in prohibition enforcement. Howard's success, however, was not achieved without cost. The announcement of the government's offer of cooperation was greeted with protests from members of Parliament and with the opposition of the British press. An editorial in the *Morning*

Post condemned the Foreign Office's "amicable dealings with the United States" and declared that concessions should not be granted until American officials offered restitution for their past infringements of British rights.[17] The *Sunday Times* concluded that the Coast Guard agreement was "as far as friendship can take Great Britain," and Chamberlain was criticized for being "too soft" on the smuggling issue.[18] The unmistakable message was that any further action by the Baldwin government was politically impossible, and this elevated the importance of the proposed informal discussion on enforcement coordination. Unless British and American officials framed a workable solution when they met in London, there would be no mutual cooperation in ending the smuggling problem.

As the first scheduled meeting neared, failure seemed preordained. State Department officials, objecting in principle to any request for new British enforcement assistance, accepted the British invitation in April with reluctance. "Mr. Kellogg," Assistant Secretary of State William Castle wrote, "agrees entirely with me that the whole business is enough to make one ashamed. We would not ask the British to help us enforce laws covering other matters and I don't see why we should turn to them to help us enforce the prohibition laws."[19] The department's lack of enthusiasm increased when Assistant Treasury Secretary Lincoln Andrews was selected to be the representative. The vainglorious Andrews regarded his mission as an independent undertaking. The press had dubbed the discussions the "London Conference," and State Department officials were repeatedly forced to deny reports that Andrews was planning to negotiate a new treaty.[20] He changed the date of departure twice and ignored State Department opposition to his plans to visit France and Germany. In frustration, Secretary Kellogg told Castle that "we had better drop the whole thing and let them go to the devil," and the fate of the London meeting was left in the uncertain hands of General Andrews.[21]

The success of the London Conference also was jeopardized by the unresolved differences over the enforcement of the liquor treaty. The United States and Great Britain continued to disagree on the use of "hypothetical" measurements. While American courts had upheld the stricter British definition, the Coolidge administration did not officially acknowledge the validity of this interpretation. The Justice Department's unwillingness to abandon claims of extratreaty seizure rights aroused the suspicion of Foreign Office officials and confirmed the uncertainty of American liquor policy. The delay in securing congressional approval for supplemental legislation to resolve the self-executing issue frustrated the efforts of U.S. enforcement officials and diminished the value of the smuggling convention. Disputes involving the treaty, however, were not part of the discussion agenda. Whatever the achievements of the London meeting, these problems remained the major cause of Anglo-American prohibition tensions in the post-treaty period.[22]

On July 14 the American delegation arrived in London. Accompanying Andrews were William Vallance of the State Department, Arthur Henderson from the Justice Department, Treasury Officer Keith Weeks, former Nassau Consul Harry Anslinger, and Admiral Frederick Billard of the Coast Guard.[23] Speaking to reporters, Andrews was unusually reserved, emphasizing the informal nature of his visit and declaring that a new liquor treaty was not under consideration. His temperate remarks immediately eased the controversy surrounding the conference, and the previously critical London press now praised the limited goals of the meeting.[24]

On the following day the delegation met with representatives of the Foreign Office, Board of Trade, Admiralty, Colonial Office, and Customs.[25] Vansittart, serving as chairman, established the general tone of the discussions in his opening remarks, reassuring the Americans that "there should be no real difficulty in reaching an understanding; any point on which understanding cannot be reached will be treated in a broad spirit of tolerance."[26] Vansittart then proposed that the agenda should reflect the issues of greatest concern to the United States, and he suggested that Andrews submit a list of priorities. Amid signs that pessimistic expectations were premature, the London Conference on Smuggling Enforcement began.

The first full session of the conference, dominated by Andrews and the Board of Trade's Hipwood, focused on the strict enforcement of shipping laws in the Bahamas. Andrews cited the misuse of British registry as the greatest obstacle to smuggling enforcement, and he requested that the British government strengthen registration regulations. Hipwood promised that violators would be prosecuted if the United States provided evidence of false registration, and he proposed dividing British ships into categories of either bona fide vessels or rumrunners, based on American intelligence reports. It would be the responsibility of honest traders, Hipwood maintained, to take additional precautions to ensure the integrity of their operation.[27]

The only note of discord at this session was the criticism voiced by Vallance and Admiral Billard over the Baldwin government's protest of seizures. Vansittart reminded them that it was their responsibility to respect treaty limits: "Otherwise, His Majesty's Government might be put in the awkward position of having to make a protest in defense of a general principle...arising out of the case of a notorious rumrunner, which we would prefer as far as she herself was concerned to throw to the wolves."[28] Andrews quickly reassured Vansittart that it was the policy of the United States to act strictly within the terms of the liquor convention, a claim not substantiated by the events of the last two years. The British delegates politely masked their skepticism. Following the appointment of a subcommittee on the Bahamas to refine the details of the proposed arrangements, the meeting was adjourned.

When the conference reconvened on July 17, there was a new sense of friendship and understanding, fostered by the success of the first session and the progress achieved by the Bahamas subcommittee. "We on our side are incapable of anything except appreciation," Andrews proclaimed, "we have nothing to offer except flowers." Even Billard conceded "how deeply we were impressed with the very frank, open and sympathetic manner in which matters were dealt with at the subcommittee meeting." [29] The delegates concentrated on the arrangement for Coast Guard visits to the Bahamas, which the Americans considered inadequate because visitation rights were too restrictive. British officials acknowledged the limitations of the agreement, and the Colonial Office was requested to consider granting the United States extended observation rights. [30] Expressing concern over law enforcement in the Bahamas, Andrews recommended that a British gunboat patrol the outer islands, and this proposal was referred to the Bahamas subcommittee. [31]

As the discussions continued, no serious disagreements disturbed this harmony. The British representatives calmly considered suggestions for specific assistance, and the American delegates accepted, without acrimony, the London government's inability to comply with a particular request. Hipwood was so impressed with American moderation that he prepared an unsolicited memorandum on additional enforcement cooperation, which he presented at the next conference session on July 20. He recommended the establishment of a working liaison between British and American officials in London and Nassau, the preparation of a blacklist of suspected smugglers, and the withholding of diplomatic support for any vessel involved in illegal activities. The major issues were settled, and Andrews and Hipwood were appointed to draft a preliminary report of the proceedings. [32]

Three days later the delegates met to discuss the final wording, and the draft was accepted with few changes. [33] Reflecting the informal status of the conference, the document was a recommendation for cooperation, not a binding agreement, and the preamble included the words "should be adopted." The delegates agreed that only Vansittart and Andrews would sign the final report, to avoid the impression that it was a formal convention, and the specific details of the arrangement would not be published. At the insistence of the Colonial Office, the Coast Guard was required to notify island authorities before visiting the Bahamas, and the Foreign Office weakened a suggestion by Hipwood to restrict the future protests of seized rumrunners. With these amendments, the draft report was sent to the State Department and the Foreign Office.[34]

Following the approval of Foreign Secretary Chamberlain and Secretary of State Kellogg, the delegates reassembled on July 27 for the signing of the final report. Unexpectedly, Vansittart, fearing parliamentary criticism, requested the addition of a statement that the conference had not broached the issue of extended seizure rights. Hipwood objected to foreclosing any subsequent consideration of Anglo-American treaty disagreements because he had, without Foreign Office knowledge, privately discussed this with Vallance.[35] But this last-minute snag was resolved when Andrews supported the Foreign Office amendment. The final report emphatically declared that "no question of policy, politics or past practice was called into question" and "there was no suggestion of any extension of the American right of search."[36]

The unpublished provisions of the agreement included recommendations for the creation of a shared blacklist of smugglers and a close liaison between Bahaman authorities and the U.S. consulate in Nassau. The delegates suggested providing the American consul in London with registry information and intelligence reports on all ships clearing Great Britain for ports between Panama and Canada with more than 500 cases of distilled spirits. No ships would be permitted to enter British ports clearing from the "high seas," and the frequent use of this practice in the Bahamas would justify prosecution. The Admiralty was requested to send a patrol boat to the Bahamas for enforcement purposes, and American assistance was recommended to secure evidence against rumrunners violating British law. Coast Guard cutters would be allowed to enter Bahaman waters for a renewable period of one year, if Coast Guard officers notified the appropriate authorities in person on their first visit and thereafter by radio. Finally, the delegates recommended that the British government continue its practice of examining all information on seizures before making any inquiries or official representations. In signing the report, Andrews expressed his gratitude and Vansittart praised American restraint. The general introductory provisions of the document were officially published the next day.[37]

When Andrews arrived in New York on August 11, the London Conference, which appeared destined for failure a month earlier, was hailed as a success by both British and U.S. officials. Andrews had secured unprecedented assistance in enforcing an American law, far beyond his expectations, and the British government was committed to shouldering the burden of these administrative measures. By attacking the source of the smuggling problem, the conference report corrected the major flaw of the liquor treaty and provided a framework for minimizing the continued difficulties that handicapped the operations of the Coast Guard.[38]

For Foreign Office officials, the outcome of the conference was equally gratifying: the British smuggling connection was weakened and the sealed-liquor concession was protected. The report's unqualified assurance that British rights under international law remained intact blunted domestic criticism, and the Baldwin government's generosity was applauded in the United States.[39] Building on the foundation of the liquor treaty, the British and American delegates expanded smuggling assistance to its practical limit.

The London agreement, however, did not eliminate smuggling as an Anglo-American concern, and the outstanding achievement of the conference was an intangible one. After six years of misunderstanding and suspicion, the discussions in July instilled a bilateral spirit of cooperation among those individuals responsible for resolving the liquor problem. The personal encounter between Anglo-American officials succeeded, where normal diplomatic channels had failed, in creating a calmer, more rational approach to liquor diplomacy. At the conference, former fanatics became trusted friends. The result was preventative and private discussions to avoid open controversy and a new mutual respect for the restraints confronting policymakers in London and Washington. What the British and American representatives finally secured was a positive basis for both the settlement of future prohibition problems and the establishment of the post-treaty harmony that had eluded them since 1924.

The larger value of the cordiality nurtured at the London meeting was reflected in the resolution of Anglo-American disagreements involving the enforcement and interpretation of the liquor convention. The treaty remained entangled in controversies over seizures beyond the one-hour limit, the use of hypothetical measurements, and the self-executing nature of the agreement—issues which the conference did not specifically address. But Admiral Billard returned to Washington with an appreciation of the Baldwin government's sensitivity to treaty abuses, and he immediately instructed Coast Guard officers not to interfere with British vessels outside the one-hour distance.[40]

Although Great Britain did not forfeit its right to protest violations of international law, the Foreign Office abided by the agreement to consider all available seizure information before taking any diplomatic action. This tempered American resentment toward what was previously perceived as Great Britain's unconditional defense of smugglers.[41] Foreign Office officials generally accepted Coast Guard seizures of established rumrunners. When forced to request an official explanation of flagrant abuses, their representations were friendly and the quick response of the State Department satisfied their objections. Within a few months, stricter Coast Guard respect for the treaty and Foreign Office restraint virtually eliminated extratreaty seizure tensions.[42]

The discussions in London also persuaded the Foreign Office to resolve the lingering dispute regarding the use of hypothetical measurements to determine treaty distance. At the conference, Vallance had informed Hipwood that the Supreme Court would settle the hypothetical issue when it ruled on the appeal of the *Quadra* seizure. On August 28, Ambassador Howard informed the State Department that the Baldwin government was prepared to accept the Supreme Court's decision. But in September, Howard was notified that the appeal was based on the evidence of a specific boat and the hypothetical question would not be considered.[43] Foreign Office officials, having conceded the possibility of two valid interpretations, informed Howard that they would no longer protest the American reliance upon hypothetical measurements to establish treaty jurisdiction.[44]

For their part, American officials attempted to ease the British government's apprehensions respecting the uncertainty over the self-executing nature of the treaty. Under Admiral Billard's instructions, the Coast Guard no longer pursued smuggling cases in those districts where the courts had denied the extension of U.S. statutes to the one-hour distance, and this restricted the Justice Department's reliance on non-treaty doctrines to support legal action.[45] The problems created by the lack of judicial support for seizure prosecution under the treaty were largely resolved in 1927 when the Supreme Court, in the *Quadra* appeal, accepted a broad interpretation of the conspiracy laws. Enforcement officials now were able to prosecute smugglers who were physically beyond the territory of the United States and engaged in a conspiracy to violate its statutes.[46]

This new sense of common purpose was apparent as the delegates implemented the specific recommendations of the London Conference. More than any other official, Hipwood sustained the spirit of the July discussions. Motivated by both the need to preserve the integrity of the liquor treaty and a warm personal regard for General Andrews, Hipwood faithfully executed the Board of Trade's extensive responsibility for British cooperation. Although the conference report was not officially adopted until the formal exchange of notes on September 29, 1926, he already had initiated information sharing with the American consulate in London and sent a checklist to all shipping registrars outlining the procedures for examining registry transfers of American and foreign vessels.[47] Hipwood also developed a blacklist of suspected rumrunners. Communicating the latest intelligence directly to Andrews, Hipwood's efforts produced the most comprehensive appraisal of smuggling operations ever written, and U.S. enforcement officials immediately adopted it as the official Anglo-American blacklist. Only three months after the conference, information sharing was an unqualified success.[48]

In Washington, Andrews paralleled these efforts. "I can hardly tell you what it means to me that we are thus in direct communications," he wrote Hipwood. "[We] are really having a wonderful time check-mating rum smugglers as this cooperative work with you allows."[49] For Andrews, the London meeting was a personal triumph, and he returned as the recognized spokesman for the Coolidge administration's liquor policy. Exploiting this new influence, Andrews created the Bureau of Foreign Control in the Treasury Department to serve as a clearinghouse for smuggling information and persuaded Secretary Kellogg to instruct diplomatic personnel to monitor smuggling activities.[50] Andrews was a dynamo of activity, regularly consulting with Hipwood, personally directing enforcement operations, and guiding all aspects of the conference proposals. Maximizing the benefits of British assistance, he established Anglo-American information sharing as an invaluable and permanent weapon in prohibition enforcement.[51]

Impressed with Andrews's dedication, Foreign Secretary Chamberlain assumed an active role in ensuring the Baldwin government's strict compliance with the London accords. British consuls in the United States, Latin America, and continental ports were instructed to share smuggling information with their American counterparts, and the governors of the Channel Islands were requested to report the movements of liquor cargoes.[52] Foreign Office officials were unable to persuade the Admiralty to send a patrol boat to the Bahamas, but they successfully pressured the other departments to honor their cooperative responsibilities.[53]

Chamberlain's involvement was particularly effective in prodding the Colonial Office to secure the support of authorities in the British West Indies and Bermuda. After a tenuous beginning in the Bahamas, officials adopted a new vigilance in suppressing rum-running, and smuggling information was regularly shared.[54] In Bermuda, official diligence prevented the reestablishment of smuggling, and when the Jamaican governor requested additional enforcement measures, the Coast Guard was invited to patrol the Grand Cayman Islands.[55] Although the liquor traffic continued to operate in the British West Indies with local support, most colonial officers conscientiously administered the London agreements in this largely hostile environment. By 1928 stricter enforcement in the Bahamas and the other islands discouraged the return of smuggling headquarters to a British possession and reduced the volume of the liquor trade. It also earned the respect of U.S. officials who now clearly delineated between the popular and the official attitude toward rum-running.[56]

The clearest evidence of the new understanding instilled by the London Conference was the cooperative effort to contain the problems created by the Coast Guard visitation agreement. Considering the public opposition in the Bahamas to the visits, any infraction was guaranteed to arouse local criticism. Admiral Billard issued strict orders to crew members that "under no circumstances will you exercise any authority and perform any overt act within foreign territorial waters."[57] But colonial authorities, in December 1926, complained that American cutters were entering Bahaman waters without making the required notification stop at Bimini. Satisfied that Andrews would correct this misunderstanding, Vansittart refused to authorize a formal protest.[58] When Bahaman officials considered suspending information sharing after further Coast Guard infractions, Andrews sent an urgent cable to Hipwood explaining that these unannounced visits were to secure emergency supplies. Foreign Office officials accepted this explanation, and the Baldwin government renewed the Bahaman agreement in September 1927.[59]

A week later, another controversy threatened cooperation. Lawrence Christiansen, a Coast Guard officer, was charged with smuggling during an official visit to the Bahamas. Island authorities demanded his extradition for violating international law and planned to prosecute him and his local coconspirator. Secretary of State Kellogg immediately acknowledged American responsibility for the incident and offered to extradite Christiansen on the lesser charge of conspiracy. In London, Colonial Office officials, irritated by repeated Coast Guard abuses, opposed a quiet settlement, but Vansittart, impressed with Kellogg's sincerity, forced the Colonial Office to accept a compromise. On June 3, 1928, Secretary Kellogg formally apologized and agreed to investigate all charges.[60] Following the Christiansen affair, Treasury Secretary Mellon reassured Ambassador Howard that the department would adopt stricter guidelines for Bahaman visits. Foreign Office officials were convinced that the Coast Guard now was exercising restraint, and this confidence was confirmed with the second renewal of the Coast Guard visitation agreement.[61]

In the summer of 1927, Andrews had retired from the Treasury Department. Foreign Office officials feared that the loss of this "moderate, tactful and helpful spirit" might jeopardize the London accords.[62] These apprehensions were unfounded; Andrews's true legacy was that the success of the London Conference was an enduring one. Officials in Washington recognized that the maintenance of British assistance was an important part of antismuggling activities, and the calm resolution of the Coast Guard visitation problems, after Andrews's departure, demonstrated the continued commitment to the goals of the conference.[63] In the two years following the London meeting, the great emotional, legal, and economic issues that had handicapped liquor diplomacy ebbed, reducing the importance of the Eighteenth Amendment as a source of Anglo-American tensions.

The London Conference, however, did not end the Anglo-American liquor problem. At the conference, British officials reaffirmed their determination to protect their country's shipping interests from the effects of prohibition. The sealed-liquor concession still rested on the mutual concessions of the smuggling convention; by accepting an expanded role in antismuggling efforts, the Baldwin government tightened the link between successful law enforcement and British shipping. The two countries now were united in a common interest, and, to this extent, the importation of illegal liquor into the United States remained both a British and an American concern. Consequently, any change in the liquor problem would continue to have repercussions in Washington and London.

Notes

[1] Austin Chamberlain, Minutes, July 24, 1925, A3821/31/45, PRO.

[2] The only complication involving the sealed-liquor provision was the various attempts by crew members to smuggle liquor aboard British liners. In March 1924 the Royal Mail Steam Packet Company's *Orduna* was seized in New York when enforcement agents uncovered a smuggling scheme directed by the ship's chief steward. Esme Howard to Foreign Office, March 14, 1924, A1675/27/45, and March 21, 1924, A2070/27/45, PRO. U.S. Attorney William Hayward decided to seize the vessel and bring a forfeiture suit against the ship. Howard to Foreign Office, March 28, 1924, A2220/27/45, May 16, 1924, A3197/27/45, and June 3, 1924, A3405/27/45, PRO. Foreign Office officials believed that the shipping line was extremely lax in enforcing the liquor guidelines within U.S. waters and refused to interfere in the case. British Consulate, New York, to Howard, May 19, 1924, A3410/27/45, PRO; Howard to Foreign Office, June 19, 1924, A3804/27/45, PRO; Foreign Office to Board of Trade, August 7, 1924, A4575/27/45, PRO; Board of Trade to Foreign Office, August 18, 1924, A4549/27/45, PRO. On October 16, 1924, U.S. District Court Judge Learned Hand ruled that there could be no libel against a vessel unless the owners were cognizant of the smuggling action, which Hayward could not establish, and the vessel was released.

The *Orduna* incident emphasized the need for strict compliance, and, throughout the post-treaty period, legitimate British shippers were never directly involved in liquor smuggling. Ashley Sparks to Thomas Royden, March 5, 1924, C/2/279, Cunard Archives; John M. Savage to State Department, November 3, 1926, 811.114/Great Britain/132, RG 59, NA; Henry Chilton to Frank Kellogg, December 6, 1926, A6717/88/45, PRO; Howard to Foreign Office, January 20, 1927, A644/88/45, March 6, 1927, A1396/82/45, and March 12, 1927, A1546/82/45, PRO; Howard to Kellogg, April 8, 1927,

A2343/82/45, and June 25, 1927, A4109/82/45, PRO; Andrew Mellon to International Mercantile Marine Company, May 12, 1927, copy in A4376/82/45, PRO. Foreign Office officials maintained pressure on the shipping lines to observe the treaty guidelines. Harry Armstrong to Chilton, October 6, 1926, A5508/88/45, and October 15, 1926, A5830/88/45, PRO; Chilton to Foreign Office, October 22, 1926, A5728/88/45, PRO; Charles Hipwood to British Shippers, December 26, 1926, copy in A6558/88/45, PRO; Board of Trade to Foreign Office, December 23, 1926, A6796/88/45, and January 13, 1927, A303/303/45, PRO; Sparks to Armstrong, March 17, 1927, A2021/303/45, PRO; Adrian Baille to State Department, April 9, 1928, 811.114/4678, RG 59, NA; Cunard Company, Executive Committee, Minutes, May 2, 1928, B/4/66/322, Cunard Archives; Howard to Foreign Office, May 10, 1928, A3419/211/45, PRO. The willingness of British shippers to assist enforcement officials contained periodic infractions of the treaty and prevented any serious diplomatic problems. The similar problems on USSB vessels reflected the inherent difficulty of controlling the actions of crew members. T. V. O'Connor to W. H. Stayton, July 23, 1926, 600/7, RG 32, NA; Treasury Department to USSB, December 12, 1928, 600/7, RG 32, NA.

[3]Howard to Eyre Crowe, January 19 and March 11, 1924, "United States" file, 24/1, Vol. 388, F.O. 800, PRO; Howard, *Theatre of Life* 2:477, 501–4; Willson, *Friendly Relations,* 333.

[4]Howard to Foreign Office, January 16, 1925, A454/31/45, PRO; Howard, *Theatre of Life* 2:504.

[5]Chamberlain to Arthur Balfour, January 7, 1925, Vol. 257/34, Chamberlain Papers.

[6]Chamberlain to Howard, March 13, 1925, A1285/31/45, PRO; *Times* (London), January 9, 1925; Howard to Foreign Office, January 12, 1925, A246/31/45, and January 16, 1925, A454/31/45, PRO; "Meeting with the British Ambassador," January 15, 1925, Folder 77b, Box 175, Hughes Papers; Kyvig, *Repealing National Prohibition,* 61–62, 71–97; Asbury, *Great Illusion,* 315–17; Sinclair, *Era of Excess,* 277; Kerr, *Organized for Prohibition,* 255.

[7]Howard to Chamberlain, July 24, 1925, A3821/31/45, PRO. See also Howard, *Theatre of Life* 2:477.

[8]Foreign Office, Memorandum, June 30, 1925, A3414/31/45, PRO; Foreign Office, Minutes, July 24, 1925, A3821/31/45, PRO; G. H. Locock to Robert Vansittart, June 18, 1925, A3152/52/45, PRO.

[9]T. Jaeckel to State Department, July 2, 1924, 811.114/3719, RG 59, NA; G. E. Chamberlain to State Department, February 3, 1925, 811.114/4292, RG 59, NA; Coast Guard to State Department, October 22, 1924, 811.114/3917, RG 59, NA; Harlan Stone to Charles Evans Hughes, February 28, 1925, 811.114/4304, RG 59, NA; Howard, *Theatre of Life* 2:504.

[10]Howard met with Hipwood in July and sent the Board of Trade a copy of his memorandum on prohibition. Howard to Austin Chamberlain, November 19, 1925, Vol. 258/737, Chamberlain Papers; Howard, *Theatre of Life* 2:502; Howard to Chamberlain, July 24, 1925, A3821/31/45, PRO.

[11]Interdepartmental Committee, Minutes, October 5, 1925, A5103/31/45, PRO. The committee held a second meeting to discuss Hipwood's proposal. Interdepartmental Committee, Minutes, October 8, 1925, A5059/31/45, PRO.

[12]Howard to Austin Chamberlain, October 22, 1925, Vol. 258/593, Chamberlain Papers; State Department, Memorandum, November 24, 1925, 811.114/Great Britain/63, RG 59, NA.

[13]State Department, Memorandum on Meeting with Esme Howard, December 2, 1925, 711.419/152, Roll 14, M581, RG 59, NA; Howard to Foreign Office, December 4, 1925, A6300/31/45, PRO; Kellogg to Mellon, December 21, 1925, 711.419/138, Roll 14, M581, RG 59, NA.

[14]Joseph Grew, Memorandum, January 14, 1926, 811.114/B.W.I./581, RG 59, NA; Howard to Foreign Office, January 6, 1926, A88/88/45, PRO; Harry Cordeaux to Howard, December 30, 1925, A36/88/45, PRO.

[15]Foreign Office to Howard, December 11, 1925, A6002/31/45, January 21, 1926, A6540/31/45, and March 6, 1926, A1064/88/45, PRO; Customs to Foreign Office, December 1, 1925, A5988/31/45, PRO; Foreign Office, Minutes, December 16, 1925, A6540/31/45, and December 30, 1925, A6539/31/45, PRO; Austin Chamberlain to Howard, January 22, 1926, A6540/31/45, PRO; Howard to Chamberlain, February 17, 1926, ibid.; Colonial Office to Foreign Office, January 11, 1926, A244/88/45, PRO; Harry Anslinger to State Department, February 2, 1926, 811.114/B.W.I./595, RG 59, NA; R. I. Campbell, Memorandum, March 2, 1926, A1206/88/45, PRO.

[16]Howard to State Department, March 29, 1926, 711.419/147, Roll 14, M581, RG 59, NA; Howard to Foreign Office, March 30, 1926, A1986/88/45, PRO.

[17]*Morning Post* (London), April 20, 21, 1926.

[18]*Sunday Times* (London), April 25, 1926; F. A. Sterling to State Department, April 29, 1926, 711.419/153, Roll 14, M581, RG 59, NA. See also *Tribune* (Nassau), May 15, 1926; William Smale to State Department, May 18, 1926, 711.419/159, Roll 14, M581, RG 59, NA; *New York Times,* May 6, 1926.

[19]William Castle to Boylston Beale, June 21, 1926, Folder 28, Box 3, Castle Papers.

[20]Kellogg insisted that William Vallance accompany Andrews to protect diplomatic interests. Green Hackworth to Kellogg, April 27, 1926, 711.419/190, Roll 14, M581, RG 59, NA; Hackworth to Joseph Grew, April 16, 1926, 711.419/145, Roll 14, M581, RG 59, NA; Howard to Austin Chamberlain, July 3, 1926, A3597/88/45, PRO; Grew, Memorandum on Meeting with Henry Chilton, April 17, 1926, 711.419/146, Roll 14, M581, RG 59, NA; Howard to Foreign Office, June 3, 1926, A3164/88/45, PRO; Campbell, Minutes, April 17, 1926, A2096/88/45, PRO.

[21]Castle to Beale, June 21, 1926, Folder 28, Box 3, Castle Papers; Kellogg to Garrad Winston, August 5, 1926, 711.419/200, Roll 14, M581, RG 59, NA; Grew to Leland Harrison, June 16, 1926, 711.419/165, Roll 14, M581, RG 59, NA.

[22]Montague Shearman, Memorandum respecting Decisions in Liquor Smuggling Cases, March 26, 1926, A1356/88/45, PRO.

[23]Robert Macatee of the American consulate in London also was detailed to the conference, and Andrews utilized the resources of the embassy. Horace Lee Washington to State Department, July 22, 1926, 711.419/211, Roll 15, M581, RG 59, NA.

[24]*Daily Chronicle* (London), July 14, 1926; *Westminster Gazette* (London), July 14, 1926; *Daily News* (London), July 14, 1926; *Times* (London), July 15, 1926; *Observer* (London), July 18, 1926.

[25]The British delegation included R. I. Campbell (Foreign Office), N. A. Guttery and W. J. Wragge (Board of Trade), H. P. Douglas and W. H. Hancock (Admiralty), L. B. Freeston (Colonial Office), and C. J. Gryles and E. S. Bertenshaw (Customs).

[26]"Stenographic Notes of Meetings between United States Officials and His Majesty's Government to Discuss Methods of Cooperation for the Prevention of Liquor Smuggling into the United States from the Sea," July 15, 1926, A4073/88/45, PRO (hereafter cited as "Steno Report"). See also William Vallance, Minutes of the London Conference Meetings, July 15, 1926, 711.419/205, Roll 15, M581, RG 59, NA. There are few Treasury reports on the actual proceedings, and the Justice Department file, 23/4440 (RG 60, NAS), was transferred to file 23/166/03, which does not exist.

[27]"Steno Report," July 15, 1926, A4073/88/45, PRO.

[28]Ibid.

[29]"Steno Report," July 17, 1926, A4073/88/45, PRO.

[30]Prior to the conference, General Andrews had suggested expanding this privilege, but this was rejected by Bahamas Governor Cordeaux. Howard to Foreign Office, July 1, 1926, A3711/88/45, PRO; Admiralty to Colonial Office, July 15, 1926, copy in A3794/88/45, PRO.

[31]Although Andrews offered to supply an American boat, Hipwood pressured the Admiralty to consider dispatching a boat to patrol the Bahamas. Hipwood to Vansittart, July 19, 1926, A3911/88/45, PRO; Foreign Office, Minutes, July 19, 1926, ibid.; Foreign Office to Admiralty, July 23, 1926, ibid.

[32]"Steno Report," July 20, 1926, A4073/88/45, PRO.

[33]The committee briefly reassembled on July 22 to discuss specific wording of the preliminary report. Copies were submitted to British officials. "Steno Report," July 22, 1926, A4073/88/45, PRO.

[34]"Steno Report," July 23, 1926, A4073/88/45, PRO; Campbell, Minutes, July 16, 1926, A3819/88/45, PRO; Sterling to State Department, July 21, 1926, 711.419/205, Roll 15, M581, RG 59, NA; Alanson Houghton to Kellogg, July 23, 1926, 711.419/194, Roll 14, M581, RG 59, NA; Foreign Office, Minutes, July 24, 1926, A3945/88/45, PRO.

[35]"Steno Report," July 27, 1926, A4073/88/45, PRO; Foreign Office, Minutes, July 27, 1926, A4041/88/45, PRO.

[36]"London Conference Report," July 27, 1926, 711.419/196, Roll 14, M581, RG 59, NA; "Steno Report," July 27, 1926, A4073/88/45, PRO. Unknown to Andrews, President Coolidge, responding to press reports, also was concerned that the American delegates were negotiating a new treaty. He wrote to Secretary Mellon and Secretary Kellogg, from New York, demanding that this unauthorized action be stopped. The Treasury Department maintained that Andrews was acting under the direction of the State Department, a claim that Kellogg denied. The State Department issued a press release denying the reports of a new treaty. Calvin Coolidge to Kellogg, July 24, 1926, 711.419/202, Roll 15, M581, RG 59, NA; Winston to Kellogg, July 26, 1926, "1925–26" folder,

Box 112, RG 56, NA; Kellogg to Coolidge, July 26, 1926, 270/21, Kellogg Papers; Kellogg to Winston, August 5, 1926, 711.419/200, Roll 14, RG 59, NA; Kellogg to Houghton, July 29, 1926, 711.406/206, Roll 15, M581, RG 59, NA. Considering the importance of the London discussions, Andrews's "orphan" status reflected a serious lack of communication within the Coolidge administration.

[37]Ibid.; Minutes of the Cabinet Meeting, July 28, 1926, 48/26, Vol. 53, CAB 23, PRO.

[38]*New York Times,* August 12, 1926.

[39]Vansittart, Minutes, July 24, 1926, A3945/88/45, PRO; Foreign Office, Minutes, July 26, 1926, A3432/88/45, PRO.

[40]Frederick Billard to J. F. Hottel, August 27, 1926, File 6093, Box 48, Records of the Intelligence Division, U.S. Coast Guard, Record Group 26, National Archives, Washington, DC (hereafter cited as RG 26, NA); Billard to Charles Root, January 13, 1927, File 6711, Box 48, RG 26, NA.

[41]Hipwood to Foreign Office, November 4, 1926, A5796/88/45, PRO; Howard to Foreign Office, February 1, 1927, A932/81/45, and February 14, 1927, A1281/81/45, PRO; Board of Trade to Foreign Office, February 15, 1927, A997/27/45, PRO.

[42]Foreign Office to Howard, May 15, 1926, A2243/88/45, PRO; Howard to Foreign Office, August 9, 1926, A4242/88/45, PRO; Foreign Office to Howard, August 16, 1926, A4264/88/45, PRO; Howard to Foreign Office, August 25, 1926, A4071/88/45, and September 14, 1926, A5087/88/45, PRO; Foreign Office to Howard, March 22, 1927, A1533/81/45, PRO; Howard to Foreign Office, June 30, 1927, A4117/81/45, PRO; Foreign Office, Minutes, July 21, 1927, A4522/81/45, PRO; Foreign Office to Howard, November 23, 1927, A6162/81/45, PRO; Howard to State Department, December 22, 1927, A45/45/45, PRO.

[43]Foreign Office to Howard, August 26, 1926, A3611/88/45, PRO; Howard to Kellogg, August 28, 1926, 711.419/223, Roll 15, M581, RG 59, NA; Howard to Foreign Office, April 9, 1926, A2113/88/45, PRO; Vansittart, Minutes, August 25, 1926, A3611/88/45, PRO; William Donovan to Kellogg, September 7, 1926, 23/3/20/51, RG 60, NAS; Chilton to Foreign Office, September 30, 1926, A5219/88/45, PRO; Foreign Office to Chilton, October 9, 1926, ibid.

[44]Kellogg to Attorney General, October 20, 1926, 811.114/*Quadra*/61, RG 59, NA; Chilton to Foreign Office, October 29, 1926, A5837/88/45, PRO; Kellogg, Memorandum, March 28, 1927, 811.114/4614a, RG 59, NA; Foreign Office, Minutes, April 13, 1927, A2284/81/45, PRO; Austin Chamberlain to Howard, March 11, 1927, A1441/81/45, PRO.

[45]Howard to State Department, December 29, 1926, A165/81/45, PRO; Howard to Foreign Office, February 7, 1927, A1076/81/45, PRO; Billard to Hottel, August 27, 1926, File 6093, Box 48, RG 26, NA.

[46]Jessup, *Law of Territorial Waters,* 268–69.

[47]Board of Trade to Colonial Office, August 7, 1926, copy in A4179/88/45, PRO; Kellogg to Attorney General, August 27, 1926, 711.419/218, and Kellogg to Howard, September 18, 1926, 711.419/229, Roll

15, M581, RG 59, NA; Howard to Kellogg, September 29, 1926, A5375/88/45, PRO; Board of Trade to Foreign Office, September 15, 1926, A4932/88/45, PRO.

[48]Hipwood to Lincoln Andrews, September 18, September 28, October 5, and October 7, 1926, copies in A5584/5584/45, PRO; Board of Trade, "British Vessels in Liquor Smuggling Traffic," August 16, 1926, copy in 811.114/Great Britain/90, RG 59, NA; Washington to State Department, October 15, 1926, 811.114/4569, and October 25, 1926, 811.114/Great Britain/122, RG 59, NA; Andrews to Hipwood, October 9, 1926, copy in A5910/5584/45, PRO; Foreign Office, Minutes, October 25, 1926, A5584/5584/45, PRO. For a summary of Hipwood's efforts see also Chilton to Kellogg, October 6, 1926, 711.419/240, Roll 15, M581, RG 59, NA.

[49]Andrews to Hipwood, October 9, 1926, copy in A5910/5584/45, PRO.

[50]Andrews to Kellogg, August 25, 1926, 811.114/Great Britain/95, RG 59, NA; American Consulate, London, to State Department, August 16, 1926, 811.114/Great Britain/88, and November 5, 1926, 811.114/Great Britain/125, RG 59, NA; State Department to American Consuls, October 20, 1926, 711.419/240, Roll 15, M581, RG 59, NA.

[51]Andrews to Hipwood, October 9, 1926, copy in A5910/5584/45, PRO; Hipwood to Andrews, September 18, 1926, copy in A5584/5584/45, PRO; Andrews to Customs Officials, November 26, 1926, copy in 811.114/Great Britain/134, RG 59, NA; Andrews to Kellogg, October 13, 1926, 711.419/242, Roll 15, M581, RG 59, NA; Andrews to State Department, December 1, 1926, 811.114/Great Britain/135, RG 59, NA; Andrews to Kellogg, April 22, 1927, 811.114/Great Britain/167, RG 59, NA; Howard to Foreign Office, January 1, 1927, A1696/82/45, PRO; American Consulate, London, to State Department, April 7, 1927, 811.114/Great Britain/164, and September 12, 1927, 811.114/Great Britain/189, RG 59, NA; Board of Trade to Foreign Office, September 15, 1927, A5436/82/45, PRO; A. J. Henderson to New York Customs House, December 3, 1926, File 6711, Box 48, RG 26, NA; Henderson to British Consulate, New York, January 10, 1927, File 6707, Box 48, RG 26, NA; American Consulate, London, to State Department, December 20, 1927, 811.114/Great Britain/203, and January 26, 1928, 811.114/Great Britain/209, RG 59, NA; "List of Suspected Ships Involved in Liquor Smuggling," March 28, 1928, 811.114/Great Britain/217, RG 59, NA; C. C. Broy to State Department, December 20, 1928, 811.114/Great Britain/246, RG 59, NA.

[52]Foreign Office, Minutes, December 23, 1926, A92/81/45, PRO; Board of Trade to Foreign Office, August 9, 1926, A4293/88/45, PRO; State Department to Chilton, October 28, 1926, 711.419/245, Roll 15, M581, RG 59, NA; Chilton to Foreign Office, November 1, 1926, A6060/88/45, PRO; Andrews to State Department, December 1, 1926, 811.114/Great Britain/135, RG 59, NA; Foreign Office to American Embassy, London, March 11, 1927, 811.114/Great Britain/160, RG 59, NA.

[53]Hipwood to Vansittart, January 10, 1927, A402/45/45, and March 7, 1927, A1487/45/45, PRO; Foreign Office to Customs, February 11, 1927, A799/45/45, PRO; Customs to Foreign Office, February 24, 1927,

A1201/45/45, PRO. The Admiralty claimed that the visits would place crew members in a difficult position because they would be enforcing local laws. Admiralty to Foreign Office, August 27, 1926, A4616/88/45, PRO; Foreign Office to Admiralty, September 7, 1926, ibid.; Admiralty to Foreign Office, December 20, 1926, A6731/88/45, PRO; Austin Chamberlain to Colonial Office, April 19, 1927, A1955/82/45, PRO; Chamberlain to Houghton, August 3, 1927, A4443/82/45, PRO.

⁵⁴Acting Governor A. C. Burns initially angered American Vice Consul Smale by refusing to make inquiries that the Colonial Office did not specifically authorize. Thomas Snow, Minutes, October 27, 1926, A5514/88/45, PRO; Vansittart, Minutes, December 14, 1926, A6628/88/45, PRO; Burns to Colonial Office, November 17, 1926, copy in A6755/88/45, PRO. Foreign Office officials were critical of Burns until they received evidence of his new vigilance. Burns to Governor of Jamaica, December 5, 1926, copy in A258/82/45, PRO; Colonial Office to Foreign Office, March 10, 1927, A1514/81/45, PRO; Vansittart to Hipwood, February 24, 1927, A1035/82/45, PRO; Foreign Office, Minutes, March 7, 1927, A1303/82/45, PRO; Foreign Office to Howard, March 9, 1927, A1356/82/45, PRO; Leslie Freestone to Vansittart, November 10, 1927, A6594/82/45, PRO; C. W. J. Orr to Colonial Office, September 3, 1927, copy in A5518/82/45, January 6, 1928, copy in A777/25/45, and May 25, 1928, copy in A3702/25/45, PRO. See also Seymour Lowman to Kellogg, October 26, 1927, 811.114/B.W.I./841, RG 59, NA.

⁵⁵L. J. Bols to Colonial Office, May 2, 1928, copy in A3701/25/45, PRO; C. D. Feak, "Coast Guard Memorandum," March 24, 1928, File 9211, Box 63, RG 26, NA; Billard, Memorandum, June 6, 1928, ibid.; Washington to State Department, January 24, 1927, 811.114/B.W.I./748, RG 59, NA; Colonial Office to Foreign Office, March 29, 1927, A1918/82/45, PRO; Foreign Office, Minutes, March 29, 1927, ibid.; "Memorandum on Interdepartmental Meeting," May 6, 1927, A2338/82/45, PRO; Howard to Kellogg, April 4, 1928, 811.114/B.W.I./885, RG 59, NA.

⁵⁶Foreign Office, Memorandum on Liquor Smuggling and the Bahamas, March 26, 1927, A1808/82/45, PRO; Austin Chamberlain to Leslie Amery, March 24, 1927, A1190/82/45, PRO; Amery to Chamberlain, April 26, 1927, A2553/82/45, PRO; Bols to Colonial Office, June 29, 1928, copy in A5384/25/45, PRO; Colonial Office, Circular, July 28, 1927, copy in A4497/82/45, and February 10, 1928, copy in A1082/250/45, PRO; State Department to Chilton, October 28, 1926, 711.419/245, Roll 15, M581, RG 59, NA; Howard to Foreign Office, January 4, 1927, A333/82/45, PRO; Howard to Kellogg, April 4, 1928, 811.114/B.W.I./885, RG 59, NA; H. T. Nugent, Memorandum, April 23, 1928, File 9284, Box 63, RG 26, NA; Feak, Memorandum, May 11, 1928, ibid.; Root, Memorandum, May 24, 1928, File 9359, Box 55, RG 26, NA; "List of Suspected Ships," March 28, 1928, 811.114/Great Britain/217, RG 59, NA.

⁵⁷Coast Guard, "Order 294," December 30, 1926, File 6707, Box 48, RG 26, NA.

⁵⁸Colonial Office to Foreign Office, January 10, 1927, A179/82/45, PRO; Foreign Office, Minutes, January 10, 1927, ibid.; Foreign Office to Howard,

January 26, 1927, ibid.; Vansittart to Howard, February 1, 1927, A587/82/45, PRO; Chilton to Robert Craigie, January 11, 1927, A469/82/45, PRO; Grew, Memorandum, February 16, 1927, 811.114/C.G.44/45, RG 59, NA; L. J. Jordan to Billard, January 28, 1927, File 6707, Box 48, RG 26, NA; Feak to Jordan, March 25, 1927, ibid.

⁵⁹Colonial Office to Foreign Office, June 21, 1927, A4335/82/45, PRO; Broy to State Department, June 21, 1927, 711.419/289, Roll 15, M581, RG 59, NA; Andrews to Hipwood, June 22, 1927, copy in A3769/82/45, PRO; Foreign Office to Howard, June 23, 1927, ibid.; State Department, Memorandum, June 24, 1927, 811.114/C.G.44/52, RG 59, NA; Howard to Kellogg, June 25, 1927, 811.114/C.G.44/54, RG 59, NA; Howard to Kellogg, August 5, 1927, A4927/82/45, PRO.

⁶⁰Christiansen's guilt was never conclusively established, and he was not disciplined. Vansittart, Minutes, October 25, 1927, A6258/82/45, PRO; Mellon to Kellogg, November 1, 1927, 811.114/C.G.44/85, RG 59, NA; Foreign Office, Memorandum, November 2, 1927, A6399/82/45, PRO; Howard to Foreign Office, November 1, 1927, A6396/82/45, and January 27, 1928, A868/25/45, PRO; *New York Times,* November 6, 1927; Colonial Office to Foreign Office, November 10, 1927, A6567/82/45, PRO; Vansittart, Minutes, November 3, 1927, A6414/82/45, and November 10, 1927, A6567/82/45, PRO; Orr to Colonial Office, December 8, 1927, copy in A25/25/45, PRO; Colonial Office to Foreign Office, March 8, 1928, A1709/25/45, PRO; Foreign Office to Colonial Office, March 27, 1928, ibid.; Foreign Office to Howard, May 16, 1928, A2975/25/45, PRO; State Department to British Embassy, Washington, June 29, 1928, A5059/25/45, PRO; J. Edgar Hoover to Mabel Walker Willebrandt, July 28, 1928, 23/100/699, RG 60, NAS.

⁶¹Howard to Kellogg, November 3, 1927, A6414/82/45, PRO; Billard to Coast Guard Commanders, October 31, 1927, copy in 811.114/C.G.44/81, RG 59, NA; Howard to State Department, September 14, 1927, A5643/82/45, PRO; Howard to Foreign Office, November 3, 1927, A6611/82/45, PRO; Howard to State Department, December 28, 1927, A204/25/45, PRO; Howard to Foreign Office, April 24, 1928, A2807/45/45, PRO; Howard to Kellogg, April 5, 1928, A2579/25/45, PRO; Mellon to Kellogg, April 19, 1928, File 9211, Box 63, RG 26, NA; Billard to Coast Guard Commanders, April 30, 1928, ibid.; Howard to Foreign Office, May 5, 1928, A3030/25/45, PRO; Kellogg to Howard, June 19, 1928, A4648/25/45, PRO; Foreign Office, Minutes, July 30, 1928, A5269/25/45, PRO; Foreign Office to Chilton, June 30, 1928, A4302/25/45, PRO; Foreign Office to Colonial Office, August 23, 1928, A5731/25/45, PRO.

⁶²Foreign Office, Minutes, June 9, 1927, A3338/27/45, PRO; Chilton to Foreign Office, May 27, 1927, ibid.

⁶³Jordan to Billard, January 28, 1927, File 6707, Box 48, RG 26, NA; Lowman to Kellogg, August 29, 1927, 711.419/292, Roll 15, M581, RG 59, NA; Bureau of Prohibition, Department of Treasury, *Statistics Concerning Intoxicating Liquors* (Washington, DC, 1928), 44.

Chapter Eight

A Surprising Finale
Canada, Hoover, and the
Burdens of Repeal, 1929–1940

Throughout the final years of national prohibition, the spirit of cooperation and the practical arrangements established at the London Conference continued to serve as the essential guide for British and American officials. Information sharing was a potent weapon against smugglers, and the blacklist of rumrunners grew. The annual renewal of the Coast Guard visitation agreement and the vigilance of colonial authorities prevented the return of an extensive liquor trade in the Bahamas. As problems arose, harmony prevailed, and when the repeal of the Eighteenth Amendment brought surprising consequences, the London agreements provided the basis for an amicable solution. A State Department report, recounting the peaceful settlement of disagreements, boasted in 1933 that "any one of the above mentioned incidents might have led to war in former days."[1]

This sustained understanding did not shield Anglo-American relations from the unpredictable nature of the smuggling problem, and the closing chapter of liquor diplomacy was characterized as much by change as it was by continuity. When Canada became the new headquarters for rumrunners, the United States looked to Great Britain for assistance, and smuggling enforcement was transformed into a triangular problem. But the Canadians, now part of the emerging British Commonwealth of self-governing dominions, were determined to control their own affairs, and officials in London were forced to reconcile the challenges of nationalism with the limitations of a declining empire. While the British government recognized the importance of protecting the liquor treaty and its sealed-liquor provision, prohibition assistance and the smuggling convention were perceived in Ottawa as symbols of Canada's position as the poor stepchild in Anglo-American relations. With Canadian support uncertain and imperial ties weakened, Foreign Office officials were forced to maintain an active guardianship of the liquor treaty. To their dismay, the liquor issue remained an enduring problem in British and American foreign relations.

The implications of a trilateral liquor problem were clearly demonstrated in early 1929. On March 21, A. W. Powell, the commander of the Coast Guard's Eighth Division in the Gulf of Mexico, sent an urgent cable to headquarters. The previous day, a Coast Guard patrol had sighted the *I'm Alone*, a Canadian vessel operated under British registry, 10.8 miles from the coast. When requested to stop, the captain of the *I'm Alone* refused, and the Coast Guard cutter, handicapped by a jammed gun and a small crew, retreated to await further orders. A careful check in Washington revealed that the *I'm Alone* was on the smuggling blacklist and had recently cleared from Belize with a liquor cargo for Bermuda, placing the vessel 500 miles off course. Powell was instructed, if satisfied that the ship was within 12 miles from the shore when boarding was refused, to use "all your forces to seize her," and he dispatched the cutters *Dallas* and *Dexter* as reinforcements.[2] After a twenty-four-hour chase in rough seas, the *Dexter* neared the vessel on the morning of March 22 and opened fire. Within a few minutes, one smuggler was dead, and the *I'm Alone* became the first foreign rumrunner to be sunk by the Coast Guard.

Compared to the seizures of the *Henry L. Marshall* or the *Grace and Ruby*, which precipitated such rancorous disputes over international law, the importance of the *I'm Alone* sinking was exaggerated by the press and in subsequent accounts of the episode.[3] The attack on the ship provided one of the high points of prohibition drama, but the incident never seriously damaged diplomatic relations between the United States and Great Britain or Canada. The facts proved so ambiguous that guilt on either side could not be established, and responsibility for the case was eagerly shunted onto a panel of less visible arbitrators. A month after the sinking, Secretary of State Henry Stimson reported that "the I'm Alone case was in the process of being buried." It quickly faded into arbitration where it was quietly debated for the next six years.[4]

As a catalyst, however, the destruction of the *I'm Alone* was significant. For British officials, the incident confirmed their apprehensions over the increasingly important position occupied by Canada in the liquor issue. Although the liquor industry in Canada had been a major supplier of American bootleggers since 1920, Great Britain gladly assumed no responsibility for Canadian smuggling.[5] The Foreign Office considered Canadian-American liquor problems to be a separate question detached from Anglo-American concerns. Canada was a self-governing dominion, not a Crown colony like the Bahamas, and enjoyed greater autonomy as a member of the evolving British Commonwealth. Indeed, the Ottawa government had negotiated its own smuggling information treaty with the United States in 1925, and two years later the newly opened Canadian legation in Washington accepted the supervision of all seizure cases involving Canadian rumrunners.[6] At the time, Foreign Office officials welcomed this transfer and were delighted to "sit back and let Canada take on this burden."[7]

By 1929 the Foreign Office began to doubt the wisdom of this policy of noninvolvement. The success of the London accords in the Bahamas brought a dramatic escalation in the Canadian liquor trade, and the Ontario city of Windsor, located a short distance from the United States across the inadequately patrolled Detroit River, became the new smuggling capital. Significantly, Great Britain's liquor industry quickly shifted its operations from the declining market in the Caribbean to the lucrative opportunities in Canada. As traffic to the British West Indies decreased, British liquor exports to Canada increased from 124,546 gallons in the first quarter of 1926 to 560,444 gallons for the same period in 1928, making this Canadian problem, at least indirectly, a London concern.[8]

The attitude of the Ottawa government toward this expansion of smuggling was uncertain. Although prohibition sentiment in Canada was strong and several provinces adopted local dry laws, smuggling was entangled in the larger and more sensitive issue of national autonomy.[9] After attempting to avoid the issue, Canada's prime minister, William Mackenzie King, finally accepted an American proposal for a conference in Ottawa on antismuggling cooperation.[10] Following these discussions in January 1929, the Canadian participants presented the prime minister with a plan for the curtailment of all liquor clearances from Canada to the United States. King, hoping to exploit the issue of smuggling assistance in future tariff negotiations with the incoming Hoover administration, delayed his approval.[11]

This uncertainty presented the British government with a difficult dilemma. At the Imperial Conference of 1926, Canada and the other dominion governments were granted more control over their own affairs as part of the transition from empire to commonwealth. From the perspective of foreign policy, the intended purpose of the commonwealth was to relieve the London government of local responsibilities and to continue the mobilization of the empire's economic resources. Guided by expediency, Foreign Office officials hoped to preserve diplomatic unity and to use the commonwealth to sustain a strong bargaining position for Great Britain within the international arena.[12]

The smuggling issue, however, demonstrated that the dominions also might limit British foreign policy options. If King's Liberal government offered substantial antismuggling concessions, the United States would expect a similar gesture from Great Britain. Whatever King decided, British interests might be jeopardized and Foreign Office officials no longer could ignore the Canadian presence in Anglo-American liquor diplomacy.[13]

The *I'm Alone* incident, coming two months after the Ottawa Conference, provided British officials with additional evidence of the frustrations created by Canadian involvement in the liquor issue. Assistant Secretary of State William Castle sent Ambassador Howard a copy of the official Treasury Department report which maintained that the behavior of the *I'm Alone* captain and "hot pursuit," the doctrine allowing extraterritorial seizures if pursuit began within the respective area of authority, justified the Coast Guard's conduct.[14] Before Howard could respond, it was established that the *I'm Alone* was operated by Canadians, and the ambassador was obliged to transfer the case to the Canadian minister in Washington, Vincent Massey. Howard reminded Massey that the case involved imperial interests. But the British ambassador was now simply a consultant, unable to control the direction of diplomatic discussions, and Massey received his instructions from Ottawa, not London.[15]

The resolution of the *I'm Alone* dispute essentially rested on the answer to three questions: Was the boat within the limits of the liquor treaty? Did the hot-pursuit doctrine apply from a distance beyond territorial waters and within one hour? Was the Coast Guard's action justified? On this third point, British and Canadian officials were in agreement that the sinking of the rumrunner was deplorable and indefensible. The other two issues, raising ancillary questions, were less easily resolved. As additional facts emerged, it was apparent that there was a major discrepancy over the distance at which the ship was first hailed. The captain of the *I'm Alone* alleged that his vessel, capable of sailing twelve miles in one hour, was never closer than fifteen miles from the shore. Coast Guard accounts, with far more convincing evidence, placed the ship within treaty limits. Relying on the captain's report, the Canadian government was prepared to include this treaty violation in its formal protest.[16]

At the Foreign Office, where the smuggling convention was regarded as the cornerstone of the government's liquor policy, officials seriously questioned the Canadian decision. The uninterrupted operation of the sealed-liquor allowance on British ships starkly contrasted with the enforcement and legal problems that confronted the United States. The *I'm Alone* case, by demonstrating the difficulty of establishing the one-hour distance, focused attention on this imbalance and threatened the treaty. Cecil Hurst warned that if it were publicly acknowledged that only fifteen miles from the shore a ship was beyond treaty jurisdiction, American critics might challenge the usefulness of the agreement.[17]

Hurst also reminded his colleagues that the League of Nations was preparing to hold a conference on the codification of international law. A growing number of legal scholars acknowledged that a state was entitled to exert limited authority over foreign vessels hovering near territorial waters for illegal purposes. When the conference met, he warned, Great Britain might be compelled to accept a modified application of this principle, further weakening American reliance on the treaty. Consequently, Ambassador Howard was instructed to request that the Canadian protest omit any details of distance and accept that the *I'm Alone* was seized under the liquor convention.[18]

Prime Minister King, pressured by the hostile reaction of the Canadian press to the sinking, was determined to argue the case in strict legal terms, and he refused to consider the Foreign Office recommendation. On April 9, Massey sent the State Department a formal protest, claiming that the *I'm Alone* was never within treaty limits and that the hot-pursuit doctrine solely applied from within territorial waters. The Coast Guard had exercised unnecessary force, Massey contended, and consequently the "extreme course adopted constitutes just ground for such redress as is now possible."[19] The Canadian government did accept an American suggestion to exercise the procedures established under Article 4 of the liquor treaty, which provided for the consideration of seizure disagreements by a joint commission. If there was no settlement, the matter would be presented for formal arbitration. While arrangements were finalized for the establishment of the commission, Foreign Office officials found some consolation in the fact that this would limit public discussion of the dispute.[20]

The referral of the *I'm Alone* case did not lessen Foreign Office apprehensions that the incident might undermine the treaty's sealed-liquor provisions. To safeguard British shipping, officials were willing to adopt whatever drastic measures were necessary to strengthen the liquor agreement.[21] Secretary of State Stimson, responding to the Canadian protest, intimated that without the hot-pursuit doctrine the treaty was of little value to the United States. When the *I'm Alone* commissioners were selected in August, the Foreign Office requested William Clark, the British high commissioner in Canada, to inform Prime Minister King that Great Britain would accept hot pursuit under the treaty. Recognizing that the ratification of an amending convention was politically difficult, it was suggested that the *I'm Alone* commissioners sign a joint report declaring that the doctrine of hot pursuit was included in the treaty, and this would be followed by an exchange of diplomatic notes sanctioning this action.[22]

In attempting to minimize the impact of the *I'm Alone* case, Foreign Office officials incorrectly assumed that the liquor treaty was as sacrosanct in Ottawa as it was in London. Canada's immediate proximity to the United States reduced the value of the sealed-liquor concession, and the treaty provided few other benefits. Canadian officials resented an agreement that authorized the extended seizure of their vessels and concurrently placed Americans violating their statutes under the normal doctrines of international law. The treaty was a perfect target for Canadian frustration, reflecting both the inequity of relations with the United States and the sacrifice of Canadian concerns for British interests. King's Liberal government was not prepared to forfeit the possibility of successful arbitration to defend the treaty, and the British proposal was rejected.[23] In frustration, Foreign Office officials hoped the *I'm Alone* commissioners would be unable to settle the hot-pursuit question, providing a later opportunity to moderate the Canadian position.[24]

Contributing to Foreign Office concern over the future of the liquor treaty was the uncertainty of the American reaction to the *I'm Alone* incident. On March 4, 1929, Herbert Hoover became the thirty-first president of the United States. Elected on a Republican platform that opposed the repeal of the Eighteenth Amendment, the victory of the dry Hoover against the wet Alfred E. Smith was perceived by the beleaguered supporters of national prohibition as a vindication of their cause. At his inauguration, Hoover unequivocally declared that "I have been selected by you to execute and enforce the laws of the country. I propose to do so to the extent of my own abilities.... To those of criminal mind there can be no appeal but vigorous enforcement of the law."[25] The following week, he began planning a reorganization of prohibition enforcement that included transferring the Treasury's Prohibition Unit to the Justice Department, tightening control over liquor permits, and unifying the border patrol.[26] On May 29, Hoover established the National Law Observance and Enforcement Commission, chaired by former Attorney General George Wickersham, to investigate federal law enforcement. Considering this early display of determination and the enforcement problems highlighted by the *I'm Alone* seizure, Foreign Office officials feared that a reexamination of American benefits under the liquor treaty would be the next focus of the president's energetic attention.[27]

The destruction of the Canadian rumrunner, however, was an unwelcome embarrassment for Hoover, not a mandate for treaty modification. Only three weeks after his inauguration, the virulent reaction of the American press to the sinking rekindled the bitter arguments of the

1928 campaign and demonstrated the eroding support for national prohibition. The incident raised serious questions about enforcement abuses, and it was exploited by the opponents of the Eighteenth Amendment as the latest evidence of the law's failure.[28] The *I'm Alone* affair forced Hoover to instruct the Treasury Department to redirect its efforts toward the "large rings and conspiracies operating with illicit liquor," and he announced that the aggressive and violent tactics of earlier enforcement efforts would be stopped. In this atmosphere of domestic hostility, any reevaluation of the liquor treaty invited criticism. Political necessity dictated moderation.[29]

State Department officials shared this view. Although Department Solicitor Green Hackworth and his colleagues believed the *I'm Alone* was within treaty limits and accepted the validity of the hot-pursuit doctrine, they were skeptical about the legality of the sinking.[30] Secretary Stimson, also harboring no illusions about the probity of Coast Guard field officers, decided to propose arbitration to avoid a prolonged public debate on this questionable action. "I suspect that the mention of arbitration in our note will be unpleasant to officials of the Treasury Department," Assistant Secretary Castle advised Stimson; "I do not believe, however, that this should be allowed to influence our decision in the matter."[31] Under these circumstances, Stimson was not prepared to consider any diplomatic initiatives based on the tenuous claims in the *I'm Alone* case.

At the Treasury Department, the affair engendered a different reaction. Unable to end smuggling and without the careful guardianship of General Andrews, Coast Guard officials became careless in respecting the limits of the liquor treaty and increasingly resentful of any criticism of their failure to enforce the prohibition laws. When the *I'm Alone* sinking was condemned by the press, rather than applauded as exemplary vigilance, enforcement officers directed their frustration at both the British government and the liquor treaty. "For six years the 'limies' have played horse with us," Coast Guard Intelligence Officer C. D. Feak wrote: "They have given us the next to worthless liquor treaties and outwardly have made us believe that they were with us heart and soul in this matter but inwardly they have trampled the spirit in the mud...when someone in the Department of State talks to me of the wonderful cooperation of the British government I feel like laughing in their face."[32]

To deflect criticism of the Coast Guard's action, enforcement officials at the Treasury Department prepared a counterattack. Commander Charles Root of the Coast Guard's Intelligence Unit advocated the denunciation of the liquor treaty unless the United States were allowed to seize smugglers at any distance from the shore. Citing Great Britain's vulnerability, Root was confident that the London government would acquiesce to protect the sealed-liquor concession. The director of the Bureau of Foreign Control, Harry Anslinger, recommended abrogating the treaty if the British refused to accept a proviso requiring a guarantee for all liquor cargo clearing for the United States. In September 1929, Anslinger's draft amendment was circulated to the other departments.[33]

If the Treasury Department's proposal accurately focused on the apprehensions of the Foreign Office, it did not reflect the attitude within the State Department. The recent resignation of Assistant Attorney General Willebrandt deprived treaty critics of their leading advocate; and Secretary Stimson, with the strong support of President Hoover, returned control of liquor diplomacy to the State Department and prevented an escalation of the bureaucratic infighting that had subverted the treaty.[34] Stimson believed that the treaty and the London Conference agreements were inseparable documents that together provided the foundation for antismuggling enforcement. The relative ease and restraint in settling the *I'm Alone* dispute demonstrated the continued importance of the liquor treaty's framework for resolving disputes over international law.[35] Stimson also was convinced that smuggling from Canada posed the greatest threat to effective enforcement. The proposal for ending liquor clearances still awaited Prime Minister King's approval, and reports from Ottawa highlighted the emotional response of the Canadian press to the *I'm Alone* sinking. As Stimson noted in his diary, "the feeling of agitation is making it impossible to get any help in our law enforcement."[36]

In addition, the secretary of state was influenced by events in Great Britain. In May the Labour party won the general election, and Ramsay MacDonald returned as prime minister. A new round of disarmament discussions between the United States and Great Britain was scheduled to begin in 1930. Three years earlier, naval talks had ended in deadlock and rekindled Anglo-American tensions.[37] President Hoover, hoping to avoid a repetition of this failure and improve diplomatic relations, invited MacDonald to hold preliminary discussions in Washington. After MacDonald agreed to this first official visit to the United States by a British prime minister, the smuggling issue was added to the agenda. Stimson was unwilling to compromise the success of these talks or to jeopardize the possibility of Great Britain's support for reducing the illegal liquor trade from Canada. It was not an appropriate moment to offend either the Canadians or the British, and Stimson refused to discuss the Treasury Department's request.[38]

When MacDonald arrived in Washington on October 4, 1929, accompanied by his principal private secretary Robert Vansittart and the new American Department chief, Robert Craigie, Anglo-American liquor diplomacy presented a strange paradox. Privately acknowledging the imbalance of the liquor treaty, British officials were willing to accept modification to preserve the right of British shipping to carry sealed liquor in American waters. Secretary Stimson, unaware of the correspondence between the Foreign Office and the Canadian government, believed that the *I'm Alone* incident weakened the ability of the United States to propose treaty amendments. As a result, the future of the liquor treaty was never discussed.[39]

President Hoover, however, did broach the subject of smuggling cooperation when the discussions began at Camp Rapidan, the presidential fishing retreat in Maryland. He suggested that Great Britain outlaw all liquor clearances to the United States.[40] Prime Minister MacDonald, despite his strong desire to strengthen Anglo-American relations, was constrained by the lack of parliamentary support for additional enforcement assistance. Any new measure, he told Hoover, "might not only provoke undesirable controversy but might well fail to pass at all."[41] MacDonald offered to expand the London accords, but he was not prepared to accept Hoover's proposal to hold a second London Conference.

Hoover and Stimson, saving their most important request for last, were not deterred by the prime minister's reluctance. "The conversation then turned to the position as between Canada and the United States," MacDonald wrote. "It soon became clear that the President and Secretary of State set much greater store on steps being taken by Canada to prohibit the export of liquor to the United States than on similar steps being taken in this country."[42] The president emphasized that unrestricted liquor clearances along the Canadian border were thwarting his new law enforcement efforts. With the British representatives scheduled to visit Ottawa, Hoover suggested that MacDonald relay this concern to Prime Minister King. MacDonald readily agreed to deliver the president's message, and Vansittart promised to inform Stimson of the outcome of their Ottawa meeting.[43]

As the prime minister's entourage departed, MacDonald could regard the results of his trip to Washington with satisfaction. Although the Camp Rapidan talks produced few tangible agreements on outstanding issues, the meeting increased goodwill between the United States and Great Britain. State Department officials were impressed with MacDonald's sincerity, and Secretary Stimson believed the visit had silenced "even the most blatant jingoes and British haters."[44] The discussions on smuggling were particularly reassuring. Minor misunderstandings were resolved, President Hoover did not express any frustration with the liquor treaty, and Secretary Stimson privately declared his opposition to any U.S. proposal for treaty modification. Moreover, Hoover's emphasis on

Canadian smuggling reduced the pressure on the British government, and MacDonald was convinced that Canadian enforcement cooperation would not encourage a demand for additional British assistance.[45]

The Camp Rapidan meeting also was unsettling. Significantly, Canada emerged as an even greater factor in Anglo-American liquor diplomacy. Without substantive action by Prime Minister King, the cordiality created by MacDonald's visit might quickly disappear, and new tensions would threaten the treaty. Canadian sensitivity to British or American pressure remained acute. Based on experience, British officials did not share President Hoover's faith in their ability to influence events in Ottawa.[46]

Fortunately for MacDonald, the Canadian attitude toward smuggling cooperation had moderated as prohibition sentiment overshadowed the concerns of national pride. The Canadian press now endorsed the curtailment of liquor exports; furthermore, when MacDonald presented President Hoover's conciliatory message, Prime Minister King agreed to introduce legislation prohibiting liquor clearances to the United States.[47] MacDonald also used the opportunity of his visit to discuss the *I'm Alone* case, stressing the need to protect the liquor treaty. King offered to consider accepting the doctrine of hot pursuit if the arbitrators ruled against the United States. Influenced by MacDonald's arguments, the Canadian government did withdraw all objections to American distance claims and acknowledged that the *I'm Alone* was within treaty limits.[48]

Returning to London, British officials were confident that the liquor treaty was secure, and they worked with Ambassador Howard's successor in Washington, Ronald Lindsay, to strengthen existing enforcement cooperation.[49] But this confidence was short-lived. In January 1931 the Canadian rumrunner *Josephine K.* was seized by the Coast Guard following a prolonged battle. The Ottawa government maintained that the seizure, clearly within twelve miles, was beyond the one-hour limit of the treaty.[50] The incident once again demonstrated the enforcement barriers imposed by the treaty. On March 24 the London *Times* reported that the Hoover administration planned to amend the treaty and substitute a twelve-mile limit for the less precise one-hour limit. Publicly, the MacDonald government calmly reassured the House of Commons that treaty modification was not under consideration. Privately, Foreign Office officials acknowledged the seriousness of the rumor and concluded that the nagging problems created by the one-hour limit must be resolved.[51]

Although the adoption of a fixed-mileage distance for the treaty represented the most dramatic change in Great Britain's liquor policy since 1923, the reconsideration of the one-hour limit provoked little soul-searching at the Foreign Office. Developments in international law made the protection of the three-mile principle a different problem than it had been eight years earlier. At the League of Nations Codification Conference in 1930, the recognition of "contiguous zones" of jurisdiction beyond territorial waters, for enforcement or customs purposes, received considerable support. The British government was defining its official position on the question, and both Foreign Office and Admiralty officials were prepared to accept this concept. Recognizing the necessity of compromise, they concluded that the creation of special exceptions to the three-mile principle would check efforts to extend the limit of general territorial authority. The corollary of this argument was that the inclusion of a mileage limit in the liquor treaty, with its narrow objective and clear preamble, would now reinforce, rather than weaken, the three-mile rule.[52]

Foreign Office officials also were concerned about changes in Canadian policy which further restricted their influence in Ottawa and undermined the results of MacDonald's visit. In the 1930 Canadian general election, King's Liberal party was defeated by the more nationalistic Conservatives. The new prime minister, Richard Bennet, had campaigned on a platform of "Canada First," promising more independence and autonomy for his country. Echoing this theme, he criticized the liquor treaty and the problematic one-hour limit.[53] Craigie and his colleagues in the American Department believed that Bennet was planning to use the upcoming *I'm Alone* discussions to secure a U.S. endorsement for a fixed-mileage treaty. If confronted with a Canadian-American joint agreement, some form of treaty modification was inevitable.[54]

Alternatively, opposing these efforts to strengthen the treaty might jeopardize the sealed-liquor concession, and this was an unacceptable risk. The worldwide economic depression, which would topple the Labour government in August and force MacDonald to form an all-party National government, engulfed Great Britain's shipping industry and depressed the transatlantic passenger service. At the same time, Congress had passed new shipping legislation in 1928 that provided generous construction loans and liberal payments for the transportation of the mails by American vessels. The following year, the U.S. Shipping Board sold the United States Lines to private interests, and these transatlantic liners were now allowed to provide liquor outside the three-mile limit. With the Cunard Company committed to the construction of a new superliner, all of these developments enhanced the continued importance of the sealed-liquor privilege.[55]

On June 26 the interdepartmental committee reconvened, and Craigie presented a Foreign Office proposal for amending the liquor treaty to include a fixed-mileage limit. Craigie argued that recognizing seizure rights at a distance equal to or greater than twelve miles would end American reliance upon the tariff acts in seizure cases, and he was confident that the Hoover administration would request Congress to extend legal jurisdiction to this same limit.[56] Board of Trade officials, who opposed the concept of contiguous zones for customs purposes, proposed extended seizure rights based on shipping tonnage to avoid weakening the British position on territorial waters. When Craigie expressed doubts that the Canadians would accept this alternative, Board of Trade representatives, primarily concerned with protecting shipping, withdrew their proposal, and the committee adopted a new seizure limit of fourteen miles. The representatives also approved an exchange of notes with the State Department to allow hot pursuit from within treaty limits and to establish a special seizure arrangement for small boats. All of these recommendations, the representatives agreed, would be shared with the Ottawa government and no action taken unless Canada or the United States initiated discussions on treaty modification.[57]

Before the committee's report was sent to Canada, Board of Trade officials had second thoughts about this shift in liquor policy. Their support for a fixed-mileage distance was predicated on the fact that it was an emergency measure to protect the treaty's sealed-liquor provision. But a recent ruling by the U.S. District Court in Rhode Island, involving the Canadian rumrunner *Mazel Tov*, concluded that seizures were not legal outside treaty limits. This unexpected reversal of earlier court decisions, which sustained seizures under U.S. customs laws, weakened the arguments for a mileage substitute.[58] Without Foreign Office approval, Board of Trade officials consulted representatives of the Admiralty and Fisheries Department and redrafted the interdepartmental recommendations. The Board of Trade then proposed offering additional search rights based on shipping tonnage, if the United States requested treaty modification, and applying the one-hour distance to faster Coast Guard vessels. Craigie, worried that the Rhode Island court's resurrection of this issue would escalate American criticism of the liquor treaty, acknowledged the Board of Trade's suggestion as an acceptable substitute.[59]

Considering the attitude toward the liquor treaty within the prohibition agencies, U.S. enforcement officials would have welcomed the Board of Trade's proposal for an extended and verifiable seizure limit. They continued to regard the treaty's restrictions as the leading cause of antismuggling failures and the *Josephine K.* and *Mazel Tov* incidents strengthened support for treaty modification. Following the *Josephine K.* seizure, Assistant Treasury Secretary Seymour Lowman vented his frustration to Secretary of State Stimson, declaring that "if the action of the Coast Guard is to be disavowed in this instance then that service might as well abandon further efforts to exercise the rights conferred" under the treaty.[60] Justice Department officials were surprised and alarmed by the District Court's *Mazel Tov* ruling and the renewed claim of treaty precedence. Faced with the prospect of relying solely on the liquor agreement for seizure libels, they maintained that the smuggling convention in its present form would handicap their ability to prosecute rumrunners, and customs officials joined this chorus of treaty criticism.[61]

Secretary Stimson, however, refused to demand British assistance, and he ignored these complaints. He was convinced that the British government would not willingly alter the treaty. State Department officials also disputed the Justice Department's contention that the liquor agreement was not exclusive, and they supported an appeal of the *Mazel Tov* decision to resolve this issue. When the Circuit Court of Appeals sustained the Justice Department's argument, the State Department insisted that the case be presented to the Supreme Court for a definitive ruling. Until the Court acted, Secretary Stimson refused to discuss any aspect of treaty modification.[62]

Stimson was equally cognizant of the domestic realities that restrained liquor diplomacy. In January 1931 the National Law Observance and Enforcement Commission had published its final report on prohibition. Although the panel recommended stricter enforcement rather than amending the Volstead Act, a majority of commissioners individually advocated some form of revision. The ambivalence of the group's findings and President Hoover's attempt to gloss over these contradictions inflamed public criticism of prohibition.[63] Antiprohibition organizations, such as the Association Against the Prohibition Amendment, now mounted a full-scale campaign to repeal the Eighteenth Amendment. Personally, the secretary of state believed that "we have reached the point of correcting the mistake of constitutional prohibition" and a new enforcement initiative was impossible.[64] Ironically, at the moment when the British government was prepared to offer the treaty changes sought by enforcement officials, the Hoover administration was both unwilling and unable to press its unsuspected advantage.

As the 1932 presidential campaign began, the debate over the Eighteenth Amendment gained momentum. President Hoover, accepting his party's nomination in August, acknowledged problems with national prohibition and endorsed a return to state liquor control under federal protection.[65] The delegates to the Democratic convention in Chicago, by adopting a wet platform, forced their nominee, New York Governor Franklin Delano Roosevelt, to declare his support for the outright repeal of the Eighteenth Amendment.[66] Along with Roosevelt's resounding victory on November 8, prohibition was rejected in eleven state referenda, the size of the wet faction in Congress was increased, and the future of the Eighteenth Amendment was preordained.[67]

For Foreign Office officials, these events added a new dimension to the question of modifying the liquor treaty. The British treaty amendments were never forwarded to Ottawa, and the delay proved advantageous when the repudiation of national prohibition in the United States persuaded Prime Minister Bennet not to press for any changes in the liquor treaty.[68] Canadian criticism of the treaty was further circumscribed when the Supreme Court ruled on the *Mazel Tov* appeal on January 23, 1933. The Court maintained that the treaty superseded the tariff acts and provided the exclusive basis for liquor smuggling seizures.[69] The following month, Congress approved a resolution repealing the Eighteenth Amendment and sent the constitutional revision to the states for ratification. With relief, the Foreign Office closed the discussions on treaty modification.[70]

British officials quickly discovered that the repeal of the Eighteenth Amendment did not end the Anglo-American liquor problem; it only altered its characteristics. The most obvious change was that the restrictions on sealed-liquor cargoes would be removed, along with the major justification for British smuggling cooperation. The diminished value of the liquor agreement was not lost on eager Board of Trade officials and, in September 1933, as the repeal amendment was considered by the state legislatures, they proposed the termination of the smuggling convention. Foreign Office officials were reluctant to consider any unilateral abandonment of the treaty if liquor smuggling persisted. After repeal, rumrunning would be a customs problem, and without the treaty the Coast Guard could rely upon the tariff laws and transform extraterritorial seizures into a generally asserted right.[71] To protect principles of international law, they concluded that Great Britain must remain an active participant in the liquor issue. The interdepartmental committee, while withdrawing its support for the hot-pursuit doctrine, endorsed the continuation of the treaty. These recommendations were sent to the Canadian government.[72]

In Washington, the official repeal of the Eighteenth Amendment in December 1933 did not bring any immediate changes in U.S. liquor diplomacy. Department Solicitor Hackworth assured Ambassador Lindsay that the treaty remained in force and no alterations in the agreement were under consideration.[73] Surprisingly, Treasury Department officials agreed. They feared that Coast Guard appropriations would decrease in the postprohibition period, and the treaty's extended seizure rights were a potentially important weapon in the difficult task of enforcing customs regulations for liquor.[74] But throughout the spring of 1934, liquor smuggling actually declined, and the British government was informed that information sharing was no longer necessary. Satisfied that the treaty was secure, Foreign Office officials welcomed the Roosevelt administration's decision to dismantle the burdensome London Conference agreements.[75]

By August this temporary lull ended, and smuggling now presented an embarrassing problem for the Roosevelt administration. The president himself encouraged this development by ignoring a recommendation that a minimal tax on liquor would discourage illegal activities. Searching for new sources of revenue, Roosevelt imposed a hefty federal tax on distilled spirits. The result was that illegal liquor remained a competitive commodity in the United States, and rumrunners, always sensitive to consumer demand, established operations in Newfoundland and the Caribbean.[76]

Treasury Secretary Henry Morgenthau, remarkably uninformed about earlier cooperation, was outraged, and he recommended barring liquor imports from Great Britain and Canada unless the two countries offered smuggling assistance. State Department officials were reluctant to press for further enforcement assistance based on arbitrary trade restrictions, and Morgenthau withdrew his plan.[77] With President Roosevelt's support, Morgenthau continued to demand additional anti-smuggling cooperation, and Secretary of State Cordell Hull proposed that the British government prosecute shipowners making false clearance declarations and deny British registry to suspected rumrunners. He also requested that Great Britain secure the extension of these restrictions to Newfoundland.[78]

Unwilling to return to a position of defending rumrunners, Foreign Office officials reassembled the interdepartmental committee in October.[79] Committee members, without the incentive of protecting the sealed-liquor concession, had little enthusiasm for expanding cooperation beyond the London Conference agreements. Unconvinced that smuggling was still a serious problem, they agreed to consider assistance only after an investigation of the smuggling trade in the Bahamas. Craigie, aware of President Roosevelt's growing impatience, pressed for the completion of the Bahaman inquiry and urged the Newfoundland government to curtail smuggling.[80] On February 23, 1935, Ambassador Lindsay informed the State Department that the Newfoundland government would enact stricter regulations and that Great Britain would expand clearance regulations in the British West Indies as well as reinstitute the suspended reports on liquor cargo. Although this did not include new enforcement concessions or any restrictions on shipping registry, Secretary Morgenthau expressed his satisfaction.[81]

Morgenthau's proposal was the last American request for additional British smuggling assistance. The *I'm Alone* dispute was settled in early 1935 after the commissioners, without addressing any treaty-related issues, ruled that the sinking was illegal and awarded compensation to the crew and the Canadian government.[82] In September, the Roosevelt administration implemented antismuggling legislation that extended the tariff laws to the one-hour limit and created a fifty-mile enforcement zone for nontreaty ships. The following year Canadian officials approved legislation enlarging customs jurisdiction and strengthening enforcement powers against Canadian vessels hovering beyond this limit. Together, these measures reduced the volume of illegal liquor imports to the United States. With the smuggling convention in force, disagreements over international law did not reappear.[83]

There was, however, a small band of rumrunners who persisted in violating U.S. revenue laws, and the Roosevelt administration was obligated to maintain its vigilance. Clearance, registry, and cargo information from Great Britain remained an important element in American smuggling enforcement. The Coast Guard Bahaman visitation agreement was renewed annually, and the blacklist of suspected lawbreakers was periodically updated. All of these cooperative arrangements continued until the beginning of World War II, when the hazards of travel in wartime finally ended the smuggling trade.[84]

The continuation of smuggling assistance following the repeal of the Eighteenth Amendment was not surprising. The final years of prohibition demonstrated the enduring nature of the liquor issue. The decision of successive London governments to safeguard the ability of British shipping to carry sealed liquor in U.S. waters closely linked Great Britain to American smuggling enforcement. Recognizing that this privilege was secure only if the liquor treaty was an effective barrier against rumrunners, Foreign Office officials were prepared to bolster the comparative weakness of U.S. treaty provisions and to protect the treaty from the perceived threat of the Canadian government's indifference. Although they achieved their objective, American expectations and the preservation of principles of international law precluded any quiet withdrawal from the burdens of the Anglo-American liquor problem when prohibition ended.

These burdens were eased by the lasting success of the London Conference agreements. The 1926 accords reduced the basic inequities of the liquor treaty and safeguarded the sealed-liquor concession, guaranteeing that the treaty remained the foundation of British and American liquor diplomacy. By resolving the difficult legal and diplomatic questions of the post-treaty period, the London Conference encouraged the harmony that minimized repercussions of Canadian intransigence and the unexpected problems after repeal. It was the salutary effect of the London Conference and its restoration of trust, rehabilitation of the smuggling treaty, and legacy of close cooperation that provided the final resolution of the Anglo-American liquor problem.

Notes

[1]State Department, "Cooperation in the Prevention of Liquor Smuggling," February 6, 1933, "Western European Affairs" folder, Box 51, "Presidential Papers-Cabinet Offices (PPCO), Hoover Papers; State Department, "Divisional Reports—Great Britain," February 25, 1933, Frame 671, Roll 166, (671/176), Microfilm edition, Papers of Henry L. Stimson, Sterling Memorial Library, Yale University, New Haven, Connecticut (hereafter cited as Stimson Papers). For examples of the continuation of the London agreements see State Department to Consular Officers, March 9, 1929, 811.114/4752, RG 59, NA; Coast Guard to British Consul, New York, "State Department—1930, 1931, 1932" folders, Box 58, RG 26, NA; Charles Dawes to State Department, April 4, 1930, 811.114/Great Britain/298, RG 59, NA; "Black List of Suspected Smugglers," February 1931, copy in 811.114/Great Britain/327, RG 59, NA; Ronald Lindsay to State Department, March 14, 1932, 811.114/Great Britain/353, RG 59, NA; Colonial Office to Foreign Office, September 26, 1932, A6413/130/45, PRO; American Consulate General, London, to State Department, March 1, 1933, 811.114/Great Britain/384, RG 59, NA; British Customs to State Department, December 31, 1933, 811.114/Great Britain/404, RG 59, NA.

[2]USCG *Wolcott,* "Log," March 20, 1929, File 10, Box 76, RG 26, NA; Coast Guard to A. W. Powell, March 21, 1929, File "A," Box 73, RG 26, NA; Powell to Captains of the *Wolcott, Dallas* and *Dexter,* March 21, 1929, File "B," ibid.; Frederick Billard to Seymour Lowman, March 25, 1929, File "A," ibid.

[3]Sinclair, *Era of Excess,* 218; Carse, *Rum Row,* 157–58; Jones, *Eighteenth Amendment and Our Foreign Relations,* 80–81; *Literary Digest* 101 (April 13, 1929): 16; *New York Times,* March 31, April 2, 8, 12, and 29, 1929; *Washington Post,* March 29, 1929; *New Republic* 58 (April 3, 1929): 183. For a different perspective of the controversy see Paul M. Holsinger, "The *I'm Alone* Controversy: A Study in Inter-American Diplomacy, 1929–1935," *Mid America* 50 (1968): 305–13.

[4]Henry Stimson, Memorandum on Conversation with Esme Howard, April 25, 1929, 592/162, Stimson Papers; William Vallance, Memorandum, December 12, 1934, 811.114/*I'm Alone*/4170, RG 59, NA.

[5]Sean D. Cashman, *Prohibition: The Lie of the Land* (New York, 1981), 30–33; Asbury, *Great Illusion,* 259–62; Sinclair, *Era of Excess,* 197–98; Peter C. Newman, *Bronfman Dynasty: Rothschilds of the New World* (Toronto, 1978), 103–22; Joseph L. Green, Memorandum, February 20, 1936, 23/37/37, RG 60, NAS.

[6]R. F. Holland, *Britain and the Commonwealth Alliance* (London, 1981), 6–8; Norman Hillmer, "The Foreign Office, the Dominions, and the Diplomatic Unity of the Empire, 1925–1929," in David Dilks, ed., *Retreat from Power: Studies in Britain's Foreign Policy of the Twentieth Century, 1906–1939* (London, 1981), 68–70, 77; Charles Evans Hughes to Auckland Geddes, March 7, 1923, 811.114/1223, RG 59, NA; British Embassy to State Department, June 19, 1923, 811.114/1595, RG 59, NA; O. D. Skelton to Mrs. Gordon Wright,

September 25, 1925, Department of External Affairs, Office of the Under-Secretary of External Affairs, Record Group 25, D1, Microfilm T-1810, Roll 48, File 582, Frame 58 (582/58), Public Archives Canada, Ottawa, Canada (hereafter cited as CAN); Richard N. Kottman, "Volstead Violated: Prohibition as a Factor in Canadian-American Relations," *Canadian Historical Review* 43 (June 1962): 106–13; Jones, *Eighteenth Amendment and Our Foreign Relations,* 60–68.

⁷Esme Howard to Foreign Office, March 4, 1927, A1565/82/45, PRO; Geoffrey Thompson, Minutes, January 20, 1929, A154/25/45, PRO; Vincent Massey, *What's Past Is Prologue* (New York, 1964), 127–28; Martin B. Cohen, "The First Legation: Canadian Diplomacy and the Opening of Relations with the United States" (Ph.D. diss., George Washington University, 1975); Robert Craigie, Minutes, December 1, 1929, A8869/25/45, PRO.

⁸Alfred Nutting to State Department, April 21, 1928, 811.114/Great Britain/222, RG 59, NA; Lowman to Andrew Mellon, September 3, 1929, copy in "June–September 1929" folder, Box 54E, PPCO, Hoover Papers; Department of Trade and Commerce, Dominion Bureau of Statistics, Canada, *The Liquor Traffic in Canada* (Ottawa, 1929), 6; Larry L. Engleman, *Intemperance: The Lost War against Liquor* (New York, 1979), 95–118.

⁹Canadian Undersecretary of External Affairs O. D. Skelton maintained that public opinion in Canada opposed further concessions to the United States. O. D. Skelton to C. B. Sissons, January 17, 1929, Microfilm T-1758, Roll 14, 150/1, CAN; Skelton to A. E. Darby, June 11, 1929, ibid., 150/7, CAN; Department of External Affairs, "United States Prohibition Enforcement," December 1928, ibid., 149/384, CAN; George P. Glazebrook, *A History of Canadian External Relations* (Toronto, 1950), 333–47, 379–95; H. Blair Neatby, *William Lyon Mackenzie King,* 3 vols. (Toronto, 1963), 2:180–91.

¹⁰Mabel Walker Willebrandt, "How Dry Is Wet Canada," *New York Herald Tribune,* September 16, 1928. Canadian and American officials held informal talks on customs problems in 1927, but Prime Minister King refused to discuss liquor smuggling pending a report by Canadian customs authorities. Skelton to Governor General's Secretary, February 14, 1927, Microfilm T-1758, Roll 14, 151/41, CAN; State Department, Memorandum on Meeting with Canadian Officials, August 30, 1927, 811.114/Canada/4414, RG 59, NA; William Phillips to Mackenzie King, November 27, 1928, Microfilm T-1758, Roll 14, 151/42, CAN; Kottman, "Volstead Violated," 113–14.

¹¹Skelton to Vincent Massey, January 12, 1929, copy in A1247/25/45, PRO; Department of External Affairs, Memorandum on the Ottawa Conference on Smuggling, January 22, 1929, Microfilm T-1758, Roll 14, 149/413, CAN; "Brief Record of Proceedings of Anti-Smuggling Conference Held at Ottawa, January 8–10, 1929, between Representatives of the United States and of Canada," ibid., 151/86, CAN; Report on Proceedings of Ottawa Conference by Canadian Representatives, February 7, 1929, ibid., 151/51, CAN; Memorandum for the Prime Minister, March 2, 1929, ibid., 149/423, CAN; Neatby, *Mackenzie King* 2:272–73, 282–88; Kottman, "Volstead Violated," 118–19.

¹²Holland, *Britain and the Commonwealth Alliance,* 8, 53–86, 208; Hillmer, "The Foreign Office, the Dominions, and the Diplomatic Unity of the Empire," 64–73.

[13]Foreign Office, Minutes, January 9, 1929, A76/25/45, PRO; Leo Amery to Foreign Office, January 3, 1929, ibid. British officials were embarrassed when the conference delegates discovered that there was no specific statute forbidding liquor exports from Great Britain to the United States. Although in practice liquor did not clear directly for the United States, British officials had long obscured from the State Department the absence of any legal restrictions. Frank Kellogg to American Consul General, London, December 20, 1928, 711.419/295a, Roll 15, M581, RG 59, NA; Albert Halstead to State Department, December 22, 1928, 711.419/297, ibid.

[14]Howard to Foreign Office, March 23, 1929, A2118/25/45, PRO; Billard to Lowman, March 25, 1929, File "A", Box 73, RG 26, NA; Howard to Foreign Office, March 26, 1929, A2202/25/45, PRO; Austin Chamberlain to Howard, March 28, 1929, A2215/25/45, PRO.

[15]Howard to Foreign Office, March 25, 1929, A2118/25/45, and April 4, 1929, A2642/25/45, PRO; Massey, *What's Past Is Prologue,* 128; Chamberlain, Minutes, March 25, 1929, A2118/25/45, PRO; Foreign Office, Memorandum, April 17, 1929, A2697/25/45, PRO.

[16]Henry Tom to Howard, March 27, 1929, A2480/25/45, PRO; Howard to Foreign Office, March 31, 1929, A2265/25/45, and April 12, 1929, A2791/25/45, PRO; Captain Gamble to Billard, March 28, 1929, File "A," Box 73, RG 26, NA. In addition to the Coast Guard's superior instrumentation, the distance was verified by the sighting of a cargo ship in the same vicinity. Coast Guard officials also claimed that the *I'm Alone*'s captain was intoxicated. Howard to Foreign Office, March 31, 1929, A2265/25/45, PRO.

[17]Foreign Office, Minutes, March 31, 1929, A2265/25/45, PRO; Howard to Chamberlain, March 29, 1929, A2478/25/45, PRO; Cecil Hurst, Minutes, April 15, 1929, A2700/25/45, PRO.

[18]Hurst, Minutes, March 31, 1929, A2265/25/45, PRO; Foreign Office to Howard, April 5, 1929, ibid.

[19]Massey to Stimson, April 9, 1929, 811.114/*I'm Alone*/76, RG 59, NA; Howard to Foreign Office, April 9, 1929, A2516/25/45, and April 12, 1929, A2791/25/45, PRO. Ignoring Foreign Office objections, Ambassador Howard endorsed the Canadian protest. Howard to Stimson, April 11, 1929, 811.114/*I'm Alone*/87, RG 59, NA; Craigie to H. F. Batterbee, April 11, 1929, A2514/25/45, PRO.

[20]Chamberlain, Minutes, April 10, 1929, A2514/25/45, PRO; Foreign Office to Dominion Office, April 11, 1929, ibid.; William Castle, Memorandum, April 11, 1929, 811.114/*I'm Alone*/107, RG 59, NA; Howard to Foreign Office, April 11, 1929, A2564/25/45, PRO; Stimson to Massey, April 17, 1929, 811.114/*I'm Alone*/111, and Massey to Stimson, April 24, 1929, 811.114/*I'm Alone*/119, RG 59, NA; Howard to Foreign Office, April 28, 1929, A2946/25/45, PRO; Dominion Office to Foreign Office, May 14, 1929, A3282/25/45, PRO; Foreign Office, Minutes, April 11, 1929, A2564/25/45, and May 13, 1929, A3219/25/45, PRO.

[21]Howard to Foreign Office, April 9, 1929, A2516/25/45, PRO; Geoffrey Thompson, Minutes, April 9, 1929, ibid.; Foreign Office, Minutes, May 8, 1929, A3052/25/45, PRO; Foreign Office, "Draft of a Letter to High Commissioner of Canada," August 1929, A3219/25/45, PRO.

[22]Canadian Legation to State Department, August 7, 1929, 811.114/*I'm Alone*/234, RG 59, NA; Howard to Foreign Office, August 8, 1929, A5238/25/45, PRO; Dominion Office to William Clark, August 15, 1929, copy in A3219/25/45, PRO.

[23]William Beckett, Minutes, September 10, 1929, A6046/25/45, PRO; Memorandum for the Prime Minister on the Sinking of the Canadian Schooner 'I'm Alone,'" Microfilm T-1813, Roll 51, 625/306, CAN. Canadian officials were willing to consider this after the *I'm Alone* dispute was resolved and if Canada were granted reciprocal seizure rights. British High Commissioner, Ottawa, to Dominion Office, August 29, 1929, copy in A5876/25/45, PRO; Dominion Office to Foreign Office, September 10, 1929, A6046/25/45, PRO. See also Canadian Legation to State Department, August 26, 1929, 811.114/*I'm Alone*/280, RG 59, NA; William Malkin, Memorandum, October 28, 1929, A7233/25/45, PRO.

[24]Foreign Office, Minutes, September 10, 1929, A6046/25/45, PRO; Foreign Office to Dominion Office, September 27, 1929, ibid.

[25]William Starr Meyers, ed., *The State Papers and Other Public Writings of Herbert Hoover*, 2 vols. (New York, 1934), 1:4–6; David Burner, *Herbert Hoover: A Public Life* (New York, 1979), 190–211; Hoover, *Memoirs* 2: 197–209; Brown, *Mabel Walker Willebrandt*, 154–73; Kyvig, *Repealing National Prohibition*, 98–103; Vaughn D. Bornet and Edgar E. Robinson, *Herbert Hoover: President of the United States* (Stanford, 1975), 82–96; Hoff-Wilson, *Hoover*, 128–29.

[26]Justice Department to Herbert Hoover, March 9, 1929, "1929 March–May" folder, box 54E, PPCO, Hoover Papers; Lawrence Richey to Willebrandt, March 23, 1929, "Prohibition Enforcement—March–July 1929" folder, Box 237, "Presidential Papers Subject File," (PPSF), Hoover Papers; Willebrandt to Hoover, March 28, 1929, "1929 March–May" folder, Box 54E, PPCO, Hoover Papers; Hoover to Attorney General, May 31, 1929, Box 228, PPSF, Hoover Papers; Hoover, *Memoirs* 2:283; Martin L. Fausold, *The Presidency of Herbert Hoover* (Lawrence, KS, 1985), 34–35, 61–62. Congress did not approve these proposals until 1930. Bornet and Robinson, *Herbert Hoover*, 87, 91; Kerr, *Organized for Prohibition*, 267–69.

[27]Hoover, *Memoirs* 2:277; Ernst Cherrington to Hoover, October 19, 1929, Box 229, PPSF, Hoover Papers; Meyers, *Papers of Herbert Hoover* 1:63–64; Bornet and Robinson, *Herbert Hoover*, 87; Fausold, *Presidency of Herbert Hoover*, 61–62, 125–29.

[28]*Literary Digest* 101 (April 6, 1929): 5; *The Outlook and Independent* 151 (April 10, 1929): 582; *New York Times*, March 31, April 2, 1929; *Washington Post*, March 24, 25, 1929; *New Republic* 58 (April 10, 1929): 213; Howard to Foreign Office, March 29, 1929, A2478/25/45, PRO; Kyvig, *Repealing National Prohibition*, 107, 116–17.

[29]Hoover to Mellon, April 8, 1929, "1929 March–May" folder, Box 54E, PPCO, Hoover Papers; Burner, *Hoover*, 219.

[30]Vallance, Memorandum, March 25, 1929, 811.114/*I'm Alone*/98, RG 59, NA; Green Hackworth to William Castle, March 29, 1929, 811.114/*I'm Alone*/99, RG 59, NA; Mellon to Stimson, March 25, 1929, 811.114/*I'm*

Alone/53, RG 59, NA; William Mitchell to Stimson, April 4, 1929, 811.114/*I'm Alone*/68, RG 59, NA; Coast Guard, Press Statement, File "A," Box 73, RG 26, NA. The absence of reliable evidence forced the Justice Department to abandon criminal proceedings against the *I'm Alone*'s captain. This further weakened the State Department belief in the ultimate validity of the American defense. Arthur Henderson to Willebrandt, April 1, 1929, 23/101/16, RG 60, NAS; Mitchell to Stimson, April 10, 1929, 811.114/*I'm Alone*/86, RG 59, NA; Vallance, Memorandum, April 9, 1929, 811.114/*I'm Alone*/81, RG 59, NA; Mellon to Stimson, April 27, 1929, Box 236, RG 26, NA.

[31]Castle to Stimson, April 13, 1929, 811.114/*I'm Alone*/109, RG 59, NA. Castle discussed this with Massey on April 11. William Castle, Memorandum, April 11, 1929, 811.114/*I'm Alone*/107, RG 59, NA; Massey to Stimson, April 24, 1929, 811.114/*I'm Alone*/119, RG 59, NA.

[32]C. D. Feak, Memorandum, March 27, 1929, File "A," Box 73, RG 26, NA. See Coast Guard, Memorandum, April 11, 1929, ibid.

[33]Charles Root to Harry Anslinger, September 23, 1929, "Treaties" file, Box II-B, RG 58, NA; Treasury Department, Draft Treaty, September 1929, ibid.; John Doran to Ogden Mills, November 6, 1929, Box 113, RG 56, NA.

[34]Willebrandt to Hoover, May 26, 1929, "May 1929" folder, Box 21, PPCO, Hoover Papers; Brown, *Mabel Walker Willebrandt,* 177–78; Fausold, *Presidency of Herbert Hoover,* 169–72.

[35]Stimson, Memorandum on Conversation with Esme Howard, April 25, 1929, 592/162, Stimson Papers; Stimson, Memorandum, June 20, 1929, 625/162, Stimson Papers; Craigie to C. W. Dixon, November 13, 1929, A7233/25/45, PRO; Root to Francis de Wolf, August 30, 1929, 811.114/4782, RG 59, NA. See also Stimson, Diary, September 30, 1930, Frame 378, Roll 2, (378/2), Diaries of Henry L. Stimson, Microfilm edition, Sterling Memorial Library, Yale University, New Haven, Connecticut (hereafter cited as Stimson Diaries).

[36]Willebrandt to Hoover, March 9, 1929, "Prohibition Enforcement" folder, Box 237, PPSF, Hoover Papers; Kellogg to Hoover, March 22, 1929, ibid.; John Hickerson, Memorandum for Incoming Secretary of State, April 8, 1929, 145/160, Stimson Papers; Lowman to Mellon, September 3, 1929, copy in "1929 June–September" folder, Box 54E, PPCO, Hoover Papers. This was further complicated by the fact that Hoover, fulfilling a campaign pledge, raised tariffs and eliminated the best incentive for Canadian antismuggling cooperation. Henry Stimson, Diary, June 22, 1929, 255/2, Stimson Diaries; Meyers, *Papers of Herbert Hoover* 1:31–37; Neatby, *Mackenzie King* 2:272–73, 282–83, 286; Phillips to State Department, March 11, 1929, 811.114/*I'm Alone*/94, RG 59, NA; Phillips to Stimson, March 29, 1929, 65/78, Stimson Papers.

[37]Mowat, *Britain between the Wars,* 351–53; James, *British Revolution* 2:215–17, 227–31; Hogan, *Informal Entente,* 218–20; J. C. McKercher, *The Second Baldwin Government and the United States, 1924–1929: Attitudes and Diplomacy* (Cambridge, England, 1984), 55–103, 169–70.

[38]Burner, *Hoover,* 290–91; Price Bell to Hoover, June 4, 1929, 033/4111/MacDonald/½, RG 59, NA; Stimson, Memorandum, September 10,

1929, 033/4111/MacDonald/40½, RG 59, NA; American Legation, Ottawa, to State Department, August 16, 1929, 811.114/Canada/4230, RG 59, NA.

[39]The press reported that the two leaders would discuss the *I'm Alone* sinking, but this was excluded from the agenda. *New York Times,* September 26, 1929; Clark to Dominion Office, November 5, 1929, copy in A8045/25/45, PRO.

[40]Stimson first suggested this to Craigie on the journey to Camp Rapidan. Stimson, Memorandum of Trip to Rapidan, October 7, 1929, 033/4111/MacDonald/95½, RG 59, NA; Robert Vansittart, *The Mist Procession* (London, 1958), 386, 390–91; Ramsay MacDonald, "Confidential Memorandum on Discussions in Washington," November 12, 1929, A7633/3895/45, PRO.

[41]Ibid. See also Leffler, *Elusive Quest,* 220–21; McKercher, *Second Baldwin Government,* 195–96; Fausold, *Presidency of Herbert Hoover,* 172–73.

[42]MacDonald, "Confidential Memorandum," November 12, 1929, A7633/3895/45, PRO.

[43]Preparing his memorandum to Prime Minister King, Hoover received an unconfirmed report that a Canadian decision was imminent. James J. Britt to Walter Newton, October 9, 1929, "Prohibition Enforcement—August–December 1929" folder, Box 237, PPSF, Hoover Papers; Hoover to MacDonald, October 9, 1929, "Disarmament—October 1929" folder, Box 998, "Presidential Papers-Foreign Affairs" (PPFA), Hoover Papers; Hoover to Stimson, October 10, 1929, 033/4111/MacDonald/105½, RG 59, NA.

[44]Stimson to Candace [Stimson], November 1, 1929, 176/79, Stimson Papers; Castle to Robert Hadfield, October 28, 1929, Folder 35, Box 4, Castle Papers; *Literary Digest* 103 (October 19, 1929): 5. For a summary of the other aspects of the discussions see Ellis, *Republican Foreign Policy,* 161–62; Burner, *Hoover,* 290–91; Hoover, *Memoirs* 2:342–48; McGeorge Bundy and Henry L. Stimson, *On Active Service in Peace and War* (New York, 1947), 166.

[45]Craigie delayed his departure to discuss a lingering dispute between the American Consul in Nassau, C. C. Broy, and Bahaman Governor Orr. Broy claimed there was a lack of cooperation, but State Department officials were not sympathetic. Kellogg to British Embassy, January 17, 1929, 811.114/B.W.I./925, RG 59, NA; Broy to State Department, January 25, 1929, 811.114/B.W.I./926½, RG 59, NA; Howard to Stimson, May 30, 1929, 811.114/B.W.I./952, RG 59, NA; Clara Borjes, Memorandum on Meeting with C. C. Broy, July 23, 1929, 811.114/B.W.I./963½, RG 59, NA; Broy, Memorandum, August 19, 1929, 811.114/B.W.I./977, RG 59, NA. Craigie's meeting with John Hickerson of the State Department was cordial, and they agreed that all minor disputes of this kind should be resolved informally by Broy and Governor Orr. Hickerson, "Memorandum of Conversation with Mr. Craigie," October 11, 1929, 811.114/B.W.I./982, RG 59, NA; Hickerson to American Consulate, Nassau, December 17, 1930, 811.114/B.W.I./998, RG 59, NA; Craigie to Dixon, November 13, 1929, A7233/25/45, PRO.

[46]MacDonald, "Confidential Memorandum," November 12, 1929, A7633/3895/45, PRO.

[47]R. H. Hadow to Dominion Office, July 31, 1929, copy in A7789/25/45, PRO; Clark to Dominion Office, August 15, 1929, copy in ibid.; Neatby,

Mackenzie King 2:288; Kottman, "Volstead Violated," 119–22; Hoover to MacDonald, October 9, 1929, "Disarmament—October 1929" folder, Box 998, PPFA, Hoover Papers; MacDonald, "Confidential Memorandum on Discussions in Canada," November 12, 1929, A7634/3895/45, PRO. King presented the proposal in February 1930; after a bitter debate, the Canadian Parliament approved the restrictions. Robert Vansittart to Stimson, October 19, 1929, 033/4111/MacDonald/105½, RG 59, NA; Skelton to King, March 11, 1930, Microfilm T-1758, Roll 14, 149/443, CAN; Massey to Skelton, April 7, 1930, ibid., 149/462, CAN. Although the *New York Times* reported that the United States would press for treaty modification unless Canada restricted exports, Secretary Stimson was already aware of King's decision. *New York Times,* January 29, 1930; British Embassy to Foreign Office, January 31, 1930, A894/10/45, PRO; Dominion Office to Foreign Office, January 30, 1930, A885/10/45, PRO; Howard to Foreign Office, February 1, 1930, A894/10/45, and February 3, 1930, A930/10/45, PRO; Leslie Frost to State Department, February 18, 1930, 811.114/Canada/4291, RG 59, NA; American Legation, Ottawa, to State Department, March 5, 1930, 811.114/Canada/4299, and March 18, 1930, 811.114/Canada/4307, RG 59, NA; Neatby, *Mackenzie King* 2:313–15; Irving Linnel to State Department, October 8, 1930, 811.114/Canada/4357, RG 59, NA; Engleman, *Intemperance,* 120–21.

[48]MacDonald, "Confidential Memorandum on Discussions in Canada," November 12, 1929, A7634/3895/45, PRO; Clark to Dominion Office, November 5, 1929, A8095/25/45, PRO; Hadow to Dominion Office, April 3, 1930, copy in A2792/10/45, and June 17, 1930, A4744/10/45, PRO.

[49]Foreign Office, Minutes, March 4, 1930, A1726/10/45, PRO; Foreign Office to Customs, April 3, 1930, A1944/10/45, PRO; Foreign Office, Memorandum, April 24, 1930, A2662/10/45, PRO; Foreign Office to American Embassy, London, May 7, 1930, A3086/10/45, PRO; Colonial Office to Foreign Office, June 21, 1930, A4355/10/45, PRO; Lindsay to Foreign Office, July 23, 1930, A5393/10/45, PRO; Colonial Office to Foreign Office, March 6, 1931, A1570/32/45, PRO; Castle to Justice Department, January 17, 1931, 811.114/*Mazel Tov*/63, RG 59, NA; British Embassy to State Department, February 6, 1931, 811.114/Great Britain/319, RG 59, NA; Castle to Justice Department, February 21, 1931, 23/101/53, RG 60, NAS; Lindsay to Foreign Office, June 5, 1931, A3703/32/45, PRO.

[50]Although the Canadian government protested the seizure, the case was settled through the normal legal channels. Coast Guard, Report on Seizure of the *Josephine K.,* January 26, 1931, copy in 23/101/62, RG 60, NAS; Frank Lee to State Department, January 27, 1931, 811.114/*Josephine K.*/122, RG 59, NA; Treasury Department to State Department, January 31, 1931, 811.114/*Josephine K.*/124, RG 59, NA; Lindsay to Foreign Office, February 2, 1931, A750/32/45, PRO; Canadian Legation to State Department, March 16, 1931, 811.114/*Josephine K.*/167, RG 59, NA; Mitchell to Stimson, June 9, 1931, 811.114/*Josephine K.*/185, RG 59, NA; Canadian Legation to State Department, August 25, 1931, 811.114/*Josephine K.*/243, and State Department to Canadian Legation, October 25, 1931, 811.114/*Josephine K.*/257, RG 59, NA.

⁵¹*Times* (London), March 24, 1931. The story was actually based on a report which first appeared in the *Baltimore Sun. New York Times,* March 24, 1931; *Baltimore Sun,* March 23, 1931; Foreign Office, Minutes, May 21, 1931, A3206/32/45, PRO.

⁵²Interdepartmental Committee on Territorial Waters, Minutes, November 30, 1930, T2802/127/377, F.O. 372, PRO; Foreign Office, Minutes, May 21, 1931, A3206/32/45, PRO; Winston C. Extavour, *The Exclusive Economic Zone* (Geneva, Switzerland, 1978), 24–41. There was a recognition within the Foreign Office that the one-hour limit was the source of treaty disagreements. Geoffrey Thompson, Minutes, March 27, 1931, A2041/32/45, PRO; Foreign Office, Minutes, May 21, 1931, A3206/32/45, PRO; Foreign Office, Memorandum, June 18, 1931, ibid.

⁵³Burner, *Hoover,* 289; Glazebrook, *Canadian External Relations,* 298–99; Neatby, *Mackenzie King* 2:333–35; Acting High Commissioner, Ottawa, to Dominion Office, January 5, 1933, copy in A555/34/45, PRO.

⁵⁴Lindsay to Foreign Office, March 5, 1931, A1788/32/45, PRO; Foreign Office, Minutes, May 21, 1931, A3206/32/45, PRO; Foreign Office, Memorandum, June 18, 1931, ibid.

⁵⁵Martin Pugh, *The Making of Modern British Politics, 1867–1939* (New York, 1982), 273–74; Mowat, *Britain between the Wars,* 379–99; James, *British Revolution,* 234–38; Kemble and Kendall, "Years between the Wars," in Kilmarx, *America's Maritime Legacy,* 160–62; Emmons, *Atlantic Liners,* 11, 56; *Washington Post,* April 11, 1929; T. V. O'Connor to H. E. Woolever, September 14, 1931, 580/129/Part 7, RG 32, NA; Chauncey Parker to Charles Turck, May 20, 1932, ibid.

⁵⁶Foreign Office, Memorandum, June 18, 1931, A3206/32/45, PRO.

⁵⁷Craigie, Minutes, June 26, 1931, A4060/32/45, PRO; Interdepartmental Committee, Minutes, June 26, 1931, ibid. The committee members also included representatives from the Treasury, Lord Chancellor's Department, Fisheries, Agriculture Ministry, Scottish Office, Dominion Office, Colonial Office, and Home Office.

⁵⁸51 Fed (2d.) 292; British Embassy, Washington, to Foreign Office, September 14, 1931, A5727/32/45, PRO; Office of the U.S. Commissioner of Customs, Memorandum, September 26, 1931, copy in 23/101/53, RG 60, NAS.

⁵⁹Board of Trade to Foreign Office, November 10, 1931, A6636/32/45, PRO; Craigie, Minutes, September 12, 1931, A5727/32/45, PRO; Foreign Office, Minutes, November 10, 1931, A6636/32/45, PRO.

⁶⁰Lowman to Stimson, April 6, 1931, 811.114/*Josephine K.*/177, and December 30, 1932, 811.114/Miss CB/56, RG 59, NA. See also the *Baltimore Sun,* March 23, 1931.

⁶¹Henderson to Lowman, November 29, 1932, 23/101/53, RG 60, NAS; George Pepper to Solicitor General, November 9, 1932, ibid.; F. X. Eble to Solicitor General, November 18, 1932, ibid.

⁶²State Department Solicitor, Memorandum, January 27, 1931, 711.419/339, Roll 6, T1252, RG 59, NA; 56 Fed (2d.) 921; Borjes, Memorandum, May 14, 1932, 811.114/*Mazel Tov*/87, RG 59, NA. See also Office of

the U.S. Commissioner of Customs, Memorandum, September 26, 1932, copy in 23/101/53, RG 60, NAS; State Department to Justice Department, November 14, 1932, 811.114/*Mazel Tov*/94, RG 59, NA.

⁶³Burner, *Hoover,* 220; Sinclair, *Era of Excess,* 364–75; Kyvig, *Repealing National Prohibition,* 112–15; Hoover, *Memoirs* 2:278; Bornet and Robinson, *Herbert Hoover,* 91.

⁶⁴Stimson to George Barclay, June 28, 1932, 70/83, Stimson Papers; "Annual Report of the Director of Prohibition," June 30, 1931, "1931 June–August" folder, Box 26, PPCO, Hoover Papers; Bundy and Stimson, *On Active Service,* 286–87.

⁶⁵Hoover, "Acceptance Speech Prohibition Statement," "Statements by Hoover—April–August 1932" folder, Box 238A, PPSF, Hoover Papers; Hoover, *Memoirs* 3:318–21; Burner, *Hoover,* 307–8; Fausold, *Presidency of Herbert Hoover,* 195–96; Bornet and Robinson, *Herbert Hoover,* 92–96.

⁶⁶Kyvig, *Repealing National Prohibition,* 156–59; Frank Freidel, *Franklin Roosevelt,* 4 vols. (Boston, 1956), 3:302–3, 340–41.

⁶⁷Kyvig, *Repealing National Prohibition,* 167–68.

⁶⁸The Foreign Office was prepared to send the Board of Trade proposals. Lindsay to Foreign Office, January 15, 1932, A496/130/45, and February 1, 1932, A851/130/45, PRO; British High Commissioner, Ottawa, to Dominion Office, December 24, 1931, copy in A199/130/45, PRO; Foreign Office, Minutes, April 14, 1932, A1957/130/45, PRO; Interdepartmental Committee, Minutes of Semi-Official Discussions on the Liquor Question, June 22, 1932, A3907/130/45, PRO; Foreign Ofice, Minutes, July 20, 1932, A4376/130/45, PRO; Admiralty to Foreign Office, September 28, 1932, A6567/130/45, PRO; Foreign Office, Memorandum, October 20, 1932, A6567/130/45, PRO; Dominion Office to Foreign Office, November 8, 1932, A7563/130/45, and Foreign Office to Dominion Office, November 25, 1932, A7563/130/45, PRO; Dominion Office to Acting British High Commissioner, December 9, 1932, copy in A8282/130/45, PRO; Dominion Office to Foreign Office, January 24, 1933, A555/34/45, PRO.

⁶⁹*U.S. v. Cook* 288 U.S. 102. The ruling forced the United States to withdraw its tariff law claims in the *I'm Alone* case. Canadian Legation to State Department, December 5, 1932, 811.114/*Mazel Tov*/113, RG 59, NA; Lindsay to Foreign Office, December 8, 1932, A8411/130/45, and January 24, 1933, A578/34/45, PRO; Justice Department to State Department, January 27, 1933, 811.114/*Mazel Tov*/155, RG 59, NA; Justice Department, "Summary of the *I'm Alone* Case," February 21, 1935, 23/101/16, RG 60, NAS; U.S. Department of State, *The I'm Alone Case Joint Interim Report of the Commissioners and Statements of the Agents of Canada and the United States Pursuant Thereto with Supporting Affidavits* (Washington, DC, 1935); *New York Times,* January 23, 1933; Foreign Office, Minutes, February 21, 1933, A1209/34/45, PRO.

⁷⁰Lindsay to Foreign Office, February 24, 1933, A1800/34/45, PRO; Foreign Office to Dominion Office, April 10, 1933, A2405/34/45, PRO.

⁷¹Board of Trade to Foreign Office, September 2, 1933, A6513/34/45, PRO; Territorial Waters Committee, Minutes, February 17, 1933,

T2894/252/380, F.O. 372, PRO; P. M. Roberts, Memorandum, September 15, 1933, A8322/34/45, PRO; William Beckett, Minutes, September 15, 1933, ibid.; British Consulate, New York, to British Embassy, Washington, November 6, 1933, A8367/34/45, PRO.

[72]Roberts, Memorandum, November 14, 1933, A8323/34/45, PRO; Dominion Office to Foreign Office, July 24, 1933, A5472/34/45, PRO; British High Commissioner, Ottawa, to Dominion Office, October 20, 1933, A8042/34/130, PRO. Foreign Office officials also were concerned that American courts might nullify the treaty after repeal. The interdepartmental committee agreed to negotiate a new treaty without a fixed-mileage limit, and there was no objection to a separate Canadian-American treaty. Territorial Waters Committee, Minutes, November 28, 1933, T13513/252/380, F.O. 372, PRO; Dominion Office to Foreign Office, July 24, 1933, A5472/34/45, and December 13, 1933, A9018/34/45, PRO; Board of Trade to Foreign Office, December 23, 1933, T13992/252/38, F.O. 372, PRO; Foreign Office to Board of Trade, January 4, 1934, A9335/34/45, PRO; Dominion Office to High Commissioner, January 25, 1934, A832/13/45, PRO. The Canadian government dropped the hot-pursuit doctrine question from the *I'm Alone* discussions, but there was no comment on the future of the treaty. British High Commissioner, Ottawa, to Dominion Office, February 22, 1934, A2515/13/45, PRO.

[73]British Embassy, Washington, to Foreign Office, December 14, 1933, A9385/34/45, PRO; State Department, Memorandum, February 19, 1934, 811.114/Great Britain/406, RG 59, NA; Vallance to Hackworth, February 19, 1934, 711.419/344, Roll 6, T1252, RG 59, NA. His opinion was subsequently affirmed in the courts. State Department to Justice Department, February 27, 1934, 711.419/344, Roll 6, T1252, RG 59, NA; Vallance to Hackworth, April 23, 1937, 711.419/367, ibid.

[74]Coast Guard, Reports on Effects of Repeal, 1933, File "B," Box 20, RG 26, NA; Hackworth, Memorandum, December 29, 1933, 811.114/Liquor/403, RG 59, NA.

[75]State Department to American Consul General, London, March 30, 1934, 811.114/Great Britain/408, RG 59, NA; British Embassy, Washington, to Foreign Office, April 11, 1934, A3115/13/45, PRO; American Consulate, London, to British Customs, May 2, 1934, A3666/13/45, PRO; John P. Hurley to State Department, August 13, 1934, 811.114/B.W.I./1239, RG 59, NA; Foreign Office to Customs, June 19, 1934, A4935/13/45, PRO; Roberts, Minutes, May 2, 1934, A3666/13/45, PRO; P. H. Gore-Booth, Memorandum, July 12, 1934, A5830/13/45, PRO; Colonial Office to Foreign Office, September 13, 1934, A7203/13/45, PRO.

[76]Treasury Department, "Preliminary Report to Secretary of Treasury on Taxation and Control of Alcoholic Liquors," October 14, 1933, copy in 811.114/Liquor/317, RG 59, NA; Coast Guard, Reports on Effects of Repeal, 1933, File "B," Box 20, RG 26, NA; British Embassy, Washington, to Foreign Office, August 30, 1934, A6942/13/45, PRO; Phillips, Memorandum, August 22, 1934, 811.114/Great Britain/420, RG 59, NA; William E. Leuchtenburg, *Franklin D. Roosevelt and the New Deal, 1932-1940* (New York, 1963), 47-48.

[77]Henry Morgenthau to Phillips, September 10, 1934, 811.114/Great Britain/420½, RG 59, NA. The Treasury Department also was preparing anti-smuggling legislation. Herman Oliphant to Vallance, October 18, 1934, 811.114/Liquor/797, RG 59, NA; Phillips, Memorandum, August 22, 1934, 811.114/Great Britain/420½, RG 59, NA; Hickerson, Memorandum, September 19, 1934, 811.114/Liquor/778, RG 59, NA; State Department, Office of Economic Advisers, Memorandum, September 19, 1934, 811.114/Liquor/779, RG 59, NA. The establishment of liquor quotas was linked to the American effort to pressure the British government to raise its pork quotas. Lindsay to Foreign Office, November 23, 1933, A8684/34/45, December 31, 1933, A43/13/45, and January 8, 1934, A269/34/45, PRO.

[78]Cordell Hull, Memorandum, September 25, 1934, 811.114/Great Britain/421a, RG 59, NA; Hackworth to Hull, September 26, 1934, 811.114/Great Britain/422½, RG 59, NA; Lindsay to Foreign Office, September 26, 1934, A7995/13/45, PRO; Morgenthau to Hull, November 2, 1934, 811.114/Liquor/808, RG 59, NA; Phillips to Lindsay, November 2, 1934, A9147/13/45, PRO.

[79]Foreign Office, Minutes, August 30, 1934, A6943/13/45, PRO; Lindsay to Foreign Office, September 13, 1934, A7330/13/45, PRO.

[80]Craigie, Minutes, October 16, 1934, A7995/13/45, PRO; Interdepartmental Committee, Minutes, October 18, 1934, A8285/13/45, PRO; Foreign Office, Memorandum, October 25, 1934, A8437/13/45, PRO; Colonial Office to Bahaman Governor, October 25, 1934, copy in A8488/13/45, PRO; B. E. H. Clifford to Colonial Office, November 21, 1934, copy in A10076/13/45, PRO; Board of Trade to Foreign Office, November 21, 1934, A9381/13/45, PRO; Foreign Office to British Embassy, Washington, December 18, 1934, A10008/13/45, PRO; Dominion Office to Foreign Office, January 8, 1935, A268/7/45, and Foreign Office to Dominion Office, January 15, 1935, A129/7/45, PRO. Phillips pressed Lindsay for a reply. Phillips, Memorandum on Meeting with Ronald Lindsay, December 14, 1934, 811.114/Great Britain/430, and January 7, 1935, 811.114/Great Britain/433, RG 59, NA; Lindsay to Foreign Office, December 19, 1934, A10913/13/45, and January 21, 1935, A5930/7/45, PRO; Gore-Booth, Minutes, January 2, 1935, A593/7/45, PRO; Phillips, Memorandum on Meeting with Ambassador Lindsay, January 22, 1935, 811.114/Great Britain/436, RG 59, NA; Raymond Atherton to State Department, January 23, 1935, 811.114/Great Britain/437, RG 59, NA; Foreign Office, Minutes, January 22, 1935, A629/7/45, PRO; Interdepartmental Committee, Minutes, January 22, 1935, A717/7/45, PRO; Cabinet, "Extract of Meeting," January 23, 1935, copy in A730/7/45, PRO.

[81]Morgenthau to Lindsay, August 5, 1935, A7231/7/45, PRO. British Counsellor D'Arcy Osborne met with Treasury officials and convinced them that registry restrictions were impractical. He also learned that the primary American concern was enforcement assistance in Newfoundland, which was the new smuggling headquarters. Harold Graves to Hickerson, January 17, 1935, 811.114/Great Britain/439, RG 59, NA; Lindsay to Foreign Office, January 12, 1935, A386/7/45, January 18, 1935, A527/7/45, and January 22, 1935, A629/7/45, PRO; Foreign Office, Minutes, January 18, 1935,

A527/7/45, PRO; Morgenthau to Hull, January 28, 1935, 811.114/Great Britain/440, RG 59, NA; Lindsay to Foreign Office, February 1, 1935, A1041/7/45, and February 7, 1935, A1209/7/45, and Foreign Office to Lindsay, February 23, 1935, A1668/7/45, PRO; Colonial Office to Bahamas, Barbados, British Honduras, and Bermuda, February 6, 1935, copy in A1204/7/45, PRO; Gore-Booth, Memorandum, March 8, 1935, A2638/7/45, PRO; Colonial Office to Foreign Office, May 27, 1935, A4789/7/45, PRO; Lindsay to Morgenthau, July 31, 1935, A1086/7/45, PRO; Craigie, Minutes, February 6, 1935, A1172/7/45, PRO; Interdepartmental Committee, Minutes, February 28, 1935, A2216/7/45, PRO; Lindsay to Foreign Office, March 23, 1935, A2271/7/45, PRO.

[82]"Joint Final Report of the *I'm Alone* Commissioners," January 9, 1935, copy in 811.114/*I'm Alone*/4302, RG 59, NA; Justice Department, "Summary of the *I'm Alone* Case," February 21, 1935, 23/101/16, RG 60, NAS; Lindsay to Foreign Office, January 10, 1935, A649/7/45, PRO. See also "Complete Record of *I'm Alone* Case," January 7, 1935, copy in 811.114/*I'm Alone*/4290, RG 59, NA. The commissioners agreed that the ship was owned and controlled by Americans, and no damages were paid for either loss of cargo or the ship. On January 22, 1935, Secretary of State Hull formally apologized for the incident and agreed to pay $25,000 to the Canadian government plus various sums to the crew members.

[83]Oliphant to Hull, February 6, 1935, 811.114/Liquor/879, RG 59, NA; Vallance, Memorandum, February 6, 1935, ibid.; British Embassy, Washington, to Foreign Office, May 15, 1935, A4671/7/45, PRO; State Department to American Consuls, August 14, 1935, 811.114/Liquor/969, RG 59, NA; American Consulate, Nassau, to State Department, October 10, 1935, 811.114/B.W.I./1318, RG 59, NA; Foreign Office to Lindsay, August 3, 1935, A7002/7/45, PRO; Foreign Office, Minutes, September 28, 1935, A8650/7/45, PRO; Foreign Office, Memorandum, October 15, 1935, A9007/7/45, PRO; Interdepartmental Committee, Minutes, November 12, 1935, A9807/7/45, and November 4, 1936, A9645/83/45, PRO; Dominion Office to Foreign Office, June 22, 1938, A4952/244/45, PRO.

[84]British Embassy, Washington, to State Department, October 18, 1935, 711.419/361, October 5, 1938, 711.419/373, and October 10, 1939, 711.419/376, Roll 6, T1252, RG 59, NA; American Consulate, Nassau, to State Department, November 21, 1936, 811.114/B.W.I./1557, January 18, 1938, 811.114/B.W.I./1609, and November 28, 1939, 811.114/B.W.I./1708, RG 59, NA; American Consulate, London, to State Department, December 19, 1939, 811.114/Great Britain/687, RG 59, NA; Colonial Office to Foreign Office, September 26, 1939, A6615/86/45, PRO; Foreign Office to Ministry of Shipping, February 10, 1940, A619/619/45, PRO; Foreign Office to British Embassy, Washington, September 18, 1940, A3934/619/45, PRO.

Conclusion

For fourteen years national prohibition was a major cloud on the horizon of Anglo-American relations. Transcending changes in the American presidency, resignations or retirements of diplomatic personnel, the rise and fall of British governments, and the political repudiation of the Eighteenth Amendment, prohibition enforcement was an enduring concern for both countries. Prohibition emerged as a diplomatic issue because it was not simply an effort to standardize American morality. Rather, it was a complex problem, raising questions of international law and economic rivalry, that was a part of the fabric of American and British foreign policy in the interwar period.

In the United States, the foreign policy challenge was to clarify the nation's role in the postwar world. This assumed the form of an independent internationalism that both recognized the necessity of maintaining an economic presence in the international arena and attempted to avoid political entanglements. But independent internationalism was a broad spectrum that included dedicated internationalists and strident nationalists, unilateralists and collectivists. It was never a permanently fixed doctrine, and these competing forces continued to debate over its precise definition. Without a clear diplomatic direction, partisan political rivalries, bureaucratic infighting, and domestic pressures emerged as important determinants in U.S. foreign policy.

The history of liquor diplomacy underscores the fact that this independent internationalism, not isolationism, was the predominant characteristic of Washington's postwar diplomacy. National prohibition initially reflected an isolationist effort to cleanse American society, but the practical ramifications of enforcing the liquor laws disclosed the limitations of this rhetoric. Smuggling shattered the belief that the United States could exist blissfully behind the imaginary walls of isolationism. If Wayne Wheeler and enforcement officials regarded the British as a

155

convenient excuse for the shortcomings of the Eighteenth Amendment, they also accepted the fact that their own country could not enforce the Volstead Act alone. Instead, they sought Great Britain's assistance in the 1924 liquor treaty, at the London Conference, in securing Canadian help, and through the uninterrupted operation of these cooperative measures. Liquor diplomacy demonstrated that the rejection of isolationism in the United States was not based solely on economic concerns. Prohibition enforcement, perhaps more than any other issue, revealed that the dismissal of this unrealistic dogma was more widespread and encompassed pragmatic political considerations.

Although isolationism was not a pervasive influence, American diplomats were not free to pursue their own policy objectives. The struggle within independent internationalism over the achievement of national goals encouraged the intrusion of domestic constraints in foreign policymaking. In Congress, this produced immigration restrictions, the first geographic extension of customs jurisdiction since 1799, and the effort to revitalize shipping. Wheeler and other prohibitionists demanded the replacement of international law with an aggressive enforcement strategy. Flexing his considerable political muscle until the middle of the decade, Wheeler delayed the adoption of seizure guidelines and circumscribed the liquor policy of the Harding administration. Concurrently, shipping interests in the United States embraced a nationalistic fervor that regarded the rebuilding of the merchant fleet as a reflection of new strength in the postwar world. Together, these domestic influences were determined to protect and extend American interests regardless of diplomatic considerations.

Domestic pressures also were manifested in the bureaucratic infighting that hampered the development of a consistent U.S. foreign policy. Much has been written about congressional-executive relations in the postwar period, but the prohibition issue illustrates the negative impact of the schisms within the executive branch itself. All of the departments involved in the formulation of liquor policy reflected the views of a particular segment of domestic opinion. While Mabel Walker Willebrandt was supported by advocates of strict law enforcement in her unilateral approach to smuggling and Albert Lasker defended shipping interests, the State Department struggled to retain control of liquor diplomacy. Overwhelmed by bureaucratic squabbling, policy vacillated between the avowed desire of State Department officials to resolve prohibition disputes through diplomacy and the determination of other executive branch departments to advance incompatible domestic interests. The result was delay, inertia, and confusion.

At the center of this bureaucratic deadlock was weak presidential leadership. Warren Harding, recognizing the enormity of the smuggling problem, offered no feasible solution and was incapable of resolving the internal disputes that paralyzed his administration. Fearing the political power of the Anti-Saloon League, he tolerated Willebrandt's subversion and sacrificed his ship subsidy plan. The handling of the Busch-Lasker affair was a colossal example of presidential mismanagement and weakened the proposition that Harding was a forceful leader during the final years of his presidency. This leadership vacuum, continued by Harding's successor, Calvin Coolidge, repeatedly allowed the prohibition enforcement agencies, the U.S. Shipping Board, and the State Department to pursue mutually exclusive goals. Liquor policy was only removed from the bureaucratic battleground when General Andrews bridged the gap between diplomacy and smuggling enforcement and when Herbert Hoover reasserted presidential leadership at the end of the decade.

For British officials, the principal postwar goal was the restoration of their nation's pre-1914 supremacy. This was a difficult task at a time when their commitments were greater than their resources. The British strategy was to stimulate foreign trade and to draw upon imperial assets to strengthen Great Britain's position. Crucial to the expansion of commercial opportunities was the maintenance of traditional dominance of world shipping and the preservation of those international law principles that guaranteed a wider application of unrestricted commerce.

Because prohibition threatened the achievement of these larger objectives, the London government could not ignore the Eighteenth Amendment. When the United States began to seize British rumrunners beyond the three-mile limit, Foreign Office officials were prepared to sacrifice Anglo-American relations to maintain their vigilant defense of international law, but the *Cunard* ruling and Secretary of State Hughes's offer to disregard the sealed-liquor restrictions in exchange for extended seizure rights injected a new dimension into this question. Altering the basic assumptions of British officials, the American treaty proposal made the simultaneous protection of Great Britain's shipping and the defense of the three-mile principle impossible.

With the effects of U.S. prohibition reaching the Liverpool docks, the liquor problem became an economic issue as the immediate protection of shipping interests outweighed the absolute preservation of international law. British shippers, like their American counterparts, enlisted the support of governmental allies to ensure that London's liquor diplomacy recognized their interests. What finally brought an accommodation was the recognition that prohibition was damaging shipping and frustrating the efforts of Great Britain to achieve its postwar objectives. Despite Foreign Secretary Curzon's inability to accept this strategic compromise, the protection of shipping was the guiding force behind the British involvement in smuggling enforcement. The cooperative measures adopted at the London Conference, and the willingness of British officials to reconcile their policy when the independence of Canada threatened the liquor treaty, reflected this reality. Following the acrimonious debate of 1923, economics, not the desire for American goodwill, served as the cornerstone of London's liquor diplomacy.

This highlights the fact that the liquor treaty was not a British concession. Officials in London appreciated the distinction between international law and international comity. On the question of American seizure rights, the Foreign Office staff steadfastly believed that their position was correct and would be supported by any international tribunal. These same officials harbored no similar confidence in the illegality of Attorney General Daugherty's ruling that restricted sealed liquor within the three-mile limit. The abrogation of international comity was a departure from standard practice; it was offensive and encouraged diplomatic friction. Yet, from the beginning, British officials privately acknowledged the technical right of the United States to exercise jurisdiction in its own waters. Therefore, in negotiating the liquor treaty and extending assistance at the London Conference, they did not compromise principles of international law for the affirmation of an assumed right. They secured a valuable privilege which was otherwise unattainable.

The operation of the liquor treaty from 1924 to 1934 also suggests that the smuggling convention was not a British sacrifice. Rather than weakening the three-mile rule, the treaty preamble bound the United States to this general principle. The treaty handicapped the U.S. Shipping Board's transatlantic challenge while British shipping continued, without interruption, to transport sealed liquor in American waters. When international support for the three-mile limit declined in the early 1930s, the London government retained its reciprocal benefits under the treaty until the repeal of the Eighteenth Amendment. While British ships openly carried sealed-liquor stores, American treaty benefits were ensnared in legal controversy and uncertainties over measurement that made it an ineffective enforcement weapon. The London government never adopted any new legislation to curtail the abuse of registry or clearance regulations, and throughout the prohibition period the British liquor industry thrived on the unrestricted export of distilled spirits. Judged on the basis of its practical ramifications, the liquor treaty was a notable victory for Great Britain.

Within this framework of British and American concerns, prohibition complicated the search for an Anglo-American accommodation in the early postwar period. British officials regarded the American abuse of international law as evidence that the United States was not prepared to assume its position as a respected member of the international community. The extension of Eighteenth Amendment restrictions to British shipping confirmed that U.S. diplomacy was a hostage of competing domestic pressures, and Foreign Office officials were unwilling to place their trust in the unreliability of American friendship. At the same time, the unwillingness of the London government to assist in the curtailment of smuggling demonstrated to American critics the inherent and calculated selfishness of Great Britain. It substantiated the fear that the British were determined to thwart American ambitions and bolstered the argument for unilateral action. The British were considered unreasonable and an unsuitable partner for the United States.

Amid an atmosphere of mutual suspicion, prohibition inflamed American anglophobia and British anti-Americanism. Consequently, the relative cordiality that characterized Anglo-American relations in the middle of the decade was only possible because the 1924 treaty reduced the emotionalism of the liquor issue. Prohibition did not prevent the resolution of other outstanding disagreements between the United States and Great Britain, nor did the return of Anglo-American tensions by 1927 disrupt the continuation of antismuggling cooperation. Prohibition, however, did delay the translation of agreement into full political harmony. Throughout 1922 and 1923 the striking feature of transatlantic diplomatic correspondence on prohibition and shipping was the intensity of bitterness and the reluctance to compromise. Prohibition demonstrated that there was no intrinsic community of agreement between the United States and Great Britain after World War I. Harmony, where it was possible, was not easily achieved.

The history of Anglo-American liquor diplomacy was significant because the liquor issue was never solely a dispute over distilled spirits. Raising questions of international law, economics, and domestic political interests, the enforcement of the Eighteenth Amendment was an enduring problem that threatened the fundamental concerns of British and American foreign policy during the interwar years. Casting a long shadow over Anglo-American relations, the liquor issue was a serious and complicated problem that demonstrated both the limits and the possibilities of diplomacy.

Bibliography

Manuscript Collections

Cambridge, England. Cambridge University. Stanley Baldwin Papers.
Columbus, Ohio. Ohio State Historical Society. Walter F. Brown Papers. MSS 12.
———. Harry Daugherty Collection. MSS 271.
———. Harry Daugherty Papers. MSS 668.
———. Simeon D. Fess Papers. MSS 283.
———. Warren G. Harding Papers. Microfilm edition.
———. Frank B. Willis. MSS 325.
———. Microfilm Edition of Temperance and Prohibition Papers. Anti-Saloon League of America. Series 7 and 8.
Liverpool. University of Liverpool. Cunard Company Archives.
London. Public Record Office. Board of Trade Correspondence. Board of Trade 196.
———. ———. Board of Trade Correspondence. Mercantile Marine Department. Mercantile Trade 9.
———. ———. Conclusions of Meetings of the Cabinet. Cabinet 23.
———. ———. Stenographic Notes of the Imperial Conferences. Cabinet 32.
———. ———. General Political Correspondence of the Foreign Office. Foreign Office 371.
———. ———. Foreign Office General Treaty Files. Foreign Office 372.
———. ———. Private Secretary Archives. Private Office Papers—Foreign Office. Foreign Office 800.
———. ———. Private Secretary Archives. Private Papers of Austin Chamberlain. Foreign Office 800.
———. ———. Private Secretary Archives. Private Papers of Arthur Henderson. Foreign Office 800.
———. ———. Private Papers of J. Ramsay MacDonald. Public Record Office 30/69.
New Haven, Connecticut. Yale University. Henry L. Stimson Diaries. Microfilm edition.
———. ———. Henry L. Stimson Papers. Microfilm edition.
Ottawa, Canada. Public Archives Canada. Department of External Affairs. Office of the Undersecretary of External Affairs. Record Group 25, D1. Microfilm edition.

St. Paul, Minnesota. Minnesota Historical Society. Frank B. Kellogg Papers. Microfilm edition.

Suitland, Maryland. National Archives. Classified Subject Files of the Department of Justice. Record Group 60.

———. ———. Charles Evans Hughes Papers.

Washington, DC. Library of Congress. Calvin Coolidge Papers. Microfilm edition.

———. National Archives. Records of the Department of Treasury. Coast Guard. Record Group 26.

———. ———. Records of the United States Shipping Board. Record Group 32.

———. ———. Records of the United States Shipping Board. Albert Lasker Files. Record Group 32.

———. ———. Central Files of the Department of Treasury. Record Group 56.

———. ———. Records of the Department of Treasury. Internal Revenue Service. Prohibition Bureau. Record Group 58.

———. ———. General Records of the Department of State. Record Group 59.

———. ———. General Records of the Department of Justice. Record Group 60.

West Branch, Iowa. Herbert Hoover Presidential Library. William Castle Papers.

———. ———. Herbert Hoover Papers.

Other Unpublished Sources

Cohen, Martin B. "The First Legation: Canadian Diplomacy and the Opening of Relations with the United States." Ph.D. dissertation, George Washington University, 1975.

Mannock, James H. "Anglo-American Relations: 1921–1928." Ph.D. dissertation, Princeton University, 1962.

Government Documents

Canada. Department of Trade and Commerce. Dominion Bureau of Statistics. *The Liquor Traffic in Canada* (1929).

Great Britain. Colonial Office. *Colonial Reports Annual.* Number 1192, "Bahamas 1922–23" (1924).

Great Britain. Parliament. *Parliamentary Papers* (Commons). Command 1703, "Licensing Statistics, 1921—Statistics as to the Operation and Administration of the Laws relating to the Sale of Intoxicating Liquor for the Year 1921" (1922).

Great Britain. Parliament. *Parliamentary Papers* (Commons). Command 1987 (1923).

Tariff Act of 1922, Statutes at Large, vol. 42 (1923).

U.S. Congress. House. Committee on Foreign Affairs. *The Treaty between Great Britain and the United States. Hearings on H. Res. 174,* 68th Cong., 1st sess., 1924.

U.S. Congress. House. Committee on Merchant Marine and Fisheries. *American Merchant Marine: Report.* Report 1112. 67th Cong., 2d sess. (June 16, 1922).

———. *Minority Views: The Subsidy Bill.* Report 1112–Part 2. 67th Cong., 2d sess. (June 28, 1922).

U.S. Congress. Senate. Committee on Commerce. House. Committee on Merchant Marine and Fisheries. *To Amend the Merchant Marine Act of 1920. Joint Hearings on S. 3217 and H.R. 10644,* 67th Cong., 2d sess., 1922.

U.S. Department of Commerce. *The Balance of International Payments of the United States in 1924* (1925).

U.S. Department of State. *Convention between the United States and Great Britain: Prevention of Smuggling of Intoxicating Liquors.* Treaties and Other International Acts Series, no. 685 (1924).

———. *The I'm Alone Case Joint Interim Report of the Commissioners and Statements of the Agents of Canada and the United States Pursuant Thereto with Supporting Affidavits* (1935).

U.S. Department of Treasury. Bureau of Prohibition. *Statistics concerning Intoxicating Liquors* (1928).

———. Internal Revenue Service. *Hearings on the Application of the National Prohibition Act to the Sale of Intoxicating Beverages on American Vessels on the High Seas* (1920).

U.S. Shipping Board. *Government Aid to Mercantile Shipping* (1922).

Court Cases

Cunard v. Mellon et al., United States Reports, vol. 262 (1924).

Frances and Louise, Federal Reporter (Second Series), vol. 1 (1925).

Frances E., Federal Reporter (Second Series), vol. 7 (1926) and vol. 13 (1927).

Grace and Ruby, Federal Reporter, vol. 283 (1923).

Grogan v. Walker and *Anchor v. Aldridge, Federal Reporter,* vol. 275 (1922).

Grogan v. Walker and *Anchor v. Aldridge, United States Reports,* vol. 259 (1923).

Henry L. Marshall, Federal Reporter, vol. 292 (1923).

Marjorie Bachman, Federal Reporter (Second Series), vol. 4 (1925).

Over the Top, Federal Reporter (Second Series), vol. 5 (1925).

Pictonian, Federal Reporter (Second Series), vol. 3 (1925).

Sagatind, Federal Reporter (Second Series), vol. 4 (1925), vol. 8 (1926), and vol. 11 (1926).

U.S. v. Cook (Mazel Tov), Federal Reporter (Second Series), vol. 51 (1931) and vol. 56 (1932).

U.S. v. Cook, United States Reports, vol. 288 (1933).

U.S. v. Ford (Quadra), Federal Reporter (Second Series), vol. 3 (1925) and vol. 10 (1926).

Other Sources

Address by the President of the United States on the Need for an American Merchant Marine. Washington, DC: Government Printing Office, 1922.

Adler, Selig. *The Uncertain Giant, 1921–1941: American Foreign Policy between the Wars.* American Diplomatic Series. New York: Macmillan Company, 1965.

Albury, Paul. *The Story of the Bahamas.* New York: St. Martin's Press, 1975.

Aldcroft, Derek H. *The Inter-War Economy: Britain, 1919–1939.* London: B. T. Batsford, 1970.

Allen, Everett S. *The Black Ships: Rumrunners of Prohibition.* Boston: Little, Brown, and Company, 1965.

Allen, Harry C. *Great Britain and the United States.* London: Odhams Press, 1954.

Allen, Herbert W. *Number Three Saint James's Street: A History of Berry's the Wine Merchants.* London: Chatto and Windus, 1950.

Andrews, Allen. *The Whiskey Barons.* London: Jupiter Books, 1977.

Anti-Saloon League of America. *Proceedings of the Twentieth National Convention: December 6–8, 1921.* Washington, DC: S. E. Nicholson (Secretary), 1922.

Asbury, Herbert. *The Great Illusion: An Informal History of Prohibition.* Garden City, NY: Doubleday and Company, 1950.

Babcock, F. Lawrence. *Spanning the Atlantic.* New York: Alfred A. Knopf, 1931.

Barbican, James. See Walker, Eric Sherbrooke.

Bell, Hugh M. *Bahamas: Isles of June.* New York: Robert M. McBride and Company, 1934.

Blocker, Jack S., Jr. *Retreat from Reform: The Prohibition Movement in the United States, 1890–1913.* Contributions in American History Series, no. 51. Westport, CT: Greenwood Press, 1976.

————. *Alcohol, Reform and Society: The Liquor Issue in Social Context.* Contributions in American History Series, no. 83. Westport, CT: Greenwood Press, 1979.

Bornet, Vaughn D., and Robinson, Edgar E. *Herbert Hoover: President of the United States.* Stanford: Hoover Institution Press, 1975.

Brander, Michael. *The Original Scotch: A History of Scotch Whisky from the Earliest Days.* New York: Clarkson N. Potter, 1975.

Brown, Dorothy M. *Mabel Walker Willebrandt: A Study of Power, Loyalty, and Law.* Knoxville: University of Tennessee Press, 1984.

Buckley, Thomas H. *The United States and the Washington Conference, 1921–1922.* Knoxville: University of Tennessee Press, 1970.

Bundy, McGeorge, and Stimson, Henry L. *On Active Service in Peace and War.* New York: Harper and Brothers, 1947.

Burner, David. *Herbert Hoover: A Public Life.* New York: Alfred A. Knopf, 1979.

Carse, Robert. *Rum Row.* New York: Rinehart and Company, 1959.

Carter, Henry. *The Control of the Drink Trade.* London: Longmans, Green, and Company, 1918.

Carter, Paul A. *The Twenties in America.* New York: Thomas Y. Crowell Company, 1968.

Cashman, Sean D. *Prohibition: The Lie of the Land.* New York: Free Press, 1981.

Clark, Norman H. *Deliver Us from Evil: An Interpretation of American Prohibition.* Norton Essay in American History Series. New York: W. W. Norton and Company, 1976.

Coffey, Thomas M. *The Long Thirst: Prohibition in America, 1920–1933.* New York: W. W. Norton and Company, 1975.

Colombos, C. John, and Higgins, Alexander P. *The International Law of the Sea.* London: Longmans, Green, and Company, 1943.

Costigliola, Frank C. "Anglo-American Financial Rivalry in the 1920s." *Journal of Economic History* 37 (1977): 911–34.

Craton, Michael. *A History of the Bahamas.* London: Collins, 1962.

Current, Richard N. *Secretary Stimson: A Study in Statecraft.* New Brunswick, NJ: Rutgers University Press, 1954.

Danielski, David J., and Tulchin, Joseph S., eds. *The Autobiographical Notes of Charles Evans Hughes.* Cambridge, MA: Harvard University Press, 1973.

Dawes, Charles G. *Journal as Ambassador to Great Britain.* New York: Macmillan Company, 1939.

Dickinson, E. D. "Are the Liquor Treaties Self-Executing?" *American Journal of International Law* 20 (1926): 444–52.

Dilks, David, ed. *Retreat from Power: Studies in Britain's Foreign Policy of the Twentieth Century.* Vol. 1. London: Macmillan Press, 1981.

Downes, Randolph C. *The Rise of Warren Gamaliel Harding, 1865–1920.* Columbus: Ohio State University Press, 1970.

Drummond, Ian M. *Imperial Economic Policy, 1917–1939: Studies in Expansion and Protection.* London: George Allen and Unwin Ltd., 1974.

Duroselle, Jean Baptiste. *From Wilson to Roosevelt.* Translated by Nancy L. Roelker. Cambridge, MA: Harvard University Press, 1963.

Ellis, Lewis Ethan. *Frank B. Kellogg and American Foreign Relations, 1925–1929.* New Brunswick, NJ: Rutgers University Press, 1961.

———. *Republican Foreign Policy, 1921–1933.* New Brunswick, NJ: Rutgers University Press, 1968.

Emmons, Frederick. *The Atlantic Liners.* New York: Drake Publishers, 1972.

Engleman, Larry L. *Intemperance: The Lost War against Liquor.* New York: Free Press, 1979

———. "Organized Thirst: The Story of Repeal in Michigan," in Jack S. Blocker, Jr., *Alcohol, Reform and Society: The Liquor Issue in Social Context.* Contributions in American History Series, no. 83. Westport, CT: Greenwood Press, 1979.

Extavour, Winston C. *The Exclusive Economic Zone.* Geneva: Institut Universitaire de Hautes Etudes Internationales, 1978.

Fausold, Martin L. *The Presidency of Herbert Hoover.* Lawrence: University Press of Kansas, 1985.

"Foreign Liquor Ships outside the Territorial Belt." *Harvard Law Review* 36 (1923): 609–15.

Freidel, Frank. *Franklin D. Roosevelt.* Vol. 3. *The Triumph.* Boston: Little,

Brown, and Company, 1952.

Fry, Michael G. *Illusions of Security: North Atlantic Diplomacy, 1918–22.* Toronto: University of Toronto, 1972.

Fulton, Thomas W. *The Sovereignty of the Seas.* London: William Blackwood and Sons, 1911.

Gardiner, Alfred G. *The Anglo-American Future.* New York: Thomas Seltzer, 1927.

Geddes, Auckland. *The Forging of a Family.* London: Faber and Faber, 1952.

Glad, Betty. *Charles Evans Hughes and the Illusions of Innocence.* Urbana: University of Illinois Press, 1966.

Glazebrook, George P. *A History of Canadian External Relations.* Toronto: Oxford University Press, 1950.

Glynn, Sean, and Oxborrow, John. *Interwar Britain: A Social and Economic History.* London: George Allen and Unwin, 1976.

Gray, David. "Bootlegging from the Bahamas." *Colliers* (June 24, 1922): 6–10.

Grew, Joseph C. *Turbulent Era.* 2 vols. Edited by Walter Johnson. Boston: Houghton, Mifflin, and Company, 1952.

Gunther, John. *Taken at the Flood: The Story of Albert D. Lasker.* New York: Harper and Bros., 1960.

Gusfield, Joseph R. *Symbolic Crusade.* Urbana: University of Illinois Press, 1963.

Haynes, Roy A. *Prohibition Inside Out.* Garden City, NY: Doubleday, Page, and Company, 1923.

Hicks, John D. *Republican Ascendancy, 1921–1933.* New American Nation Series. New York: Harper and Bros., 1960.

Hillmer, Norman. "The Foreign Office, the Dominions, and the Diplomatic Unity of the Empire, 1925–29," in Dilks, David, ed., *Retreat from Power: Studies in Britain's Foreign Policy of the Twentieth Century.* Vol. 1. London: Macmillan Press, 1981: 64–77.

Hinman, George W. "Diplomatic Victory over Rum." *American Review* 3 (1925): 418.

Hoff-Wilson, Joan. *American Business and Foreign Policy, 1920–1933.* Lexington: University of Kentucky Press, 1971.

———. *Herbert Hoover: Forgotten Progressive.* Boston: Little, Brown, and Company, 1975.

Hogan, Michael J. *Informal Entente: The Private Structure of Cooperation in Anglo-American Economic Diplomacy, 1918–1928.* Columbia: University of Missouri, 1977.

Holland, R. F. *Britain and the Commonwealth Alliance, 1918–1939.* London: Macmillan Press, 1981.

Holsinger, Paul M. "The *I'm Alone* Controversy: A Study in Inter-American Diplomacy, 1929–1935." *Mid America* 50 (1968): 305–13.

Hoover, Herbert. *The Memoirs of Herbert Hoover.* Vol. 2. *Cabinet and Presidency.* New York: Macmillan Company, 1952.

———. *The Memoirs of Herbert Hoover.* Vol. 3. *The Great Depression.* New York: Macmillan Company, 1953.

Howard, Esme. *Theatre of Life.* 2 vols. London: Hodder and Stoughton, 1936.

Hughes, Charles Evans. "Recent Questions and Negotiations." *Foreign Affairs* 2 (February 1924): 1–7.

———. *The Pathway of Peace: Representative Addresses.* New York: Harper and Bros., 1925.

Hulen, Bertram D. *Inside the Department of State.* New York: McGraw-Hill, 1939.

Hutchins, John G. B. "The American Shipping Industry since 1914." *Business History Review* 28 (June 1954): 105–13.

Hyde, Charles Cheney. "Charles Evans Hughes," in *The American Secretaries of State and Their Diplomacy.* Vol. 10: 221–402. Edited by Samuel Flagg Bemis. New York: Pageant Book Company, 1958.

Hyde, Francis E. *Cunard and the North Atlantic, 1840–1973.* London: Macmillan Press, 1975.

James, Robert Rhodes. *The British Revolution: British Politics, 1880–1939.* Vol. 2. London: Hamish Hamilton, 1977.

Jessup, Phillip C. *The Law of Territorial Waters and Maritime Jurisdiction.* New York: G. A. Jennings Company, 1927.

Johnson, Willis F. *George Harvey: A Passionate Patriot.* Boston: Houghton, Mifflin, and Company, 1929.

Jones, Robert L. *The Eighteenth Amendment and Our Foreign Relations.* New York: Thomas Y. Crowell Company, 1933.

Kerr, K. Austin. *Organized for Prohibition: A New History of the Anti-Saloon League.* New Haven: Yale University Press, 1985.

———. "Organizing for Reform: The Anti-Saloon League." *American Quarterly* 32 (Spring 1980): 37–53.

Kett, Joseph F. "Temperance and Intemperance as Historical Problems." *Journal of American History* 67 (March 1981): 878–85.

Kemble, John H., and Kendall, Lane C. "The Years between the Wars: 1919–1939." In *America's Maritime Legacy: A History of the United States Merchant Marine and Shipbuilding Industry since Colonial Times,* 149–74. Edited by Robert A. Kilmarx. Boulder, CO: Westview Press, 1979.

Kilmarx, Robert A., ed. *America's Maritime Legacy: A History of the United States Merchant Marine and Shipbuilding Industry since Colonial Times.* Boulder, CO: Westview Press, 1979.

Kottman, Richard N. "Volstead Violated: Prohibition as a Factor in Canadian-American Relations." *Canadian Historical Review* 18 (June 1962): 106–13.

Kyvig, David E. *Repealing National Prohibition.* Chicago: University of Chicago Press, 1979.

Lawrence, Samuel A. *United States Merchant Shipping Policies and Politics.* Washington, DC: Brookings Institution, 1966.

Leffler, Melvyn P. "Political Isolationism, Economic Expansionism, or Diplomatic Realism: American Policy toward Western Europe, 1921–1933." *Perspectives in American History* 8 (1974): 413–61.

———. *The Elusive Quest: America's Pursuit of European Stability and French Security, 1919–1933.* Chapel Hill: University of North Carolina, 1979.

Leuchtenburg, William E. *Franklin Roosevelt and the New Deal, 1932-1940.* New American Nation Series. New York: Harper and Row, 1963.

Link, Arthur S. *Wilson: Confusions and Crises, 1915-1916.* Princeton: Princeton University Press, 1964.

———. *Wilson: The Struggle for Neutrality, 1914-1915.* Princeton: Princeton University Press, 1961.

Lockhart, Robert Bruce. *Scotch.* London: Putnam, 1951.

Longmate, Norman. *The Waterdrinkers: A History of Temperance.* London: Hamish Hamilton, 1968.

Lythgoe, Gertrude C. *The Bahama Queen.* New York: Exposition Press, 1964.

McCoy, Donald R. *Calvin Coolidge: The Quiet President.* New York: Macmillan Company, 1967.

McDowall, Robert J. S. *The Whiskies of Scotland.* 3rd ed. London: John Murray, 1975.

McKercher, J. C. *The Second Baldwin Government and the United States, 1924-1929: Attitudes and Diplomacy.* Cambridge: Cambridge University Press, 1984.

Massey, Vincent. *What's Past Is Prologue.* New York: St. Martin's Press, 1964.

Masterson, William E. *Jurisdiction in Marginal Seas.* New York: Macmillan Company, 1929.

Merz, Charles. *The Dry Decade.* Garden City, NY: Doubleday, Doran, and Company, 1930.

Meyers, William Starr, ed. *The State Papers and Other Public Writings of Herbert Hoover.* 2 vols. Garden City, NY: Doubleday, Doran, and Company, 1934.

Middlemas, Keith, and Barnes, Joseph. *Baldwin.* London: Weidenfield and Nicolson, 1969.

Moray, Alastair. *The Diary of a Rum-Runner.* London: Philip Allan and Company, 1929.

Mosley, Leonard. *The Glorious Fault: The Life of Lord Curzon.* New York: Harcourt, Brace, and Company, 1960.

Mowat, Charles L. *Britain between the Wars: 1918-1940.* Chicago: University of Chicago Press, 1955.

Murphy, James, comp. *Speeches and Addresses of Warren G. Harding President of the United States.* N.p., 1923.

Murray, Robert K. *The Harding Era: Warren G. Harding and His Administration.* Minneapolis: University of Minnesota Press, 1969.

———. *The Politics of Normalcy: Governmental Theory and Practice in the Harding-Coolidge Era.* New York: W. W. Norton and Company, 1973.

Neatby, H. Blair. *William Lyon Mackenzie King.* Vol. 2. *The Lonely Heights.* Toronto: University of Toronto Press, 1963.

Newman, Peter C. *Bronfman Dynasty: Rothschilds of the New World.* Toronto: McClelland and Stewart, 1978.

Nicholas, Herbert G. *The United States and Great Britain.* Chicago: University of Chicago Press, 1975.

Nicolson, Harold. *Curzon: The Last Phase, 1919–1925.* New York: Houghton, Mifflin, and Company, 1934.

Noggle, Burl. *Into the Twenties: The United States from Armistice to Normalcy.* Urbana: University of Illinois Press, 1974.

Odegard, Peter H. *Pressure Politics: The Story of the Anti-Saloon League.* New York: Columbia University Press, 1928.

Offner, Arnold A. *The Origins of the Second World War: American Foreign Policy and World Politics, 1917–1941.* New York: Praeger Publishers, 1975.

Our Merchant Marine. Washington, DC: National Merchant Marine Association, March 1923.

Parrini, Carl P. "Anglo-American Corporatism and the Economic Diplomacy of Stabilization in the 1920s." *Reviews in American History* 6 (1978): 379–87.

———. *Heir to Empire: United States Economic Diplomacy, 1916–1923.* Pittsburgh: University of Pittsburgh Press, 1969.

Perkins, Dexter. *Charles Evans Hughes and American Democratic Statesmanship.* Library of American Biography Series. Boston: Little, Brown, and Company, 1956.

Phillips, William. *Ventures in Diplomacy.* Boston: Beacon Press, 1952.

Pollard, Sidney. *The Development of the British Economy, 1914–1950.* London: Edward Arnold Ltd., 1962.

Pugh, Martin. *The Making of Modern British Politics, 1867–1939.* New York: St. Martin's Press, 1982.

Pusey, Merlo J. *Charles Evans Hughes.* 2 vols. New York: Macmillan Company, 1951.

Reeves, Ira L. *Ol' Rum River: Revelations of a Prohibition Administrator.* Chicago: Thomas S. Rockwell Company, 1931.

Rose, Kenneth. *A Superior Person: Curzon and His Circle of Friends.* London: Weidenfield and Nicolson, 1969.

Ross, James. *Whiskey.* London: Routledge and Kegan, 1970.

Rowland, Peter, *Lloyd George.* London: Barrie and Jenkins, 1975.

Russell, Francis. *The Shadow of Blooming Grove: Warren G. Harding in His Times.* New York: McGraw-Hill, 1968.

Russett, Bruce M. *Community and Contention.* Cambridge, MA: MIT Press, 1963.

Safford, Jeffrey J. *Wilsonian Maritime Diplomacy, 1913–1921.* New Brunswick, NJ: Rutgers University Press, 1978.

"Self-Execution of Treaties under the Constitution." *Columbia Law Review* 26 (1926): 859–70.

Shaw, Albert, ed. *The Messages and Papers of Woodrow Wilson.* 2 vols. New York: Review of Reviews Corp., 1924.

Sinclair, Andrew. *Prohibition: The Era of Excess.* Boston: Atlantic Monthly Press, 1962.

———. *The Available Man: Warren Gamaliel Harding.* New York: Macmillan Company, 1965.

Speeches of Senator Warren G. Harding of Ohio. Washington, DC: Republican National Committee, 1920.

Sprout, Harold and Margaret. *Toward a New Order of Sea Power: American Naval Policy and the World Scene, 1918–1922.* Princeton: Princeton University Press, 1940.

Steuart, Justin. *Wayne Wheeler: Dry Boss.* New York: Fleming H. Revell Company, 1928.

Swarztrauber, Sayre A. *The Three Mile Limit of Territorial Seas.* Annapolis: Naval Institute Press, 1972.

Tate, Merz. *The United States and Armaments.* Cambridge, MA: Harvard University Press, 1948.

Taylor, Arnold H. *American Diplomacy and the Narcotics Traffic: 1900–1939.* Durham, NC: Duke University Press, 1969.

Thorpe, D. R. *The Uncrowned Prime Ministers.* London: Darkhorse Publishing, 1980.

"The Three Mile Limit as a Rule of International Law." *Columbia Law Review* 23 (1923): 472–76.

Tillman, Seth P. *Anglo-American Relations at the Paris Peace Conference of 1919.* Princeton: Princeton University Press, 1961.

Trani, Eugene P., and Wilson, David L. *The Presidency of Warren G. Harding.* Lawrence: Regents Press of Kansas, 1977.

Van de Water, Frederic F. *The Real McCoy.* Garden City, NY: Doubleday, Doran, and Company, 1931.

Vansittart, Robert. *The Mist Procession.* London: Hutchinson and Company, 1958.

Vinson, John Chalmers. "Charles Evans Hughes." In *An Uncertain Tradition: American Secretaries of State in the Twentieth Century,* 128–48. McGraw-Hill Series in American History. Edited by Norman A. Graebner. New York: McGraw-Hill, 1961.

———. *The Parchment Peace: The United States Senate and the Washington Conference, 1921–22.* Athens: University of Georgia Press, 1955.

Walker, Eric Sherbrooke [James Barbican]. *The Confessions of a Rum-Runner.* London: William Blackwood and Sons, 1927.

Walworth, Arthur C. *America's Moment: 1918.* New York: W. W. Norton and Company, 1977.

Waters, Harold. *Smugglers of Spirit: Prohibition and the Coast Guard.* New York: Hastings House Publishers, 1971.

Watt, D. Cameron. *Succeeding John Bull: America in Britain's Place, 1900–1975.* Cambridge: Cambridge University Press, 1984.

Watt, D. L. *Personalities and Policies: Studies in the Formulation of British Foreign Policy in the Twentieth Century.* London: Longmans, Green, and Company, 1965.

Wesser, Robert F. *Charles Evans Hughes: Politics and Reform in New York, 1905–10.* Ithaca: Cornell University Press, 1967.

Wheeler, Post, and Rives, Hallie E. *Dome of Many-Coloured Glass.* Garden City, NY: Doubleday and Company, 1955.

Willebrandt, Mabel Walker. "How Dry Is Wet Canada." *New York Herald Tribune.* September 16, 1928.

———. *The Inside of Prohibition.* Indianapolis: Bobbs-Merrill Company, 1929.

Williams, William A. "The Legend of Isolationism in the 1920s." *Science and Society* 18 (1954): 1–20.

Willoughby, Malcolm F. *Rum War at Sea.* Washington, DC: U.S. Coast Guard, 1964.

Willson, Beckles. *America's Ambassadors to England, 1785–1928: A Narrative of Anglo-American Diplomatic Relations.* Freeport, NY: Books for Libraries Press, 1928.

———. *Friendly Relations.* Boston: Little, Brown, and Company, 1934.

Wilson, Ross. *Scotch: The Formative Years.* London: Constable and Company, 1970.

Wright, Quincy. "The Prohibition Amendment and International Law." *Minnesota Law Review* 7 (1922–23): 28–39.

Young, Kenneth. *Stanley Baldwin.* London: Weidenfield and Nicolson, 1976.

Zeis, Paul M. *American Shipping Policy.* Princeton: Princeton University Press, 1938.

Index

Admiralty, 78, 112, 114, 117
American Bar Association, 78
American Review, 89
American Steamship Owners Association, 38
Anchor v. Aldridge, 34, 46; enforcement of, 41, 42; opposition to, 60–61. *See also* Transshipment of liquor
Anchor Line, 33, 34
Andrews, Lincoln C.: appointment, 96; British respect for, 116, 118; and implementation of London agreements, 117, 118; at London Conference, 111, 112–14; role in prohibition enforcement, 117, 118, 133, 157
Anglo-American relations: after World War I, xv–xvi, 4; and disarmament, 134; Hughes support for improvement in, 15; impact of prohibition on, 21, 62, 68–69, 101, 108–9, 155–59; improved by London Conference, 115, 119; in 1923, 59–60; post-treaty strains in, 89, 90, 101, 108–9; role of Canada in, 127–42; shipping as an issue in, 31–32, 33, 35–37. *See also* Anglophobia; Anti-Americanism
Ango-Japanese alliance, 15, 59
Anglophobia, xvi, 59–60; in Congress, 19; encouraged by smuggling, 4, 108–9, 158–59; and shipping rivalry, 36; of Willebrandt, 19
Anslinger, Harry, 112, 134
Anti-Americanism, xvi, 5; *Cunard* ruling strengthens, 46, 62; encouraged by prohibition enforcement, 5, 60, 158–59; as impediment to enforce-

ment cooperation, 64, 110–11
Anti-Saloon League, 39; criticizes Harding administration, 23, 25, 61, 157; influence, 22–23, 45, 47, 157; opposes liquor on ships, 32, 33, 37, 38, 42–43, 45; support for liquor treaty, 81, 93; Wheeler's leadership of, 22. *See also* Prohibitionists (United States); Wheeler, Wayne B.
Antismuggling cooperation, 64–66, 67–68, 109–10. *See also* Liquor Treaty; London Conference; Prohibition enforcement
Araunah decision, 17–18, 19, 20, 21, 67. *See also* Constructive presence concept
Association Against the Prohibition Amendment (AAPA), 94, 139
Australia, 79

Bahamas: attitude toward smuggling in, xiv, 3, 4–5, 62–63; and British liquor policy, 66, 67, 109; Coast Guard visitation agreement, 110, 113, 114, 117–18, 127; concern for American annexation of, 66, 109; decline in smuggling from, 62–63, 129; discussed at London Conference, 112, 114; economic conditions in, 1–2; enforcement of London agreements in, 117–18; financial benefits of smuggling to, 3; lax enforcement by officials in, 3–5, 8, 24–25, 62–63; liquor smuggling from, 2, 4–5, 8, 24, 109, 141. *See also* Nassau; Smuggling of liquor

173